Socratic Seminars in High School

Teach students how to engage in thoughtful discussions about a text. Socratic Seminars are highly effective at helping students read closely and think critically about what they've read. They also teach students how to participate in authentic discussions. This practical book from bestselling authors Victor and Marc Moeller is your go-to guide for getting started! It will help teachers who are new at Socratic Seminars and provide fresh ideas to teachers who are experienced with the format. Part I provides guidelines on how to prepare students for discussion and how to form good discussion questions. Part II includes ready-to-use lesson plans organized by compelling themes to engage students. The lesson plans include unabridged literary and nonfiction reading selections from classic and contemporary authors, as well as suggested film pairings.

Authors featured in this book include . . .

- William Faulkner
- Abraham Lincoln
- Mike Royko
- Isaac Asimov
- Aldous Huxley
- Andrew Postman
- Gina Berriault
- Gene Siskel
- Judith Guest
- President Obama
- Anton Chekhov
- Robert Frost
- John Cheever
- And more!

Victor J. Moeller is an English professor at McHenry Community College in Illinois.

Marc V. Moeller teaches English at Prairie Middle School in the Barrington Community Unit School District in Illinois.

Socratic Seminars in High School

Texts and Films That Engage Students in Reflective Thinking and Close Reading

Victor J. Moeller and Marc V. Moeller

Routledge
Taylor & Francis Group
NEW YORK AND LONDON

First published 2015
by Routledge
711 Third Avenue, New York, NY 10017

and by Routledge
2 Park Square, Milton Park, Abingdon, Oxon, OX14 4RN

Routledge is an imprint of the Taylor & Francis Group, an informa business

Portions of this book were previously published as Socratic Seminars and Literature Circles, 2001

Library of Congress Cataloging-in-Publication Data

Moeller, Victor J., 1937–
Socratic seminars in high school : texts and films that engage students in reflective thinking and close reading / Victor Moeller, Marc Moeller.
pages cm
Includes bibliographical references.
1. Questioning. 2. Literature—Study and teaching (Secondary).
I. Moeller, Marc V., 1970– II. Title.
LB1027.44.M64 2014
371.3′7—dc23
2014007663

ISBN: 978-1-138-02318-5 (hbk)
ISBN: 978-1-138-02319-2 (pbk)
ISBN: 978-1-315-77662-0 (ebk)

Typeset in Bembo
by Apex CoVantage, LLC

Please be aware that some of the topics covered in this book may be considered challenging and sensitive, in order to engage students and stimulate debate. Teachers should use their best judgement regarding appropriateness when planning lessons, taking into account their own students' beliefs, levels of maturity, and personal experiences.

Contents

Please note that the Answer Key for the exercises in this book and some bonus activities can be found in the online Teacher Resource, available free at www.routledge.com/books/details9781138023192

Meet the Authors

Victor J. Moeller has taught College Rhetoric, English and American literature, and Philosophy in public and private high schools and colleges. As an in-service field instructor of the Chicago Great Books Foundation for 14 years, he conducted teacher-training courses in 36 states and became Minnesota Area Director of professional development. Since 2007, he has been Reader for the AP English Literature and Language Exam and consultant for the College Board of Evanston, Illinois. All of Moeller's textbooks define, illustrate, and demonstrate how to implement the Socratic method of teaching and learning in the humanities. Moeller has Master's degrees in English, Education, and Philosophy. He currently teaches at McHenry County College, Crystal Lake, Illinois, and Elgin Community College, Elgin, Illinois.

Marc V. Moeller has taught courses in high schools and middle schools ranging from AP English, Composition, English literature to English as a second language. He has a Master's degree in education from National Louis University of Chicago. He readily admits that the greatest impact on his teaching career has been Victor Moeller, his father and mentor. Marc Moeller currently teaches English at Prairie Middle School in Barrington, Illinois, and may be reached by **email at victormoeller.com**

Preface

- "Students enter school as question marks and graduate as periods." Neil Postman
- "Reading is the only art form in which the audience plays the score; no other art requires the audience to be a performer." Kurt Vonnegut
- "When we read too fast or too slow, we understand nothing." Blaise Pascal
- "Reading and writing without discussion is like cooking without eating." Tom Romano
- "If you do not read, you will know only what you think." John Cheever
- "Authentic learning begins when teachers challenge students with real questions—problems about meaning that demand solutions." Victor Moeller
- "In training a child to activity of thought, above all things we must beware of 'inert ideas'—that is, ideas that are merely received into the mind without being utilized, or tested, or thrown into fresh combinations. Education with inert ideas is not only useless it is above all things, harmful." Alfred North Whitehead
- "Good discussion calls for the best teachers and I am convinced furthermore that it accomplishes more than any other form of teaching." Jacques Barzan
- "For Socrates, teaching was not merely asking a series of questions . . . He wanted to make every pupil realize that truth was in the pupil's own power to find, if he searched long enough and hard enough, refusing all 'authoritative statements' and judged every solution by reason alone. This system is the most difficult, the least common, and yet the most thorough way to teach." Gilbert Highet
- "The ideal Socratic Seminar occurs when the teacher is able to resort only to questions—when there is no declarative teacher-talk, but only the asking of questions . . . The more the seminar is an experience of

active learning for the students, the sooner they will become active learners in their reading of texts for future seminars and the sooner they will be able to engage in learning by themselves without the help of teachers, which is the ultimate goal of all teaching." Mortimer Adler

- "Good schools promote the habit of respectful skepticism . . . Asking questions captures our minds more readily than memorizing somebody else's answers to yet somebody else's questions." Theodore Sizer
- "What students most need to learn in schools is how to learn. The emphasis must be on the *how* of learning rather than the *what*." Neil Postman

Dear Colleague,

If you agree with most or at least some of the above statements, you have found a kindred spirit. As I shake your hand and get a chair for you, let me explain briefly how this book will help you become a better teacher. Everything in this text is based on the assumption that students, not teachers, are the primary agents in learning. The corollary is that authentic learning is active learning. The consequence is that students become responsible for their own learning.

I have been writing this book in my imagination for the last thirty years. It describes, illustrates, and explains how to engage in the Socratic method of discussion and learning. However, just as no book on tennis, for example, cannot make you a good tennis player so neither can a book, by itself, make you a proficient teacher. Nevertheless, with sustained effort, practice, experimentation, guidance, and willingness to learn from your mistakes, and use of video film, you can learn how to become an active learner along with your students. Better yet, take a Basic Leader Training Course from the Great Books Foundation of IL or the National Paideia Center Teacher Training Program of NC. See also online teacher conferences: for help with collaborators and colleagues **www.englishcompanion.ning.com**

For another important resource, check out my English Student Home Page. If you have questions, comments, or suggestions, I would love to hear from you since it is, after all, for teachers like you that this book has been written.

Sincerely,
Victor Moeller

Acknowledgments

"We are as pygmies standing on the shoulders of giants."
St. Bernard of Clairvaux

I must give credit where it is due. Much of what I know about the **Socratic method** of teaching, I learned during my fourteen years as an in-service instructor for the Great Books Foundation and from my mentor Mortimer Adler. While most of the ideas that I present here are my own since I have developed and refined them over the last forty years in the classroom, the seminal ideas are found in Adler's writings (see References) and in the training manuals of the Great Books Foundation, Chicago. VJM

Copyrights

PART I

The Socratic Method

Memorandum

TO:
FROM:
RE: On reading and writing
DATE: First semester

NOTE: Write me a personal letter about your previous reading and writing experience in high school English classes. This background information will help me to better understand how I may help you in this class. Please answer each numbered group of questions in a paragraph.

1. For you, is **writing** in school, difficult, enjoyable, or somewhere in between? What is the best essay, letter, story, or poem that you have ever written? What is the best sentence that you have ever read or written?
2. How important is **reading** in your life? Do you read regularly? What is the last book that you read? Have you ever read a book more than once? If so, why? What is the most important or memorable book that you have ever read? Why? While reading, do you ever make notations in the margins? Why do some books deserve and require more than one reading while others are not worthy of even a first reading?
3. Did your previous teachers **lecture** mostly or conduct **discussions**? Which did you prefer? If so, why so? If not, why not? Would you like to co-lead a discussion in this class? If so, why so? If not, why not?
4. What do you hope to get out of this class? Try to be as specific as possible. Do you have any particular concerns about this class? If so, what are they?
5. Finally, is there anything that I should know about you that may be an obstacle to your work in this class? For example, having a part-time job would hinder greatly your ability to write essays and to complete frequent reading assignments.

CHAPTER

1 Two Models of Teaching

If Good Teaching is a Dialogue, Why Does the Monologue Continue to Dominate?

Robert Benchley once remarked that: "There are two kinds of people—those who classify things and those who don't." Since I belong to the first group, I tend to classify teachers according to those who still employ the lecture model of learning and those who daily engage their students in active learning. I do so not only because most of my former teachers assumed that they were the most important part of the learning process but also because the lecture method continues to dominate in too many classrooms even today. In contrast, the Socratic teacher knows that the student is the most important part of the learning process.

Take my high school American literature teacher, Marc Prosser. He began most lessons by stating the objective: "By the end of this class you will be able to identify the characteristics of the 'code hero' in Hemingway"—and then, anticipating the so-what looks on our faces, explained the relevance or importance of this knowledge: "Hemingway's concept of the 'code hero' will give you standards by which to judge your own ideas of heroism." The class proceeded as a lecture. Mr. Prosser knew what a code hero was and he was going to tell us, tell us that he told us, and then ask us to tell him what he had told us. Our job as students was to "pay attention," that is, to be receptive and passive and to take careful, detailed notes. We were not to interrupt his lecture with comments; however, we were allowed to ask questions for elementary clarification. For example, "What do you mean by pragmatic?" or "Who is James L. Roberts?" or "Why do you call this stuff literary criticism?" His authority was supreme, his answers all we needed to know on those subjects. After all, he had a Master's degree.

His lessons concluded with an objective test. "I am the tester, and you are the testees," he would say, and never would we break from those roles. However, "to be fair"—another of his pet phrases—he "entertained" questions before the test. If we had none, Mr. Prosser judged his lesson a success. In the end, we were to trust that Mr. Prosser knew best even when we did not know what he was talking about. "Someday you will understand, and all will be clear," he would reassure us.

What I eventually came to understand, thanks to my college contemporary literature professor, Kenelm Basil, was that there was a better way to teach. Mr. Basil was a Socratic teacher if ever there was one. He began each lesson not by telling us what we were going to learn (he was not certain that we would learn anything although that was, of course, his fondest hope) but by posing a major problem about the meaning the day's assigned *text* (a work of art whether written, created, or performed). He began always with a basic question of interpretation, wrote it on the board, and then asked each of us to write down our own initial answers on scrap paper. For example, "According to Vonnegut's story, 'Harrison Bergeron,' is the desire to excel as strong as the tendency to be mediocre?" Because he kept his own opinions to himself—he was not a participant but a leader—he asked only follow-up questions on our comments, Mr. Basil convinced us over time that he really did not have a single correct answer in mind. Indeed, the class soon realized that more than one correct answer was possible because evidence from the story supported differing views. In short, our teacher began the discussion with a real question, the answer to which he himself was uncertain of or even had no answer at all.

As students, we had to be active: clarifying our answers, testing others' answers for supporting evidence, resolving conflicting answers with evidence, and listening for more opinions. Learning in Mr. Basil's classroom was not about receiving ideas but about wrestling with them. The test of truth was reason and evidence, not teacher authority. The lesson concluded with a resolution activity since, after all, questions are quests for answers. We were asked to review our original responses and then to write a paragraph or a brief essay stating our comprehensive answer to the basic question. Most importantly, Mr. Basil strove not for group consensus or truth by vote, but rather for individual understandings: "Given the answers that you have just heard in discussion, what now is *your* solution?"

Liberation at last! I no longer had to sit dutifully silent while someone told me what I could just as easily have read for myself, found in a library, or researched on the Internet. I no longer had to parrot the teacher's interpretations. More important, Mr. Basil challenged me to think independently and to become responsible for my own ideas. The responsibility for learning had been placed in my hands and along with it, the joy and personal satisfaction of arriving at my own insights. I had learned to live with doubt and to uncover questions that answers hide. In short, I had learned how to learn.

Do not misunderstand. Most so-called Socratic teachers do not conduct discussions the way Mr. Basil did. Many have not mastered the art of fostering reflective, independent thinking. Such teachers confuse the right to express an opinion with the notion that any opinion can be right. Toleration of any and all ideas becomes the goal, and brain storming—that pathetic analogy—gets enthroned as the method. As one mindless person put it, "Don't we all know that everything is relative and that there are no absolutes?" Except, of course, his opinion.

Others, the pseudo-Socratic teachers, offer little more than a disguised lecture. These teachers pretend to conduct open discussions but have specific answers in mind. They tip their hands in several ways: by asking leading questions ("How can you honestly think Vonnegut would agree with you?"), by allowing opinions that they agree with go unchallenged or unsubstantiated, by developing a single line of argument on but one side of an issue, by injecting their own opinion into the discussion ("I believe that you have all overlooked important information on page six"), by commenting on student answers ("That's very good, James. I'm so proud of you" or, "Maria, I think you had better reconsider your answer. You are missing something"), and finally, by attempting to arrive at group consensus ("I would like to see a show of hands. How many think the desire to excel is as strong as the tendency to be mediocre?") If what I have said about these would-be Socratic teachers is not true, how else are we to explain these examples of common student and teacher behaviors?

Teacher: Whenever I try to have discussion, my students clam up. Only one or two contribute. They just don't get the point. I *have* to tell them.

Student: My answer is correct, isn't it Mrs. Jones?

Teacher: Discussion is a waste of time. I have to cover the curriculum.

Student: But Mrs. Jones, what *is* the right answer?

Teacher: My students' test scores have to improve. I don't have time for the luxury of endless discussions. I have 130 students. Get real.

Student: Why do you keep asking questions when you know the answers?

Teacher: Students don't know how to ask good questions and anyway, discussions are just too messy.

Student: Just let me alone and give me my C. I don't mess up your class.

Teacher: My students cannot be trusted to think for themselves. They keep coming up with silly answers.

But isn't that just the point? The lecturing teacher fails to understand that wrong answers are a necessary part of the learning process when real thinking takes place. In contrast, the authentic Socratic teacher recognizes and accepts false turns and "silly" answers as inevitable when students have the freedom to be wrong—*and* right. After all, thinking *is* difficult and students resist it like a plague. Any teacher will recognize immediately the common cop-outs: "I don't know," or "Why did you call on me?" or "I wasn't doing anything," or "Who cares?" or "What difference does it make?" and "Ask somebody else." In the end, if thinking were easy, there would be more of it.

The fundamental difference between Mr. Prosser and Mr. Basil comes down to who is finally responsible for learning. Mr. Prosser's approach implies that the teacher is, while Mr. Basil's suggests that students should be. Can anyone convince students they are responsible for their own learning other than students themselves? And is it not usually through discussion, dialogue, and problem solving—not through lecture—that students come to realize what they *have* and *have not* learned?

Not long ago, I heard James Howard of the Council for Basic Education state on National Public Radio, "Education is what you have left after you have forgotten everything you learned in school." I wonder what Mr. Prosser would make of that statement. I know what Mr. Basil would do with it.

Two Models of Teaching and Learning

Didactic Passive Learning (Master–disciple)	Socratic Active Learning (Engaged inquiry)
1. Teacher centered: based on the assumption that the teacher is the primary agent in learning.	1. Problem centered: based on the assumption that the student is the primary agent in learning.
2. Teacher's role: to impart the results of experience, personal study, and reflection.	2. Teacher's role: to uncover the question that the answer hides. To be a co-learner.
3. Primarily deductive: the usual methods are lecture, story telling, use of analogy, and aphorism.	3. Primarily inductive: the usual methods are discussion, dialogue, and problem solving.
4. Test of truth: authority and experience.	4. Test of truth: reason and evidence.
5. Learning is the reception of ideas.	5. Learning is a conflict of ideas: a thesis, antithesis, and a synthesis that results in new knowledge (Hegel).
6. Student's role: to be passive, open, receptive, trusting, and unquestioning.	6. Student's role: to be active, questioning, critical, and discriminating—learning to trust one's own judgment (independent thinking).
7. Evaluation is factual recall of data—commonly in the form of objective tests (right and wrong answers).	7. Evaluation is application of understanding interpretation of data—commonly in an essay, speech, journal, or a review.
8. Ultimate goal: wisdom viewed as the internalization of truths and beliefs.	8. Ultimate goal: wisdom viewed as an informed ignorance (knowing what one does not know—the Socratic paradox).

While the article illustrates the importance of the Socratic method for active learning, the didactic model still has *a necessary but ancillary role* since teachers must sometimes provide organized information not accessible other ways. A comparison–contrast outline of two generic lesson plans reveals important differences.

Lesson Plan Models

Didactic Infusion	**Socratic** Discovery
1. Focus: motivator.	1. Focus: attention grabber.
2. Objective: what students will be able to do by end of the lesson.	2. Objective: to solve problems. What students learn cannot be stated in advance.
3. Purpose: why lesson is important, useful and relevant.	3. Purpose: to increase understanding and enjoyment of the group task by developing the habit of independent, critical, and reflective thinking.
4. Input: new information or activities.	4. Input: basic questions of interpretation and the co-leader's related, prepared follow-up questions of interpretation.
5. Modeling: verbal or physical example of acceptable finished product or process.	5. Modeling: the co-leaders follow the four Rules of Socratic discussion.

Didactic Infusion	**Socratic** Discovery
6. Checking for understanding to determine if students have the information needed to complete the task.	6. Checking: co-leaders ask spontaneous follow-up question for clarification, substantiation, more opinion, consistency, implication, relevance, and resolution.
7. Guided practice: task done independently in small groups with teacher help.	7. Guided practice: students learn how to rely on their own judgment about which answers are good, better, or best, and to distinguish the false from the true.
8. Closure: summary of what should have been learned. Objective is restated.	8. Closure: a written or oral resolution to problem(s) of interpretation.

CHAPTER

2 What is the Socratic Method of Teaching and Learning?

> "The role of the teacher is to uncover the question that the answer hides."
>
> James Baldwin

Let us begin at the source. Like so many students before him and even those today, Socrates' student Meno is exasperated by his teacher's refusal to "just tell him" what to do, what the truth is, and in their dialogue, whether or not virtue can be taught. Meno is astounded when Socrates openly admits that not only does he not know whether virtue can be taught but also that he does not even know what virtue is. "What!" Meno asks: "Is this the report we are to take home about you?" In characteristic manner, Socrates challenges his student to rephrase the question, to reflect on it, and to arrive at his own answers. In so doing, Socrates helps Meno to wrestle with the implications of the problem that he has posed for their discussion. Indeed, Socrates makes a point of asserting his own ignorance: "All I can say is that I have often looked to see if there are any [teachers of virtue], and in spite of all my efforts, I cannot find them . . . . I do not know what virtue is and, not only that, you may say also, that to the best of my belief, I have never yet met anyone who did know" (Rouse 29). Meno leaves confounded that his teacher, his master and guide, refuses to confirm what Meno believes he already knows.

Nevertheless, when Socrates' reputation for wisdom continues to grow, another impetuous student, Chaerephon, goes to the oracle of Delphi to ask if anyone is wiser than Socrates. The priestess of Apollo, Pythia, replies that no one is. When Socrates hears the answer, he is genuinely puzzled: "I have no wisdom, small or great. What can she mean when she says that I am the wisest of men?" (Rouse 426). But why does Socrates take the oracle's word at face value? Could the god also have meant that no one was wiser than Socrates because wisdom is not to be found among men? Socrates is even more explicit about his ignorance in the defense of his life at his trial, *The Apology.* After questioning another who claimed to be wise, Socrates concludes, "I am better off than he is—for he knows nothing, and thinks that he knows; I neither know nor think that I know. In this latter particular, then, I seem to have the slight advantage over him" (Rouse 327). What we have here is the great paradox of learning: you must first know what you want to know or recognize what you do not know. Is this confusing? Only at first. What Socrates suggests is that the first step to learning is knowing how to ask an honest question—one that you have no answer to or one that you have several answers to but none of which satisfy. In short, unless you have questions, you cannot learn. As learning begins, the more you know, the more you realize that you do not know. Such is the Socratic paradox.

But what about the Socratic method? The phrase is as elusive as a greased pig. What does this method mean to the teacher in the trenches? For some, unfortunately, it means no more than asking a lot of questions—rapidly and indiscriminately. For others, it means conducting an interview. And for still others it means cross-examination. A few even seem to believe that there is something mystical about the Socratic method—that some teachers are born with it or that there really is no common method at all that other teachers can acquire. Nevertheless, all of these notions miss the mark because they fail to capture the Socratic concept of teaching *and* do not recognize that the Socratic method can be explained, applied, and evaluated. Furthermore, there is no "official" Socratic method since even today there is no consensus about Socrates' method as recorded in the dialogues of his most brilliant student, Plato. Nevertheless, based on my career with the Great Books Foundation and my mentor Mortimer Adler as well as my extensive experience in the classroom, I am confident enough to assert my own conception of a Socratic method in the following exposition.

What is the Socratic method? It is an exercise in "reflective thinking" that, according to John Dewey, has two elements: *doubt*—a problem about meaning which initiates it—and *an act searching* for a solution(s) to solve that problem.

How is it done? It is conducted mainly by *asking* *<u>prepared questions</u>* (the problems which are the focus of discussion) and *spontaneous follow-up questions* which develop the ideas being considered with a view to achieving resolution.

Why is it done this way? It is done this way to achieve the goal or purpose of this kind of engaged learning: to increase the groups' *and* the co-leaders' understanding (comprehension) of the text under discussion. *As a result*, there will be also an increase in enjoyment—that is, the satisfaction of discovering one's own answers and finding new meaning(s) in the selection.

Co-leaders are student pairs, teacher pairs, or teacher–student pairs who have been trained in the following method of discussion. But why do you need co-leaders? For several reasons. (1) Thinking continuously, keeping track of ideas, and deciding which answers to develop with spontaneous follow-up questions requires a high degree of concentration. Two leaders provide more mental power and ordinarily do a better job than a single leader. (2) Two leaders provide a good model of teamwork by working together just as the participants are expected to work together in solving the problem. Co-leaders also instill in the group a belief that they can learn from each other, and a willingness to assume a share of responsibility for the outcome of the discussion. Also, a pair of co-leaders are less likely to be viewed as "authority" figures. (3) To follow up ideas and, at the same time, to observe and to recognize those who want to speak and to invite the reluctant to participate, two sets of eyes and ears are needed. Finally, (4) co-leaders need one another to prepare properly for discussion. A co-leader ought never to say to his or her partner, "It is your question, sink or swim with it." On the contrary, it must be *our* previously agreed-upon prepared questions that are the focus of discussion; it must also be *our* spontaneous follow-up questions that develop and provide the structure needed for authentic learning to happen in discussion. In sum, the Socratic method begins with a *problem* (a prepared interpretive question), continues as a *process* of asking spontaneous follow-up questions, and results in a *product*—a resolution, increased understanding and enjoyment of the text.

The Four Rules of Socratic Discussion

1. **First, no one may participate who has not read the selection before discussion.** The ticket of admission is that everyone has read the selection carefully. For this reason, before discussion the leader(s) begin with a plot-check quiz—that is, a list of factual questions that anyone can readily answer if he or she has done the reading. Those who have not done the reading are limited to the role of spectators. For less-able readers, this rule can be obviated on occasion by making the first reading an oral one in class. Another helpful technique is to conduct textual analysis, at times, when a group is not well prepared or read the test only once.
2. **Second, participants must support answers with textual evidence.** Without evidence, discussion soon becomes a matter of sheer conjecture wherein one idea begins to sounds as good as another. Without evidence participants have no way of deciding which answers are better than others and which are wrong. Evidence turns mere opinion into interpretation. After all, there are right and wrong answers in discussion just as some interpretations are better than others.
3. **Third, participants may not introduce outside authorities but may discuss only the assigned readings.** This rule also ensures that

everyone has equal access to the same information upon which everyone has to base his or her answers. The logical starting point for discussion is the reading itself. In their *Theory of Literature* (page 127), Warren and Wellek get to the heart of the matter: "The natural sensible starting point for work in literary scholarship is interpretation and analysis of the works of literature themselves. After all, only the works themselves justify all our interest in the life of an author, in his social environment, and the whole process of literature. But curiously enough, literary history has been so preoccupied with the setting of a work of literature that its attempts at analysis of the works themselves have been slight in comparison with the enormous efforts expended on the study of their background."

Furthermore, students learn to become responsible for their own ideas when they do not try to justify them by appealing to an authority—another book or another person. They must learn to rely on their own judgment about the meaning of the *text* (a work of art whether written, created, or performed).

4. **Most importantly, the co-leaders may ask only questions.** The moment the co-leaders begin making statements during discussion, the atmosphere changes from independent thinking and mutual inquiry to attempts to please the leaders. Even worse, the vociferous can quickly turn discussion into an argument or debate. Furthermore, no matter how well intentioned, leaders' comments hinder participants' opportunity to think independently and freely. And finally, the co-leaders' primary role to develop and relate ideas becomes practically impossible when one or both become participants.

CHAPTER

3 Lesson Plan 1

Active and Close Reading

1. **Focus:** How important is reading in your life? Do you enjoy reading? If so, why so? If not, why not? (Brief discussion or journal.)
2. **Objective:** To develop and to apply the techniques of Active and Close Reading.
3. **Purpose:**
   - To increase our mutual understanding (comprehension) and, as a result, our enjoyment of reading.
   - To develop the habit of independent and critical thinking.
4. **Input:** Oral reading: "Active and Close Reading"
5. **Modeling, checking, and guided practice:** As you go over the handout, answer any student questions or emphasize any ideas as needed. *Model* your notations on the poem by Robert Frost after you have asked them to make their own notations. *Compare notations*: what they thought was important, what they didn't understand, what they liked or disliked, agreed or disagreed with, whatever they think related (connections). *Read silently the first page* of "Reunion" by John Cheever in preparation for the following Lessons (2–5). Ask students for examples of their notations on page 1.
6. **Closure:** *Assignment*: To be able to understand the illustrations used in the next four lessons, please read twice the short story by Cheever, "Reunion." On the first reading, make notations on what is important, what you don't understand, what you like or dislike, agree or disagree with, and whatever you find related. On the second reading, convert some of your notations into at least eight questions. Include a line number for each question.

Active and Close Reading

"I read slower than I write."

John Updike

"Reading is the only art form in which the audience plays the score; no other art requires the audience to be a performer."

Kurt Vonnegut

"When we read too fast or too slow, we understand nothing."

Blaise Pascal

"The person who does not spend as much time in actively and definitely thinking about what he has read as he has spent in reading, is simply insulting the author."

M. Arnold

A first step for participating in the Seminar is reading the selection. Far too many students read neither actively nor closely—not only because they have not learned how to discriminate among the various purposes of different kinds of reading but also because they have not been taught how to read actively. Here is a method that I have found productive if employed continually by teacher and student.

The phrase "active and close reading" suggests immediately two ideas. First, some books and stories deserve to be read closely, slowly, and actively—not only because we would miss many of their implied meanings but also because we must learn to recognize meanings other than our own in what we peruse. Second, there are times when how fast we read or how much we read is of no importance. What *is* important is that we learn **to reflect** on what we read and learn how to carry on a conversation with the author. We converse with an author when we question always the text.

The purpose of active and close reading is to learn to read interpretively—to pay attention not merely to *what* an author says but to *why* he says it in the *way* that he does. In short, the purpose in reading is not merely trying to recall what happens in a story, for example, but to think about why things happen as they do. With nonfiction, active readers take particular note of an author's choice of words (diction), use of sentence structure (syntax), and his or her organization of ideas.

Some books and stories like those that we will be reading, can be **interpreted in several ways.** And no individual, adult or child, teacher or student, ever thinks of *all* of the possible interpretations in a given selection. As a result, no one can tell you what is *the* correct interpretation of a story, poem, or play—not even, believe it or not, not even the author! However, this does *not* mean that all interpretations are equally good or correct. On the contrary, some interpretations are better than others and some are wrong. How can this be so? The answer is that some interpretations have more evidence to support them which makes them more plausible. Other interpretations are more comprehensive—that is, they explain more of a text than does another view. Still other interpretations are wrong: either there is no evidence to support them or the evidence offered is contradicted by some other statement of the author. But what about the author? Why doesn't he or she have the last word about what was "really meant"?

Thomas Mann, in the extraordinary afterword of his novel, "The Making of *The Magic Mountain*" (page 725) says:

> I consider it a mistake to think that the author himself is the best judge of his work. He may be that while he is still at work on it and living in it. But once done, it tends to be something he has got rid of, something foreign to him; others, as time goes on, will know more and better about it than he. *They can often remind him of things in it he has forgotten or indeed never quite knew.*

Just as no one can tell you what is *the* correct interpretation nor what your interpretation must be, so also no one can tell you **what details** in your reading are important. Meaning can begin anywhere—even with what someone else might regard an insignificant detail. Whatever furnishes you with clues for arriving at your own interpretation, that is what is important. In short, what is important varies from reader to reader.

In addition, to interpret a work for yourself does *not* require that you first read about the author's life, or about the times in which the author lived, nor review general introductory or background statements. Instead, readers can begin by noting their responses to a story and then trying to convert as many of them as possible into questions. But to engage in this process fruitfully, readers must learn to respect their own responses—that is, to take seriously their thoughts and feelings about a book.

Forming good questions whose answers can yield a great deal of meaning about a story requires at least **two readings**. Roland Barthes, the eminent French literary critic, maintains that, "He who reads a story only once is condemned to read the same story his whole life." On the **first reading**, the readers' main interest should be to note their responses in writing—that is, to make notations. Tom Romano, a New York high school English teacher, says that: "Reading without writing [here, notations] is like cooking without eating." During the **second reading**, readers note new responses and pay special attention to those notations that they can convert into questions.

Unless readers learn to put their responses into writing by making notations as they read, they will have few questions—or, if there are any questions at all, they will be so general that they could be asked of any story. Such generic questions yield little new knowledge and yet without questions, no one can increase his understanding of the material. The first step to learning then is, paradoxically, knowing what you want to know—that is, asking real questions.

As American philosopher and educator Mortimer Adler explains in his classic essay on "How to Mark a Book," a notation is any response to the text that a reader puts into writing. Notations take various forms: underlining what is important, circling key words, drawing lines to make connections between similar parts, comments, personal, emotional reactions, reminders, and even nascent questions. As John Ruskin so aptly remarked, "No book is worth anything which is not worth much; nor is it serviceable until it has been read and reread, and loved, and loved again, *and marked*." Serviceable is the key word.

Experienced readers have found that whenever they mark up a text, they usually refer to one or more of **four sources** for formulating questions:

1. **Whatever they think is important** (for whatever reason).
2. **Whatever they don't understand.** Not understanding something is more than circling unfamiliar vocabulary (although it includes this). It also means making notations about a character's motivation, for example, or why the story begins or ends as it does, or what the author means by a certain statement or the inclusion of a certain scene, and so on.
3. **Whatever they like or dislike, agree or disagree with.** In other words, active readers are also careful to note their emotional responses. For Louise Rosenblatt (*Literature as Exploration*, Part II), this step is crucial—what the reader brings to the text.
4. **Whatever they think is related**—one part of the text to another. A chief concern of the second reading is looking for connections or patterns among various parts of the reading. For example:
   (a) The repetition of the same word or phrase.
   (b) The reoccurrence of similar actions.
   (c) Contrasting words or actions.
   (d) The place of something in the text (organization).

As with so many things, whatever we get out of an enterprise is proportionate to the effort we put into it. So too with reading. Unless we learn how to become thoughtful, active, and close readers, we will continue to miss many of the implications of what we read and, as a result, lose the pleasure of increasing our understanding of the text.

Directions: Mark up the poem below by questioning what you think is important, circling key words, drawing lines to make connections, comments, and personal emotional reactions.

"The Road Not Taken"

Robert Frost

Two roads diverged in a yellow wood,
And sorry I could not travel both
And be one traveler, long I stood
And looked down one as far as I could
To where it bent in the undergrowth;

Then took the other, just as fair,
And having perhaps the better claim,
Because it was grassy and wanted wear;
Though as for the passing there
Had worn them really about the same,

And both that morning equally lay
In leaves no step had trodden black.
Oh, I kept the first for another day!
Yet knowing how way leads on to way,
I doubted if I should ever come back.

I shall be telling this with a sigh
Somewhere ages and ages hence:
Two roads diverged in a yellow wood, and I—
I took the one less traveled by,
And that has made all the difference.

First Reading: Notations

1. Whatever you think important:
   The narrator really would like to have taken both roads (line 3).
   The narrator admits the two roads were really about the same (10).
   The narrator is talking about a major decision (16).

2. Whatever you don't understand:
   Why isn't the title about the road less traveled?
   Why will the speaker be telling about his decision with a sigh?

3. Whatever you like or dislike, agree or disagree with:
   Whenever I make an important decision, I too sometimes wonder what would have happened if I had chosen differently.

4. Whatever you think is related:
   (a) The repetition of the same word or phrase.
   First and eighteenth line.
   (b) The reoccurrence of similar actions.
   Choosing to look back on a previous choice.
   (c) Contrasting words or actions.
   Speaking about a decision and making that decision.
   (d) The place of something in the text (organization).
   Which word(s) of the last line need(s) emphasis?

Second Reading: Notations Converted into Questions

1. Why isn't the title of the poem "The Road Less Traveled"?
2. Why is the choice of the less traveled road made on a fall morning? (lines 1, 11)
3. Why would the narrator like to have taken both roads? (2, 13)
4. Why does the narrator say that one road had "perhaps" the better claim? (7)
5. Why does the narrator admit the two roads were really much the same? (10)
6. Why is there an exclamation point at the end of line 13?
7. Does the narrator sigh out of satisfaction or regret? (16)
8. Will the narrator be telling of his choice to others or only to himself? (16)
9. Why does the narrator think he will be speaking of his decision in the distant future?

On Reading Nonfiction

But what about nonfiction? Do these active reading techniques for fiction apply equally to nonfiction? Yes and no. The same basic techniques of making notations, writing questions, and so on apply also to nonfiction which is commonly defined as "all forms of prose that purport to be factual" and use exposition, argumentation, and fictions only to illustrate. However, with factual prose, particular attention must be given to: (1) identifying the author's thesis (what) and purpose (why); (2) his audience (who); (3) his style (how) of writing—diction, syntax, vocabulary, and use of examples; (4) the structure and organization of ideas; (5) the relationships among the principal sections of the text; and (6) above all, his tone or attitude towards his topic must be determined. As the College Board people continually remind us, "To miss the tone is to miss the meaning."

Textual Analysis

Textual analysis is a detailed examination of a particular passage in which you try to determine the author's meaning line by line and sometimes word by word. *This technique is a good way to get into a reading when the group has not read well enough to participate in an interpretive discussion. The teacher models close reading orally.* In addition to being a remedial device, when co-leaders use textual analysis, they model what should be happening during the first and second readings. Finally, textual analysis is also effective even when the group is doing well in discussion; in this situation, textual analysis builds on ideas already expressed to draw out more meaning from specific passages that help to resolve the basic question. Textual analysis involves four steps in this order:

1. **Select a passage** that you want to examine closely and have a group participant read it aloud. Oral reading is not only an important aid to understanding but also an indicator of a student's level of comprehension of what he or she is reading.
2. **Identify the speaker of the passage,** the narrator. It may be the author speaking directly to you, a fictional narrator, an anonymous narrator, or a character speaking to another character.
3. **Identify the context of the passage.** If you have chosen a passage other than the beginning or the conclusion of the story, try to get a rough idea of where you are in the selection. In short, ask factual questions about what happened just prior to the passage and what happened just after it.

4. **Review the passage line by line and even key words.** This step is the heart of textual analysis and the most important. Go over the difficult passage, line by line, freely *asking questions of fact or of interpretation* about the meaning of words, phrases, and sentences about which you are uncertain of the answer. Freely turn to other sections of the reading that you think are related to the passage being explored. After you have reviewed the entire passage, return to your basic question by restating or rephrasing it and then continue the discussion.

Reading Assignment

To be able to understand the examples used in the following pages of exposition, please read twice the short story by **John Cheever, "Reunion"**. On the first reading, make notations on what is important, what you don't understand, what you like or dislike, agree or disagree with, and whatever you find related—one part of the story to the other. On the second reading, convert some of your notations into questions.

"Reunion"

John Cheever

The last time I saw my father was in Grand Central Station. I was going from my grandmother's in the Adirondacks to a cottage on the Cape that my mother had rented, and I wrote my father that I would be in New York between trains for an hour and a half, and asked if we could have lunch together. His secretary wrote to say that he would meet me at the information booth at noon, and at twelve o'clock sharp I saw him coming through the crowd. He was a stranger to me at—my mother divorced him three years ago and I hadn't been with him since—but as soon as I saw him I felt that he was my father, my flesh and blood, my future and my doom. I knew that when I was grown I would have to plan my campaigns within his limitations. He was a big, good-looking man, and I was terribly happy to see him again. He struck me on the back and shook my hand. "Hi, Charlie," he said. "Hi, boy. I'd like to take you up to my club, but it's in the Sixties, and if you have to catch an early train I guess we'd better get something to eat around here." He put his arm around me, and I smelled my father the way my mother sniffs a rose. It was a rich compound of whiskey, after-shave lotion, shoe polish, woolens, and the rankness of a mature male. I hoped that someone would see us together. I wished that we could be photographed. I wanted some record of us having been together.

We went out of the station and up a side street to a restaurant. It was sill early, and the place was empty. The bartender was quarreling with a delivery boy, and there was one very old waiter in a red coat down by the kitchen door. We sat down, and my father hailed the waiter in

Reproduced with permission see Acknowledgments

a loud voice. "Kellner!" he shouted. "Garcon! Cameriere! You!" His boisterousness in the empty restaurant seemed out of place. "Could we have a little service here!" he shouted. "Chop-chop." Then he clapped his hands. This caught the waiter's attention, and he shuffled over to our table. "Were you clapping your hands at me?" he asked. "Calm down, calm down, sommelier," my father said. "If it isn't too much to ask of you—if it wouldn't be too much above and beyond the call of duty, we would like a couple of Beefeater Gibsons."

"I don't like to be clapped at," the waiter said.

"I should have brought my whistle," my father said. "I have a whistle that is audible only to the ears of old waiters. Now take out your little pad and your little pencil and see if you can get this straight: two Beefeater Gibsons. Repeat after me two Beefeater Gibsons."

"I think you'd better go somewhere else," the waiter said quietly.

"That," said my father, "is one of the most brilliant suggestions I have ever heard. Come on, Charlie, let's get the hell out of here."

I followed my father out of that restaurant into another. He was not so boisterous this time. Our drinks came, and he cross-questioned me about the baseball season. He then struck the edge of his empty glass with his knife and began shouting again. "Garcon! Kellner! Cameriere! You! Could we trouble you to bring us two more of the same."

"How old is the boy?" the waiter asked.

"That," said my father, "is none of your Goddamned business."

"I'm sorry, sir," the waiter said, "but I won't serve the boy another drink."

"Well, I have some news for you," my father said. "I have some very interesting news for you. This doesn't happen to be the only restaurant in New York. They've opened another on the corner. Come on, Charlie."

He paid the bill, and I followed him out of that restaurant into another. Here the waiters wore pink jackets like hunting coats, and there was a lot of horse tack on the walls. We sat down, and my father began to shout again. "Master of the hounds! Tallyhoo and all that sort of thing. We'd like a little something in the way of stirrup cup. Namely, two Bibson Geefeaters."

"Two Bibson Geefeaters?" the waiter asked, smiling.

"You know damned well what I want," my father said angrily.

"I want two Beefeater Gibsons, and make it snappy. Things have changed in jolly old England. So my friend Duke tells me. Let's see what England can produce in the way of a cocktail."

"This isn't England," the waiter said.

"Don't argue with me," my father said. "Just do as you're told."

"I just thought you might like to know where you are," the waiter said.

"If there is one think I cannot tolerate," my father said, "it is an impudent domestic. Come on, Charlie."

The fourth place we went to was Italian. "Buon giorno," my father said. "Per favore, possiamo avere due cocktail americani, forti, forti. Molto gin, poco vermut."

"I don't understand Italian," the waiter said.

"Oh, come off it," my father said. "You understand Italian, and you know damned well you do. Vogliamo due cocktail americani. Subito."

The waiter left us and spoke with the captain, who came over to our table and said, "I'm sorry, sir, but this table is reserved."

"All right," my father said. "Get us another table."

"All the tables are reserved," the captain said.

Reproduced with permission see Acknowledgments

"I get it," my father said. "You don't desire our patronage. Is that it? Well, the hell with you. Vada all'inferno. Let's go Charlie."

"I have to get my train," I said. "I'm terribly sorry." He put his arm around me and pressed me against him. "I'll walk you back to the station. If there had only been time to go up to my club."

"That's all right, Daddy," I said.

"I'll get you a paper," he said. "I'll get you a paper to read on the train."

Then he went up to the newsstand and said, "Kind sir, will you be good enough to favor me with one of your Goddamned, no good, ten-cent afternoon papers?" The clerk turned away from him and stared at a magazine cover. "Is it asking too much for you to sell me one of your disgusting specimens of yellow journalism?"

"I have to go, Daddy," I said. "It's late."

"Now, just wait a second sonny," he said. "Just wait a second. I want to get a rise out of this chap."

"Goodbye, Daddy," I said, and I went down the stairs and got my train, and that was the last time I saw my father.

CHAPTER

4 Lesson Plan 2

Three Kinds of Questions

1. **Focus:** *Overview*: Review several individual questions written on "Reunion" (previous assignment) by asking someone to answer each question orally. Does the answer turn us into the story? If yes, it is factual OR interpretation. If we cannot disagree about the answer because it is given, it is factual ("What does it say?"). If we can disagree about the answer answer, it is interpretation ("What does it mean?"). If the answer *takes us outside the story*, ("Is it true?"), it is evaluation.
2. **Objective:** To identify and write questions of fact, interpretation and evaluation.
3. **Purpose:**
   - To increase our mutual understanding (comprehension) and, as a result, our enjoyment of the reading.
   - To develop the habit of independent and critical thinking.
4. **Input:** Explain and illustrate the three kinds of questions (see handout). Have students write in on their handout the examples displayed on the projector.
5. **Modeling, checking, and guided practice:** Have students complete (in pairs or individually) Exercise 1 on Three Kinds of Questions. Review as a class the type of each question to check for understanding. To reinforce student understanding of the three kinds of questions, have them compose orally for review two or three sequences of related questions.
6. **Closure:** Have students *combine and revise* (in pairs) the questions that they wrote individually on "Reunion." Hand in one sheet with two names of their ten best questions. Grade and return at the next class.

Three Kinds of Questions

"What does it say? What does it mean? Is it true?"

Mortimer Adler

When did you first realize the importance of the kinds of questions that you ask your students? Was it when you were puzzled about why some questions fell flat while others provoked immediate response? Was it when you suddenly realized your questions were not clear? Was it when you knew that you placed too much emphasis on factual or memory questions? Was it when you got into "bull sessions" as a consequence of emphasizing evaluative questions? Whatever the moment of insight, few teachers would deny the importance of writing and asking good questions. On the other hand, my experience has been that while teachers recognize that questioning is an art, they also too often are at a loss not only about how to write good discussion (interpretive) questions but also about how to sustain them in discussion.

Mortimer Adler, the eminent American philosopher and education reform leader, first formulated the three kinds of questions in 1948 in *A Guide for Leaders of Great Books Discussion Groups.* He asked: "(1) What does the author say? (2) What does he mean? (3) Is it true; does it have relevance to you here today? *Fact, Interpretation, Evaluation*—these are the three levels of questions" (8). In 1956, Benjamin Bloom edited a *Taxonomy of Educational Objectives: Cognitive Domain*, which classified eight educational objectives that used examples of questions for each kind of thinking: knowledge (memory), comprehension, translation, interpretation, application, analysis, synthesis, and evaluation. Ten years later, Norris Sanders popularized Bloom's taxonomy for social studies teachers with useful illustrations in his *Classroom Questions: What Kinds?*

But do teachers need eight kinds of questions? Not in my experience. Too often have I been in workshops where teachers get into vigorous and pointless arguments about identifying types of questions. Bloom's and Sanders' work has its value for developing standardized tests, but for classroom discussion, their added distinctions are not needed since it becomes evident in discussion that translation, application, analysis and synthesis can be put under the umbrella of interpretation. Knowledge or memory questions are factual and evaluation is about personal values and/or experience. In other words, classroom teachers do well enough, as do most of my colleagues, to recognize the vital difference between *the purpose* of each type of question: to check for recall (factual). To check for understanding (interpretation). Or to check for personal relevance and application (evaluation). Here is how I explain and illustrate the three kinds of questions for my students.

Three Kinds of Questions

1. **Factual:** A factual question has but one correct answer. It asks the reader to recall something that the author said or to read a passage from the text where an answer can be found. Its answer depends more on memory than thinking.

   For example: *How does Charlie's father insult the first waiter?*

   Note: Sometimes a factual question does require some thinking to answer correctly but it is still factual because only one answer is possible based on a careful reading of the text.

   For example: *Does Charlie's father like to insult "domestics"?*

2. **Interpretation:** An interpretive question has more than one correct answer because a difference of opinion about meaning is possible. It asks the reader to explain *what the author means by what is said.* The answer depends more on thinking than on memory or recall.

   For example: *Why does Cheever have Charlie's father insult several people during the visit with his son?*

3. **Evaluation:** An evaluative question asks one to think about his or her own values **or** experiences. Such questions sometimes ask readers to consider how they would act in a situation similar to one a character in the story finds himself/herself in if they have had a similar experience.

   For example (common experience): *Have you ever insulted a waiter or a clerk?*
   Or, for example (values): *Are waiters as important as doctors or lawyers?*

   Note: The **test** for distinguishing between the three types of questions is to begin answering the question itself for a half minute. If you begin talking about the text, the question is factual or interpretive. If it has but one answer, it is factual; if it can be answered in more than one way, *if you have to explain your answer,* it is interpretive. If you begin to talk about your own experiences or values, if you go outside the text, it is evaluation.

Three Kinds of Questions

"REUNION" EXERCISE 1

Directions: First, answer each question briefly on your own paper. Second, in the left margin identify the type of each question: print FACT for factual, INT for interpretation, and EVAL for evaluation.

1. Why does Charlie make no value judgments about his father's conduct in the several restaurants they visit?

2. Does Cheever want us to feel sorry for Charlie because his father is so pathetic or to admire the restraint of a son who has discovered that his father is a buffoon?

3. Even before his father arrives for their visit, is Charlie aware of his Father's defects?

4. To what extent is a child stamped with the personality of his parents or of his early environment?

5. Was Charlie's meeting with his father in Grand Central Station, NY the last time that he saw him?

6. Why do Charlie and his father keep moving from one restaurant to another?

7. Why is the title of the story "Reunion" rather than "A Reunion" or "The Reunion"?

8. Why does Charlie's father speak in several foreign languages?

9. Why does Cheever conclude his story by echoing the first sentence?

10. Do you believe that the story could have been concluded in a better way?

CHAPTER

5 Lesson Plan 3

Qualities of Good Discussion Questions

1. **Focus:**	Why do some questions elicit immediate response and even controversy while others fall flat or meet with apathy or indifference? (Brief discussion or journal topic.)
2. **Objective:**	To illustrate, identify, and write good discussion questions that are clear, specific, interpretive, answerable, and, most importantly are *real questions*, that questions that have the vital element of doubt about the answer.
3. **Purpose:**	○ To increase our mutual understanding (comprehension) and, as a result, our enjoyment of the reading. ○ To develop thc habit of independent and critical thinking.
4. **Input:**	Review Six Qualities of Good Discussion Questions.
5. **Modeling, checking, and guided practice:**	Have students complete (in pairs or individually) on Qualities of Good Questions. Review as a class what is good about or lacking in each question. A good question will elicit at least two different, plausible answers based on the text.
6. **Closure:**	Review examples of good student questions that have been revised (previous assignment). Discuss briefly each question to elicit at least two different plausible answers. Ask for supporting textual evidence for each answer.

Qualities of Good Discussion Questions

"What are you asking me, Mr. M—?"

As a teacher or student, you must have been puzzled at times about why some questions in class fall flat while others evoke immediate response. While student inattention and unwillingness to think may explain some of the lack of response, we must also look at the quality of the questions that we ask. Some questions are so general or unclear that no one could hope for a reasonable response. In short, those questions that evoke next to no response may lack one of the important qualities of good prepared discussion questions while those that generate ideas for discussion may have all the necessary qualities. Here is how I explain and illustrate the six characteristics of good discussion questions:

A Checklist of the Qualities of Good Discussion Questions

1. **Clear:** A clear question says what it means so that no one has to guess what the questioner has in mind. A question that is not clear is like asking someone to find something but not telling him/her what to look for. If the question has to be explained or if it cannot be rephrased, it is not clear. In short, the effort in discussion should be expended on trying to solve the problem, not in trying to figure out the question!
2. **Interpretive:** Since the primary aim of engaged inquiry is to increase your own and the group's understanding of the reading, center on questions of interpretation. Factual questions do not generate discussion since they have but one correct answer and when questions of evaluation become the focus of discussion, it readily becomes a bull session.
3. **Specific:** A good discussion question must be specific, that is, tailor-made so that it could be asked only of one reading and not of another. This is not a matter of being picky or merely naming a character but a matter of being precise—that is, of pinpointing a problem about meaning.
4. **Doubt:** There must be doubt in the mind of the person who formulated the question for it to function in discussion. Without the vital element of doubt about the answer to the question, there can be no increase in understanding or insight. A question has the element of doubt **either** when the questioner can think of no answer at all **or**, as is the case more commonly, when the questioner can think of more than one answer but

none seem fully satisfactory. In this case, doubt is a matter of degree; it is not complete.

5. **Answerable** on the basis of the text alone. Avoid questions that go outside the text and ask a reader to offer a speculative answer, that is, one that cannot be supported one way or another from the text itself. Such questions are unsatisfactory because there is no way to judge which answers are plausible.
6. **Care or concern:** The co-leaders must ask questions that interest them, not what they think might interest someone else. This personal quality adds an intensity to discussion.

Qualities of Good Discussion Questions

"REUNION" EXERCISE 2

Directions: At the left of each question, on your own paper, mark GOOD if it has the qualities of a good discussion question. If the question lacks one of the needed qualities, mark it:

- NC if the question is NOT CLEAR.
- NS if the question is NOT SPECIFIC and could be asked of any story.
- LD for LACKS DOUBT because it cannot be answered in more than one way.
- NI for NOT INTERPRETIVE because it is factual or evaluative.
- NA if it is NOT ANSWERABLE on basis of the text alone.

1. What was Cheever's purpose in writing this story?

2. Will Charlie ever see his father again?

3. Why does Charlie refer to his father's limitations even before their meeting?

4. Does Charlie's father enjoy badgering those he calls "domestics"?

5. Why did Charlie's father get angry when he ordered a Bibson Geefeater?

6. What is Charlie's father sorry about just before his son boards the train?

7. Did Cheever intend to portray the conduct of Charlie's father as rude?

8. Have you ever been embarrassed by your father's conduct in public?

9. The language, which is repetitious–does it show Charlie's dad's sarcasm and superiority?

10. Why does Charlie's father act like that?

11. What is ironic about Charlie's description of his father as "mature"?

12. Why hadn't Charlie seen his father for three years?

13. Where did the story really take place?

14. Based on this meeting, does Cheever want us to conclude that Charlie has accepted or rejected the father that he met for lunch?

15. What is the relationship between Charlie and his father?

CHAPTER

6 Lesson Plan 4

Basic Interpretive Questions

1. **Focus:**	Why do some interpretive questions generate so much more discussion than others? (Brief discussion or journal topic.)
2. **Objective:**	To illustrate and to learn how to write clusters of related interpretive questions (basic questions).
3. **Purpose:**	◦ To increase our mutual understanding (comprehension) and, as a result, our enjoyment of the reading. ◦ To develop the habit of independent and critical thinking.
4. **Input:**	Review the handout on the four qualities of basic questions and how to develop them. Illustrate the qualities of a basic interpretive question with the basic question on "The Road Not Taken." (According to Frost, has the narrator's choice of the less traveled road been for better or worse?) Emphasize that the question is a real issue because sufficient evidence supports either side. In short, either answer could be correct depending on each individual's interpretations of the poem.
5. **Modeling, checking, and guided practice:**	Have students complete (in pairs or individually) **Exercise 3** on basic questions. Review individual answers as a class. As needed, discuss disagreements.
6. **Closure:**	Conduct a demonstration discussion of the basic question on "Reunion." (Based on this meeting, does Cheever want us to conclude that Charlie has accepted or rejected his father as the kind of person he has discovered him to be?) Ten minutes before the end of discussion, ask your

students to write their individual resolutions to the basic question in a paragraph. Answers must be supported with evidence from the story.

Basic Interpretive Questions

After you have conducted several discussions, you will observe sooner or later that some interpretive questions require you to look at many lines and passages of a reading and give rise to a number of other related questions about the author's meaning. Those interpretive questions that consistently lead to sustained discussion (about thirty minutes per question) are *basic questions.*

Consider the difference between these two questions on John Cheever's story "Reunion." (1) When Charlie first meets his father, why does he think of his mother sniffing a rose? and (2) Does Cheever want us to conclude that Charlie has accepted or rejected his father as the person he met for lunch? Both questions are interpretive, but the first is fairly easy to resolve. You could probably find some satisfactory answer just by rereading the first paragraph of the story.

> *Charlie may recall his mother sniffing a rose in contrast to his father's male rankness. He may also remember he has not seen his father in three years.*

In contrast, to answer satisfactorily the second question, you would likely have to explore a number of related questions.

> For example: *Why does Cheever begin and end his story by telling us that this was the last time Charlie saw his father? Early in the story, why is Charlie so concerned about growing up to be like his father? Why does Charlie make no value judgments about his father's rude conduct? Why is the title of the story "Reunion" rather than, "A Reunion," or "The Reunion"?* and so on.

These additional questions, and others you might think of that have something to do with whether Charlie has accepted or rejected his father, would obviously take a great deal more time to answer than would the first question about why Charlie's father tells him that he's sorry. In short, the second question is **basic** because it deals with a major issue or problem in the story that requires you to interpret a great deal of the story before you could answer it satisfactorily.

Centering discussion on basic questions has two advantages. First, they add a new dimension to thinking about interpretive questions because they require you to organize more facts and ideas to deepen your understanding of the story. Second, basic questions yield a more comprehensive and integrated explanation of the author's meaning than you would have discussing interpretive questions that cover an assortment of unrelated topics or problems about meaning.

But how do you find and write basic questions for discussion? There are two methods: (1) begin by choosing any interpretive question that you care about and then try to write a number of questions that are related to it and help explore its implications; and (2) after you have written at least twenty interpretive questions on the reading, look for a pattern or common topic that some of them seem to be related to. Whether you write a basic question deductively—from the general to the specific (1)—or inductively—from the specific to the general (2)—the goal is to formulate a **cluster** of related questions.

Hence, a basic question is *a cluster of at least eight related interpretive questions each one of which is a distinct problem for discussion.* In short, each sub-question or follow-up question is an aspect or a piece of a comprehensive answer to the basic question. Like all interpretive questions these follow-up questions should have the qualities of any good discussion question.

In short, the basic question is the **problem**, the focus of discussion; the cluster is the co-leaders' **plan** to solve it, and the reading selection is the **source** of information needed to resolve it. The following models, one from the Frost poem and the other from the Cheever short story, illustrate the characteristics of a good basic question.

"The Road Not Taken"

According to Frost, has the narrator's choice of the less traveled road been for better or worse?

If it has been for the better, then:

1. Why is the title of the poem about the road *not* taken?
2. Why does the narrator wish that he could have taken both roads? (line 2)
3. Why does the narrator say the road less traveled had "perhaps" the better claim? (7)
4. Why is there an exclamation point at the end of line 13?
5. Why does the narrator say that he will be telling us about his choice of the less traveled road with a sigh? (16)
6. Does the last line of the poem refer to a good or bad difference?

If it has been for the worse, then:

7. Does the title of the poem refer to the road less traveled or to the road that most people would have taken?
8. Why does the narrator admit, in retrospect, both roads were really about the same? (10)
9. Why does the narrator say he kept the choice of the first road for another day? (13)
10. Why does the narrator say he will be telling about his choice "ages and ages hence"?
11. Why is there a dash after "I" in line 18?
12. Is the narrator trying to convince himself that he has made the better choice in taking the road less traveled?

"Reunion"

Based on this meeting, does Cheever want us to conclude that Charlie has accepted or rejected his father as the person that he met for lunch?

If he has accepted him, then:

1. Why does *Cheever* begin and end his story by telling us that this was the last time Charlie saw his father?
2. Why does *Charlie* end his story of his reunion with his father by telling us that this was the last time that he saw him?
3. Early in the story, why is Charlie so concerned about being like his father?
4. Even before going to several restaurants, why does Charlie refer to the limitations of his father?
5. What limitations does Charlie accept in his father by the end of the story?

If he has rejected him, then:

6. Why does Charlie make no value judgments about his father's rude conduct during their encounter?
7. Why is the title of the story "Reunion" rather than "A Reunion" or "The Reunion"?
8. Why did Charlie want a photographer to record his meeting with his father at the train station?

9. Does Cheever want us to think it was funny or sad when Charlie's father ordered "Bibson Geefeaters"?
10. When Charlie reminded his father that he has to catch a train, why does his father tell him that he was "terribly sorry"?

The following exercise (Exercise 3) will help you and your students test their understanding of the four characteristics of a good basic question: (1) all questions in the cluster are interpretive; (2) all are related to the problem; (3) none are repetitious but each is a distinct problem; and (4) the cluster has at least eight questions.

Good Basic Questions

"REUNION" EXERCISE 3

Directions: On your own paper, put an X next to any question in the cluster of this basic question which lacks any of the six qualities of a good discussion question. Put NR if the question is not related; or put R if the question is repetitious. Put GOOD next to any follow-up question that is interpretive, related, and another part of the basic question.

Based on this meeting, does Cheever want us to conclude that Charlie has accepted or rejected his father as the person that he has discovered him to be?

1. When Charlie says he has to catch a train, why does his father say he is "awfully sorry"?

2. Why is Charlie's father rude to so many people?

3. Why were Charlie's parents divorced?

4. Was Charlie looking forward to seeing his father at the train station?

5. Why does Charlie make no value judgments about his father's rude behavior?

6. What is the significance of the title of the story?

7. Why does Cheever end his story by echoing the opening sentence?

8. Why does Charlie's father have his secretary set up the meeting with his son?

9. Why does Charlie meet his father in a train station?

10. Early in the story, why is Charlie concerned about becoming like his father?

11. Why do Charlie and his father go to several different restaurants?

12. Why don't Charlie and his father talk about anything personal or important?

13. Why does Charlie refer to the limitations of his father that could affect him?

14. According to the author, is it funny or sad when the father orders "Bibson Geefeaters"?

15. Why doesn't Charlie comment on his father's rudeness?

16. Why does Charlie end his story by saying it was the last time he saw his father?

17. Why does Charlie want a photograph of this reunion with his father?

18. What evidence is there that Charlie accepted or rejected his father as he is?

19. Has one of your parents embarrassed you in public because of his/her behavior?

20. What are the approximate ages of Charlie and his father?

Three Levels of Perception: On Writing Questions That Have Real Doubt

To avoid writing and asking questions that lack real doubt in the minds of the co-leaders, they must begin at their deepest level of perception or understanding of the text. To do so, they must sometimes write a question based on an assumption or even a hypothesis (a guess at meaning). In short, not all questions should be neutral or void of any previous understandings or interpretations. The following questions illustrate the three levels of doubt or degrees or perception.

1. **Neutral:** The leaders question the significance of a fact, a detail, an event, the choice of vocabulary, a sentence, or a phrase. (What is the meaning of X?)

   Examples:

   Why is the title of Frost's poem about the road not *taken?*
   Why does Charlie say nothing about his father's rude behavior?

2. **Assumption**: The leaders' question is based on a prior interpretation; the question is not neutral but based on a previous understanding. (Because X seems to be true, how do we explain Y?)

   Examples:

   Why could Frost's title also refer to the road less traveled?
   Why does Charlie make no value judgments about his father's rude conduct?

3. **Hypothesis:** The leaders' question is a guess at meaning or an attempt to explain something in light of something else. The level of doubt here is in the *maybe*—what *may* be true. (Does X explain Y?)

   Examples:

   Is the title about the road not taken because it refers to the road that most other people would have taken?
   Does Charlie make no value judgments about his father's rude behavior to avoid a confrontation?

Note: It is important to distinguish questions based on assumptions or hypotheses from leading questions. Leading questions by definition lack doubt and indicate or hint at the answer expected. Leading questions always have telltale words or phrases in them: really, honestly, truly, or a negative. Leading questions never have a place in Socratic discussion.

CHAPTER

7 Lesson Plan 5

Spontaneous Follow-up Questions

1. **Focus:**	What is the difference between a prepared and a spontaneous follow-up question? For example? Note: a prepared follow-up (cluster questions for a basic question) is always interpretive while spontaneous follow-ups can be factual, interpretive, or even evaluative in special situations (e.g., lack of response).
2. **Objective:**	To become a good co-leader who listens actively to the answers of participants and asks appropriate follow-up questions.
3. **Purpose:**	To illustrate the purpose and kinds of good spontaneous follow-up questions and to practice and to develop the skills needed to be a good co-leader of discussion.
4. **Input:**	Explain the purpose and use of different kinds of spontaneous follow-up questions by reviewing the one-page handout on the Guidelines.
5. **Modeling, checking, and guided practice:**	Have students complete (in pairs or individually) **Exercise 4** on follow-up questions. Review individual answers as a class. Emphasize that there is no such thing as a perfect follow-up to a response; any follow-up is satisfactory as long as it gets a participant (or another participant) to reflect on and develop the answer. An unsatisfactory follow-up ignores the answer and goes on to another idea.
6. **Closure:**	Review the summary sheet on how to handle common problems in discussion: Scenarios of Discussion Review.

Spontaneous Follow-up Questions

> "The role of the teacher is to uncover the question that the answer hides."
>
> J. Baldwin

Why do some discussions fail even when you know the group has read carefully and that you began with a good interpretive question? Without doubt, such discussions so often fall flat, go nowhere, become chaotic, or degenerate into bull sessions because the leader(s) do not listen to what they hear. As a result, they miss opportunity after opportunity to follow-up on the ideas of the participants. A further consequence is that because answers are not developed, no one has any sense of satisfaction or gain in understanding.

The chief role of the co-leaders in discussion is to direct traffic, that is, to direct and control the flow of ideas among the participants. Co-leaders fulfill this role by introducing **prepared** questions to initiate discussion, basic or otherwise, **and** by asking **spontaneous** follow-up questions **to develop** and **to connect** ideas that help solve the problem(s) under discussion. By following these guidelines, you will lead an effective discussion that increases your own and the group's understanding of the reading. As a result, you will also increase your mutual enjoyment of the reading, the ultimate goal of the Socratic Seminar.

1. If you remember that there is no such thing as a perfect or ideal follow-up question, you will not make your role more difficult by trying to second-guess yourself. In other words, there several distinct kinds of follow-up questions that could be asked at any given moment of discussion. *The kind of follow-up question asked in a specific situation depends on the leader's purpose.*

   Is it (a) **to clarify**? Example: "What did you mean when you said ____?" or "Could you explain more of what you mean by ____?"

   Is it (b) **to substantiate**? Example: "Upon what in the reading are you basing your answer?" or "How do you know? What in the reading gave you that impression?"

   Is it (c) **to get more opinion**? Example: "Maria, do you agree with John's idea that ____? If so, could you explain? If not, why do you disagree?

   Is it (d) **to test for consistency**? Example: "Sarah, if what you say is correct, then how do you explain ____?"

   Is it (e) **to relate** a response to the prepared question? Example: "Brian, how does what you have said help answer our question about ____?"

Is it (f) **to draw out the implications** of a response? Example: "Ryan, are you saying ____?" or "By X do you mean Y?"

Or finally, is it (g) **to resolve** the prepared question? Example: "John, at this time what is your best answer to our question about ____? Or, "Laura, what different answers have you heard so far to our basic question?"

2. Many more ideas are heard in discussion than can ever be pursued or developed. It is unrealistic, pointless, and even impossible to try to keep track of *everything* that is said in discussion. (It simply cannot be done unless you record your discussions. I can recommend no better way to improve your leadership skills and those of your students than to record a discussion and then to critique it later.)
3. As a result, co-leaders must make conscious **choices** about what they want to (a) pursue, (b) table, or (c) ignore in any given response or series of responses. In short, the leaders' responsibility is to make choices which guide or direct the discussion—that is, which keep the responses of the participants relevant to the prepared question(s) presently on the floor.
4. How often must a leader make a choice about what to pursue, to table, or to ignore? Experience shows that the co-leaders must ask an **average** of one follow-up question **for every two or three responses**. Unless the leaders maintain this average by asking enough follow-up questions, discussion soon reverts to a series of random, unrelated, off-the-cuff comments characteristic of mundane conversation.
5. Following these guidelines leads to two important conclusions. First, good discussion **does not** consist in asking the "right" or perfect follow-up question at the "right" time since there is no such thing **but rather** in the effectiveness of the overall **pattern** of the follow-up questions asked. Second, the co-leaders' role in discussion is **to develop** and **to connect** the ideas of the participants to the prepared questions under consideration. In this way, resolution is achieved, new insights discovered, and enjoyment increased.

The following practice exercise on follow-up questions on the "Reunion" will help you to understand and illustrate for your students the kinds and purposes of good follow-up questions. The purpose of this exercise is to help you and your students to think about how they (as co-leaders) would deal with common situations that often come up in discussion. For example, what follow-up question could a leader ask when: (1) there is no response at all; (2) the response ignores the question; (3) the response has multiple ideas; (4) the response is wrong; (5) the participant does not understand the question; (6) the response is incoherent (not clear); or when the participant tries to dismiss the question because he/she doesn't want to think about it? See Scenarios of Discussion Review (pages 52–53) for suggestions.

Spontaneous Follow-up Questions

"REUNION" EXERCISE 4

Directions: Each group below consists of a question and a response during discussion. After each response, write in what you consider to be a good follow-up question. Remember the purpose of any follow-up question (which can be factual, interpretive, or even evaluative) is to get the participant **to reflect** on his or her answer so that the co-leaders help him or her to **develop it.**

1.

Leader: Why doesn't Charlie seem to object to his father's rudeness?

John: I think he does object inside. I believe he really wanted to tell his father that he was acting like a jerk.

Follow-up question:

2.

Leader: Why does Cheever begin and end the story by telling us that this was the last time Charlie saw his father?

Maria: Maybe he means that Charlie never saw his father again.

Rachael: It could also mean that during this visit Charlie discovered the truth about his father.

Follow-up question:

3.

Leader: Early in the story, why is Charlie concerned about being like his father?

Katie: He may already be somewhat aware that his father has problems. He does refer to his "limitations."

Follow-up question:

4.

Leader:	Why is the title of the story "Reunion" rather than "A Reunion" or "The Reunion"?
Tony:	I don't have a clue. Call on somebody else.
Mary:	Who cares?!

Follow-up question:

5.

Leader:	Does Cheever want us to think it is funny or sad when Charlie's father orders "Bibson Geefeaters"?
Melissa:	Neither. I think Cheever thinks the father is pathetic.

Follow-up question:

6.

Leader:	At the end of the story, what does his father mean when he told Charlie that he was "terribly sorry"?
Richard:	I think he means that he wasn't able to buy his son a newspaper?

Follow-up question:

7.

Leader:	During their visit why doesn't Charlie's father speak with his son about anything personal or important in their lives?
Maria:	I wonder why Charlie's parents got a divorce.
Roger:	I think Charlie was kinda cool.

Follow-up question:

8.

Leader:	Why does Cheever have Charlie's father insult the newspaper man as his son leaves to get on the train?
Buster:	To leave no doubt in the reader's mind that Charlie's father is a total jerk.
Roger:	The guy just can't help himself.
Rita:	He says he wants to get a rise out of him.

Follow-up question:

Scenarios of Discussion Review: How to Handle Common Problems

1. **No response at all** (which is not uncommon in early discussions). **Three solutions:** (a) *repeat* the question to give the participant time to think; (b) *rephrase* the question to give the student time to think; (c) ask a related *factual* question; (d) ask a related *interpretive* question; (e) ask a related question of *evaluation*; or (f) as a last resort, call on another student.
2. **Answer is unsupported** (an opinion) or an evaluation based on experience or personal values. **Three solutions**: (a) ask for textual evidence; (b) ask a follow-up question on that evidence; or (c) ask another student to agree or disagree.
3. **When a student does not understand the question:** rephrase it or ask another student to explain it.
4. **When the response ignores the question** (not uncommon in early discussions when students may have trouble focusing): repeat the question.
5. **When the answer is not clear** (not uncommon in early discussions for students who are not accustomed to explaining their ideas in a group). Without intimidation, the leader must get clarification. For example, "Maria, could you explain more of what you mean by ____?"
6. **A wrong answer** (an interpretation which cannot be supported by evidence or which is contradicted by other evidence.) **Three solutions:** (a) ask for supporting textual evidence that ____; (b) ask someone else if they agree (if they agree, ask for evidence); (c) ask a follow-up question for consistency—for example: "If that is so, how do you explain"? (Note: The leader must not try "to help" the students by telling them that they are wrong. To do so makes them wonder when they will be corrected next and, as a result, dampens future responses, or, just as bad, the leader becomes the authority when the only authority in discussion is the text. In short, participants must learn to judge for themselves, as in life, which answers are right or wrong, satisfactory, good, better, or best.)
7. **Multiple responses. Three solutions:** (a) follow-up on one of them but do not ignore them all by merely calling on another student; pursue whatever seems the most interesting or relevant to you; (b) table, on your seating chart, one or two ideas that you do not immediately pursue but come back to them later; (c) ask another student which response they agree with. The leader's role is to develop and connect answers to the basic question, not merely to invite students to speak by calling on them by name.

8. **Assumption in the prepared question is challenged** (more common when students become more independent thinkers). **Three solutions:** (a) ask for supporting evidence from the text; (b) get another opinion; or (c) ask a follow-up question about the evidence from the text for your assumption.

CHAPTER

8 Lesson Plan 6

Preparing Students For Discussion

1. **Focus:** What questions do you have at this moment about co-leading a discussion? Brief discussion.
2. **Objective:** To answer your questions about co-leading. To dispel student doubts about being good co-leaders. To develop their confidence as co-leaders.
3. **Purpose:** To prepare you to be effective co-leaders so that everyone will increase their understanding and enjoyment of the readings.
4. **Input:**
   - Review the Criteria for Choosing Texts for Socratic Discussion.
   - Review Guidelines for co-leading.
   - Review Use of Seating Chart.
   - Review Guidelines for Preparing Questions.
   - Review Guidelines for Spontaneous Questions.
   - Review Criteria for Critique of Discussion.
5. **Modeling:** With a teacher or student co-leader, conduct a twenty-minute demonstration discussion of a poem. Suggestion: W. H. Auden, "The Unknown Citizen."
6. **Checking:** Review the demonstration discussion by having students raise questions about how the ten criteria from the critique sheet were or were not applied.
7. **Guided practice:** Review the demonstration discussion by having students suggest ways that the discussion could have been improved.
8. **Closure:** Do you still have any questions about co-leading that were not answered satisfactorily?

What is a Socratic Seminar?

> "The role of the teacher is to uncover the question that the answer hides."
>
> James Baldwin

The Seminar is a series of extended discussions focused on a single topic, theme(s) or series of readings that may or may not be related. The seminar is conducted by a teacher or a teacher-team, or co-led by students who have been trained in the Socratic method of learning (Lessons 1–6). Its usual length is a full class period of sixty or ninety minutes, three to five days a week.

Before students begin to co-lead discussions, an entire period should be given to review and explanation of these fundamentals: The Criteria for Choosing Texts for Socratic Discussion (pages 73–75) to be sure that co-leaders understand the purpose of each rule—particularly the rule about asking only questions.

The Guidelines for Co-leading Socratic Discussion (page 57) must also be reviewed to ensure that students clearly understand their role and the purpose of discussion. Before discussion, student co-leaders must meet to refine and agree upon the questions that they plan to use in their discussion of the day's assigned reading. See Guidelines for Pre-discussion (page 60).

An important part of the Guidelines for Discussion that must also be reviewed in preparation of Lesson 6 is the Use and Importance of the Seating Chart.

Finally, students must understand that discussion will be evaluated in three ways: (1) the teacher's completion of the Criteria for Critique of Discussion (page 59) during the meeting; (2) an oral and/or written resolution of the basic question(s) at the end of the discussion; and/or (3) a formal follow-up essay (due a few days later) on one of the basic questions or commentaries on four of ten key quotations from the text, that explain its context (who and when) and theme (overall meaning).

Since the Seminars often make use of one or more available film versions, this sequence is recommended:

1. On day one, begin with a review of the cast of characters of the poem, short story, novel, or play and then follow up with a few opening scenes of the film to associate the main characters with a face in the minds of the student audience.
2. Before viewing each of the following scenes of the story, begin with a plot-check quiz of the first reading. After viewing the video of each act, students do a second reading and then write interpretive questions in pairs, as co-leaders. See Guidelines for Writing About Film (page 55).

3. The Seminar itself is always a full-period discussion of two to four basic interpretive questions which may take more than one day depending on the time allowed (60, 90, or 120 minutes). In the beginning, the teacher(s) conduct(s) *demonstration discussions* to model what will be expected of the students when they co-lead. In the following seminar discussions, to ensure that time is not wasted on questions that are not basic, clear, and specific, the teacher assigns each pair of co-leaders one of the approved basic questions from the lesson plan and then has them write eight to ten prepared follow-up questions directly related to the problem of interpretation. Each prepared follow-up question must be documented with a specific reference (act, scene, and line in a play, page reference in short stories or novels, and line in a poem) to allow the group, during discussion, to get into textual analysis. At the end of discussion, students hand in their prepared follow-up questions (one paper with two names) for a teacher grade or revision.

Resolution and Evaluation

4. The seminar concludes in two ways:
   (a) With an **oral resolution** after about twenty to thirty minutes of discussion on each of four basic questions (about one to two hours). The co-leaders:
      - repeat the basic interpretive question
      - call on members to repeat the answers they remember hearing
      - check if anyone in the group has an answer* that has not yet been repeated, or discussed in the first place
      - have members of the group compose their final answer (orally or in writing)
      - ask the members to identify memorable ideas heard during discussion that led them to develop their thinking, change their mind, or revise their initial answer to form their final conclusion.

   (b) With a **written resolution**—an essay exam which is either half-page commentaries on four of ten key quotations of the novel, short story, poem, or play, **or** a resolution in class to one of the basic questions previously discussed.

Note: At the beginning of discussion the co-leaders state the basic question and gives the group at least five minutes to write down an initial answer *to give them time to think*. As elementary as this practice should be to any teacher, without giving the group time to gather their thoughts, discussion too often begins with "I don't know", "Because that's the way the author wrote it", "To make money," and other flippant nonsense that sets the wrong tone. The second reason for having the group write down an initial answer enables them to recall it and bring it up during the resolution activity.

Guidelines for Discussion and Writing about Film

Exercise 1: Make notations on what is important, what you do not understand, what you particularly liked (emotionally) and/or disliked, and on what is related (one part of the original story to another), making connections).

Exercise 2: Make notations on what has been *added, omitted, and retained* from the original story.

Exercise 3: List ten *important differences* between the movie and the short story, play or the novel.

Exercise 4: List ten *important similarities* between the movie and the short story, play, or the novel.

Guidelines for Exercises 3 and 4

1. Each difference or similarity between the movie and the text (short story, play, or novel) must be written *as a complete sentence*.
2. In each sentence, refer to *both* the movie and the story.
3. *No two sentences may begin the same way*; the sentence openings must be varied.
4. Number each difference or similarity and skip a line between each sentence.
5. Circle the numbers of what you regard as the three most important differences or similarities. *Rank in order of importance.*
6. Use ink (no pencil, ever), write on standard paper (no spiral, ever), and put the proper heading on the upper right-hand corner.
7. Avoid wordiness; try to be as concise as possible. Use active voice.

Glue Words for "differences"

but, however, unlike, in contrast, although, as if, on the other hand, still, nevertheless, yet, rather than, despite, in spite of, instead of, contrary to

Glue Words for "similarities"

similarly, in like manner, just as, in the same way, like, as, equally, similar to

Glue Words for "ranking"

first, second, finally, more importantly, most importantly, another, furthermore, moreover, in addition, again, of primary importance, the least, the greatest

Models

1. Unlike the emphatic conclusion of Faulkner's "Barn Burning" ("He did not look back"), in the film version, Sarty looks back as he sees his family moving on to another farm.
2. Like the novel, the film version of *The Great Gatsby* portrays Nick Carraway as attracted to and yet repelled by Gatsby's character and values.

Seminar

GUIDELINES FOR CO-LEADING

When you co-lead a fifteen minute discussion of an assigned reading, please follow these **guidelines** to insure that discussion is truly shared inquiry.

1. Sit next to your co-leader and make out a **seating chart** from your position in the group.
2. Have the group **write down** your prepared question, basic or otherwise, on a piece of paper and give them two or three minutes to jot down a brief initial response. Participants need time to think and to note ideas that they may wish to bring up later in discussion.
3. Observe the **Criteria for Choosing Texts for Socratic Discussion.** Remember it is vital that you and your co-leader limit yourselves to asking only questions. You must avoid statements of any kind. Unless you do so, the group will begin looking to you for approval or even disapproval and drift away from thinking for themselves. Indeed, whenever a leader begins making statements, however well-intentioned, the discussion soon becomes a disguised lecture or it may even revert to an argument.
4. Begin the discussion by calling on someone **by name** to give his or her answer. You must address all questions by name to control the flow of discussion. Although participants may speak up freely without being called upon, you must recognize them by name to direct the group's attention.
5. Make every effort to **call on everyone** in your group at least once or twice. Put a mark next to the name on your seating chart every time that you call on someone to respond. Try to avoid the extremes of calling on the same few participants too often or of not calling on someone at all.
6. **For every two or three responses**, you and your co-leader should be asking a spontaneous follow-up question to develop the ideas given and to keep the group's thinking focused on your prepared question.
7. At the end of fifteen minutes (minimum) or thirty minutes (maximum), ask your group to recall briefly the different answers that have been given to your prepared question. Note these answers briefly on your seating chart and hand in at the end of class.
8. The answers to your prepared question noted on your seating chart are the degree to which you have increased your own and the group's understanding of the reading. This is **resolution**, which is an individual matter (not group consensus or truth by vote).

Importance and Use of the Seating Chart

At the beginning of each discussion, it is important that co-leaders make a seating chart from their position in the group that is seated in a circle. The seating chart has three important functions:

1. **It locates each participant and enables the co-leaders to call on each one by name. Preface all questions by name.**
   - This helps you to control the discussion.
   - If all have responsibility for a question, usually, none do.
   - It gives the person called on a few seconds to think of an answer. In theory, everyone should be prepared to speak all the time, but in practice, it seldom happens.
   - It enables you to call on those less likely to speak up on their own. Throwing a question out to everyone usually results in the verbally aggressive taking over the discussion.
2. **It enables the co-leaders to involve all participants more or less equally.**
   - During a twenty to thirty minute segment of discussion, the co-leaders should try to call on everyone at least once, ideally twice.
   - The co-leaders should ask an average of one follow-up question for every two or three responses.
3. **It enables the co-leaders to exercise their three options: to ignore, to table, or to pursue responses.**
   - Next to the names of the participants, the co-leaders can jot down those ideas they pursue immediately and table those for later discussion.
   - Because it is impossible to follow-up on every idea in discussion, co-leaders must make a conscious choices about what they pursue immediately, table for later, or ignore. Unless they do so, they will begin to tag end—to pick up on the last remark of the last participant. When this happens, discussion becomes mundane conversation.

Seminar

CRITERIA FOR CRITIQUE OF A DISCUSSION

Co-leaders: ______________________________ and ______________________________
English ____
Reading ____ Date ______________
Question: ____
____
____

Code: Good (10) Pretty good (5) Needs improvement (0)

1. Did the leaders initiate discussion by beginning with a **good interpretive question?**	10	5	0
2. Did the leaders call on **all** participants at least once?	10	5	0
3. Did the leaders **average** one follow-up question for every two or three responses?	10	5	0
4. Did the leaders **avoid making statements** or asking leading questions?	10	5	0
5. Did the leaders seek **clarification** as well as **substantiation** when necessary?	10	5	0
6. Did the leaders **co-lead**? Did they share equally the task of asking follow-up questions?	10	5	0
7. Did the leaders get answers to **questions on the floor** before moving on to new ideas?	10	5	0
8. Did the leaders **stick to** their prepared question?	10	5	0
9. Did the leaders **pick up ideas** from the participants for follow-up questions or did they rely too much on their list of prepared follow-up questions?	10	5	0
10. Did the leaders **resolve** their prepared question?	10	5	0

Guidelines for Pre-discussion

PREPARING DISCUSSION QUESTIONS WITH YOUR CO-LEADER

1. Before meeting with your co-leader, each of you should have written fifteen to twenty interpretive question with a page reference for each. Page references make it easy for both of you to turn to that part of the text that gave you the idea for the question. Page references also assure you that your question is specific.
2. Begin pre-discussion by checking the wording of your questions. Do this by applying the Checklist for Qualities of Good Discussion Questions (H). If you cannot revise a question to fit these six characteristics, drop it. If you have trouble getting to your deepest level of understanding, (writing questions that have real doubt for you) review "Three Levels of Perception: On Writing Questions That Have Real Doubt" (Chapter 6, page 47).
3. At this point you should decide if you want to go with a list of at least ten good interpretive questions (arranged in any order that seems logical to you) or decide on writing a basic question similar to those that you have found in the following lesson plans at the end of this lesson. Indeed, you may want to try out one of the suggested basic questions that lack prepared follow-up questions to see if together you can come up with a cluster of at least eight questions of your own.
4. Agree upon the question that you want to use to open your discussion. Do not be overly concerned with your choice of an opening question. Any question that you both genuinely care about will be suitable.

PART

II

Socratic Seminars

CHAPTER

9 Socratic Seminars and Films

An Overview: Great Books Common Core Curriculum

This course applies the Socratic method of teaching and learning to a series of seminar discussions that focus not only on select readings but also on comparison–contrast discussions of those readings. It does so because a movie version of a story is itself an interpretation that its author may or may not agree with. As a result, new interpretations often arise that would not otherwise have been considered. Additionally, our understanding and enjoyment of a story is increased.

The course is also a balance of contemporary authors: John Updike, Antonio Monda, Robert Frost, C. S. Lewis, and Andrew Postman and members of the greatest faculty in the world—authors of the Great Books of the Western World: Fyodor Dostoevsky, Anton Chekhov, Abraham Lincoln, Khalil Gibran, Aldous Huxley, George Orwell, John Steinbeck, William Saroyan, William Faulkner, and Kurt Vonnegut.

Why Great Books? Why these Great Books? Great Books, according to Matthew Arnold, are "the best that is known and thought in the world." G. K. Chesterton maintains that Great Books are always relevant because they are timeless—they can be read and reinterpreted by each succeeding generation in light of its own experience. Great Books are those that generation after generation reads and rereads because of their universal themes, boundless interpretations, inspired and memorable language, and timeless wisdom. In short, some books become great because they endure. And they endure because the human race endures.

Chapter 10: Lesson Plan 7: Why Would Someone Choose to Live Without Friends?

Aristotle begins his treatise on friendship with the startling statement that "Without friends no one would choose to live." C. S. Lewis begins his Chapter 4 on Friendship in *The Four Loves* with an astonishment equal to

Aristotle's: "Very few modern people think Friendship a love of comparable value [to Affection or Eros] *or even a love at all.*" As a result, many if not a majority of people today would dismiss out of hand Aristotle's assertion that "no one would choose to live without friends." **Emerson**, on the other hand, in his renowned essay **On Friendship,** asserts that: "There are two elements that go to the composition of friendship . . . *One is Truth.* A friend is a person with whom I may be sincere. Before him I may think aloud . . . The other element of friendship is tenderness . . . Can another be so blessed, and we so pure, that we can offer him tenderness?" In short, "the only way to have a friend is to be one."

Given Emerson's description of differing kinds of friendship, our discussions will apply them by examining the unlikely bond between William Forrester, a seventy-year-old recluse who has remained confined in his own ghetto, and a sixteen-year-old neighborhood boy who meets Forrester on a dare to invade his apartment. ***Finding Forrester*** (DVD) narrates and Illustrates how the relationship between Forrester and Jamal Wallace began in confrontation, mellowed into an acquaintance, survived a near fatal crisis, and grew into a lifelong friendship that endured until Forrester's death.

Chapter 11: Lesson Plan 8: How Important is a Brother or Your Country in Your Life?

During World War II, when **William Faulkner** was at the apex of his career as a national author, he wrote "**Two Soldiers**" and its sequel, "**Shall Not Perish**." Both stories are told from the viewpoint of a nine-year-old narrator—Pete's brother. In "Two Soldiers," much to the dismay of his anxious parents, nineteen-year-old brother, Pete, is determined to join the US Army. And his little brother is just as determined to join him—regardless of his age. Indeed, Evan runs away from home and begins walking the thirty miles to the Army recruiting station in Memphis. When these two brothers find each other, only then do they realize the depth of their brotherhood. Basic question: why does Faulkner regard Evan as much a soldier as his brother Pete?

The sequel to "Two Soldiers," "Shall Not Perish," is a title that anyone who has memorized the most renowned speech of our sixteenth President, would recognize it immediately as an allusion to Abraham Lincoln's Address at Gettysburg. According to Pulitzer Prize winner, Gary Wills, The **Gettysburg Address** were "the words that changed America." When Lincoln proclaimed that our nation was "dedicated to the proposition that all men are created equal," he so shocked some journalists, one of them expressed his self-righteous disgust in the next edition of the Chicago Tribune.

"**Are you a bumper-sticker patriot?**" echoes Tom Paine's bitter ridicule of the "sunshine patriots" of our Revolutionary War. Like Faulkner in his "Shall Not Perish," **President Obama** gave our nation a profound reminder of the meaning of patriotism today in his **speech** at Independence, Missouri, June 30, 2008.

Chapter 12: Lesson Plan 9: Is Technology as Much a Curse as a Blessing?

While Bradbury's vision of the future of technology is always skeptical and cautionary and even alarming, **Isaac Asimov** is nearly always optimistic and eager to extol its virtues. In his sequence of related stories on the history of robotics, ***I, Robot,*** the narrator, Susan Calvin who joined U.S. Robots and Mechanical Men in 2008, traces the development of robots from rather crude machines through increasing sophistication until they become virtually indistinguishable from humans in 2050. The first story, "**Robbie,**" (of *I, Robot*) takes place before Susan Calvin joined U.S. Robots in 1998. She is present in the story as a teenage girl who observes people asking questions of the first talking robot that has been put on public display. Robbie is a nursemaid for eight-year-old Gloria Weston who can do all the things a human companion could do, except talk, and, he has much greater patience. As in "The Veldt," the parents, George and Grace Weston, disagree about Robbie's place in their daughter's development. George regards Gloria's companion as "the best darn robot money can buy" even it cost him a half year's income. Grace, on the other hand, is so worried about "that terrible machine," she wants to get rid of it. She knows it cannot be healthy that Gloria prefers to play with Robbie, rather than other children. During his two years with Gloria, Robbie does not leave his charge for a moment. But Grace Weston also fears that something "might go wrong" with Robbie. After all, he is a machine and machines can and do sometimes fail. Our basic question then becomes: With whose attitude towards Robbie does Asimov want us to agree—with George's or with Grace's? Ample evidence in the story makes this a legitimate issue.

Although, the **2004 movie** version of Asimov's collection of short stories, ***I, Robot,*** was a commercial success, it failed to impress Asimov loyalists. While some critics defend it as a story in its own right, others point out that the screenplay, by Jeff Vintar and Akiva Goldsman, has but one explicit connection with Asimov's original story—the "Three Laws of Robotics": (1) a robot may not injure a human being or, through inaction, allow a human being to come to harm; (2) a robot must obey orders given it by human beings except where such orders would conflict with the First Law; and (3) a robot must protect its own existence as long as such protection does not conflict with the First or Second Law. The Three Laws become the organizing principle and unifying theme for Asimov's *Foundation Trilogy*. The movie's chief departure from Asimov (whose stories are almost devoid of violence) is its action scenes involving police and crowds fighting or evading mobs of rampaging robots. "Robot as menace," is precisely the kind of story that Asimov abhorred. In contrast, Asimov's robot stories were the first to treat robots as useful creations that could have positive interactions with humans.

Although Asimov's focus is on the history of robotics in the stories of *I, Robot,* they all assume that space travel has become commonplace and available to virtually everyone—regardless of social or financial status. But what about the dawn of the space age when Sputnik joined "the sublime company of the heavenly bodies" in our solar system fifty years ago? On October 4, 1957 two contemporary authors—Hannah Arendt, a German–American political theorist, and an anonymous spokesman for the Smithsonian—reported this historic event in remarkable contrast. Arendt is euphoric while the Smithsonian is cynical. With the advent of the millennium, James Gleick was asked to reassess the historic significance of Sputnik. These "**Three Viewpoints on Sputnik**" will give your students a rare opportunity to understand and to explain the reasons for such differing estimations.

Suggestion: Before discussion, have your students do a brief rhetorical analysis of each article by answering four questions: (1) What is each writer's *thesis*? (2) *How* does the tone of each passage differ? (3) *Why* does the tone of each passage differ? and (4) What is each writer's *purpose* (review your answer to question 3)?

Chapter 13: Lesson Plan 10: Can We Forget That We Are Human?

Aldous Huxley, George Orwell, Neil and Andrew Postman all reply with an resounding yes! Huxley and the Postmans believe that we will lose our humanity by amusing ourselves to death. Orwell believes that we will succumb to totalitarianism.

In 1958, **Aldous Huxley** wrote a sequel to his best-known work, ***Brave New World,*** entitled, *Brave New World Revisited*. Were he alive today, I am sure he would write yet another estimation of his 1932 novel. It remains relevant today because so many of its predictions of life in the twenty-sixth century have been realized already in our twenty-first century: the implications of human cloning, propaganda, brainwashing, chemical persuasion, overpopulation, subliminal advertising, hypnopaedia (conditioned sleep-learning), consumerism and, most importantly, his answer to Eric Fromm's question about whether it is possible that we can forget that we are human.

Basic questions: Why is science and technology a public danger as well as the foundation of happiness in the brave new world? Why does Mustapha

Mond's "experiment" to assimilate John the Savage into the brave new world fail? Why does Huxley have John counter Mustapha Mond's defense of the brave new world with many references to Shakespeare?

The 1980 and 1998 made for TV movie versions of the novel raise another basic question: Would Huxley reject the 1998 film but approve the 1980 interpretation of his story?

Unlike Huxley, his mentor, **George Orwell** was not concerned with self destruction but with the external threat of totalitarianism. According to Erich Fromm, "George Orwell's ***1984*** is the expression of a mood as well as a warning. Its mood verges on despair for the future of humanity and the warning is that unless the course of history changes, men all over the world will lose their most human qualities, will become soulless automatons, *and will not even be aware of it*." Perhaps the basic question of the entire novel is its focus on the human condition: Can human nature be changed in such a way that mankind will forget its longing for freedom of choice and conscience, for dignity, for integrity, for love? In short, can we forget that we are human?

Whose vision of the future, Orwell's or Huxley's, is more relevant today? Should our greatest concern be from without (Orwell) that we would be overcome by tyranny or from within (Huxley) that we will be done in by our trivial culture and our infinite capacity for distraction?

Additional basic questions: Why do Winston and Julia continue to rebel against the Party even though they both know that in the end they will be defeated? Why is Winston Smith so confident that hope for the future (the overthrow of the Party) must lie with the Proletariat?

***Amusing Ourselves to Death*:** Public Discourse in the Age of Show Business (1985) by **Neil Postman** began with a lecture Postman gave to the Frankfurt Book Fair (1984) when participating in a panel on Orwell's *1984* and the contemporary world. In the introduction to his book, Postman held that the contemporary world was better reflected by Aldous Huxley's *Brave New World* whose society was inundated by its "infinite capacity for distraction" than by Orwell's *1984*'s devastating portrayal of totalitarianism. In 2005, Postman's son **Andrew** reissued the book in a 20th anniversary edition. His lengthy introduction brings his father's cautions up to date while he recounts his exchanges with his students in classroom encounters.

Chapter 14: Lesson Plan 11: How Important is God in Your Life?

When I asked my neighbor this question, his prompt reply was that God is as important to him as the "Great Spirit" is to Chief Joseph. When I asked another neighbor he replied: "Which God? God is a generic word, isn't it? And since it means the supreme being, there can be only one supreme being. God. Right?" Yes of course, I replied. Let me rephrase the question. Which one and only God do you believe in? Again, he replied promptly. "Jesus is Lord! Son of God the Father and His Holy Spirit." When I asked another neighbor the same question, he recited the Shama: "Hear, O Israel: the Lord our God, the Lord is One." And, as expected, a Muslim at school told me, "There is no God but Allah and Mohammed is his prophet."

Are these but different names for the same God? In short, are the various religions but different paths to the same God who wears different masks? There are as many who want to believe that as there are those who vehemently affirm that their god is the only god (Martin Buber) and that all others are false. And rightly so. How can there be more than one true God? related question inevitably arises: Why is it that some people are so passionate, indeed consumed, about seeking God while others are indifferent, apathetic, uninterested, and in a word, unaware of any need to seek God? In his recently published *Do You Believe?*, New York filmmaker Antonio Monda, conducts a series of candid interviews with eighteen cultural icons that range from Jane Fonda and Spike Lee to Martin Scorsese and Elie Wiesel. He asks each to reply to five basic questions: Do you believe in God? If so, what is your image of God? What happens to you after death? Do you pray? and Do you think religious believers are deluded? Responses range from Yes and No to Well . . .?

Finally, why did professional atheists like Sigmund Freud and Bertrand Russell in their day, and today Sam Harris and Richard Dawkins, regard God as a delusion?

John Updike's "Pigeon Feathers" is the first of two short stories about two very different fundamentalist Christians. David Kern is entirely questioning, while Sarah Ruth (in "Parker's Back") is entirely unquestioning and fanatic. Because teenage David Kern is so obsessed with death, he begins to question his own, his parents, and his pastor's beliefs in an afterlife. He regards Reverend Dobson's concept of heaven as a "betrayal of Christianity" because he describes it as a place where souls sleep until the Day of Judgment. David also cannot understand why his grandmother thinks that Heaven will be no more than being reunited to her dead husband. David is equally disappointed when his mother tells him the beauty of nature is "evidence" of God. To increase his anxiety, David cannot begin to fathom why his father looks forward to death. In short, David concludes, if there is no afterlife, this life has no purpose. Is he right? These and other questions about the immortality of the soul raise this central basic question of interpretation: Is David Kern so obsessed with death because he fears his own extinction or because belief in an afterlife is not enough for him?

Bertrand Russell, a notorious celebrity atheist, gave a renowned speech in London (1927), On "Why I am not a Christian," that provides a stark then-and-now contrast with **Hans Kung,** today's greatest living theologians, and his equally famous witness, "Why I am Still a Christian."

Chapter 15: Lesson Plan 12: How Does Someone Cope with the Death of a Child?

The title of this chapter alludes to the title of **James Agee's** Pulitzer Prize winning autobiographical novel of 1957, **A Death in the Family.** In Part Three (Ch. 14–20) seven-year-old Rufkus poignantly recounts the sudden, accidental death of his loving father. The story raises several basic interpretive questions for Socratic discussion: How do Rufus and Catherine cope with the sudden death of their father? Why does Rufus reject the explanation that his father died because God put him to sleep and took him home? Why does Rufus feel so guilty about telling his classmates "My Daddy's dead"? How does Uncle Andrew help Rufus cope with the sudden death of his father? Why does Uncle Andrew tell Rufus that the Miraculous butterfly has "more of God in him than that priggish, mealy mouthed son of a bitch [Father Jackson]"? And why does Agee reveal that Rufus understands more about his father's death than what he is told?

The **1963 DVD,** ***All the Way Home*** (title taken from the last sentence of the novel) runs 110 min. B/W. In **2002, PBS Masterpiece Theatre** televised its own version of *A Death in the Family.*

Gina Berriault's "The Stone Boy" recounts the poignant story of a ten year-old boy who accidentally kills his older brother, Eugene, while picking peas on their farm. Because Arnold delays for some time and does not return promptly home for help, he becomes a "stone boy" apparently devoid of grief. Even his parents and close relatives do not know how to reach out to the traumatized boy. When Arnold does finally turn to his mother at night, she sharply turns him away evidently unable to cope with her own pain. When she realizes her mistake, and "humbly" asks her son why he knocked at her door at night, he replies flatly, "I didn't want nothing." Berriault then concludes her grim story with this line: "Then he went out the door and down the back steps, his legs trembling from the fright his answer gave him." When asked in an interview if she was pleased with the screenplay, she replied: "Not really. I was ultimately disappointed in the way that the film turned out." She explained that the screenplay was her attempt to answer the question that students most frequently asked her, "What's going to happen to Arnold?" However, Gene Siskel gives the movie three stars because it has Arnold saved by the loving care of his grandfather who is able after time to return Arnold to his family

Judith Guest's book and movie version of ***Ordinary People*** provides an alternative to Berriault's focus on Arnold and his family's failure to understand his as well as their own grief. Judith Guest centers her story on two older brothers—"Buck" who was killed when a sudden storm came up while he and his brother Conrad were sailing on Lake Michigan. When Conrad became so depressed that he attempted suicide by slashing his wrists, his father is able to save him. After an eight-month stay in a psychiatric hospital, Conrad returns home to resume life at school. However, he continues to have unresolved conflicts with his parents. Because his mother Beth has never gotten over Buck's death, Conrad's failure to save Buck festers into an abiding guilt. When Beth and Calvin's marriage begins to fail, he and Conrad come together in mutual support after Beth finally decides to leave Calvin. Three basic questions stand out: (1) Who or what was most instrumental in Conrad's learning how to cope with his brother's death?; (2) Why does Judith Guest have Calvin ask the question, "How does a Christian deal with grief?"; and (3) Why does Beth leave Calvin in the novel but in the movie he leaves her?

President Obama, in his speech to the parents of the victims at Newtown, Connecticut, "**Unconscionable Evil**" revealed the power of his eloquent rhetoric; he spoke as a parent, confidentially, to parents who must somehow cope with what is any parent's greatest nightmare—the loss of a child. By beginning with the words of Paul to Corinthians who had lost heart, Obama set the tone of his message and spoke as a Christian who knows that God is always aware of us—even in our most horrendous moments—even when we may not be aware of Him and mistakenly think that He is absent. Like Job, who never lost his trust in the God who-shows-up—even when he had lost everything (his children, his health, his status, and his wealth), Obama recognizes (as Job learned) that there is no "answer" to the paradox of how God can be good and yet tolerate evil. We, like grown-up children, must trust Him as children who depend utterly on their parents and trust them unconditionally and absolutely. In short, "In the face of unconscionable evil," we must rely on our love for one another, and bear one another's burdens (Gal 6:2). Nevertheless, as good as Obama's eloquent and compassionate rhetoric is, his concluding statement that "God has called them all home" is bad theology. God did not call anyone home that day. A madman sent them home.

Chapter 16: Lesson Plan 13: Do We all Have the Same Unconditional Right to Life?

In a remarkable article (*New York Times Magazine,* December 17, 2006) on "The Super Rich and the Rest of Us," Peter Singer asks: "What should we donate to reduce poverty, disease and death in the developing world?" He begins by posing a basic question: "What is a human life worth?" and answers: "Most of us would agree that the value of a human life would be in the millions." In so doing, is he implying that those who would put a price tag on human life believe that the right to life is conditional? In other words, that we do not *all* have the same right to life.

In some countries today, the dominant cultural ethic asserts that the lives of unborn children matter less when weighed against the needs and choice of their pregnant mothers. When the state puts someone to death, has it concluded that *some* human life is dispensable after all? And when other governments propose that those in declining health are less worthy of continued care, has the state again concluded that the right to life is not absolute and universal but conditional? Abortion, death penalty, and euthanasia. While each issue, remains always controversial, each will demand everyone's attention at some time in his or her life.

This teaching unit focuses on one of these life-changing moments of decision, the death penalty. **Anton Chekhov's "The Bet"** begins with a heated argument about capital punishment among guests at a dinner party hosted by a wealthy banker. Most of the journalists and scholars in the group disapprove of the death penalty because they regard it as immoral in a Christian society and that it should be replaced by life imprisonment. However, the banker forcefully maintains: "I don't agree . . . I have not tried either the death penalty or imprisonment for life, but if one may judge *à priori,* the death penalty is more moral and more humane than imprisonment for life. Capital punishment kills a man at once, but lifelong imprisonment kills him slowly. Which executioner is the more humane, he who kills you in a few minutes or he who drags the life out of you in the course of many years?"

Just as forcefully a young lawyer of twenty-five counters: "*Both* are equally immoral . . . for they both have the same object—to take away life. The State is not God. It has not the right to take away what it cannot restore when it wants to." On being asked to explain, he adds: "The death sentence and the life sentence are equally immoral, but if I had to choose between the death penalty and imprisonment for life, I would certainly choose the second. To live anyhow is better than not at all." At this point, the banker suddenly loses his temper, bangs his fist on the table and challenges the lawyer to put up or shut up: "It's not true! I'll bet you two million you wouldn't stay in solitary confinement for five years." The impulsive lawyer responds by enquiring why five years? Why not fifteen? Are both men half drunk or is it a matter of pride and saving face? Nevertheless, "this wild, senseless bet was carried out." As a result, the remainder of the story raises this basic question: Does Chekhov want us to agree with the banker that capital punishment is more humane than life imprisonment?

Three outstanding films also raise the issue of the death penalty in equally dramatic and urgent terms: ***Dead Man Walking***, ***A Short Film on Killing***, and ***Compulsion***. Unlike so many films on the death penalty that are transparently against it, these three films are so balanced, pro and con, that those who support the death penalty are certain all three are a defense of capital punishment while those who oppose it are just as convinced each is a condemnation of the death penalty. As a result of their controversial bipolar stance, these films always engender lively and thoughtful discussion.

According to Michael Wilmington, movie critic for the *Chicago Tribune*, "Not since Krzysztof Kieslowski's film has a motion picture about capital punishment been so disturbing and compelling as *Dead Man Walking* which gives pain and personality to both sides of the issue." Indeed. In *Dead Man Walking,* starring Sean Penn and Susan Sarandon, Tim Robbins directs a film that explores theological and theological issues not commonly raised. Is all life sacred or is some dispensable? Matthew Poncelet (Penn) has been convicted, without any doubt, of killing two teenagers. When he appeals to Sister Helen Prejean (Sarandon) for help, she agrees to write and even to visit him on death row. However, when she also visits the victims' families of Hope Percy and Walter Delacroix, they assume that she has joined their side and will stop her counseling meetings with Poncelet. Startled, she refuses, and adds that she plans to continue because "Jesus said that every person is worth more than their worst act." Enraged, Hope's father orders the nun to leave his home. This rejection shakes Sister Prejean to her core, challenging her faith which in turn prompts us to reevaluate our own stance on the value of the death penalty.

Two movie reviews, one pro and one con, add to the discussion of the basic question of interpretation that focuses on the issue of whether or not *Dead Man Walking* is as balanced as director Tim Robbins claims.

A Short Film About Killing, one of ten in Krzysztof Kieslowski's magnum opus on the Decalogue, also claims to illustrate a balanced presentation of the death penalty controversy. It relates the brutal story of a twenty-year-old psychopath, Jacek Lazar, who murders a taxi driver for no evident reason. When he is defended by an idealistic lawyer, Piotr Balicki, who has never handled a death penalty case before, Jacek is promptly convicted and sentenced to death by hanging. After Jacek's execution, (which takes as much screen time as the murder—nearly four minutes) Piotr rages, "I abhor it! I abhor it!" Hence, the basic question about both films which confronts their audiences is: In its dramatization of the death penalty, is *A Short Film About Killing* as balanced, pro and con, as *Dead Man Walking*?

Based closely on Meyer Levin's novel and transcripts of the sensational **Loeb–Leopold** murder case of 1924, director Richard Fleischer's 1959 film, ***Compulsion*** is one of a kind. The second half of the movie is taken directly from defense attorney Clarence Darrow's riveting courtroom presentation. Chicago attorney Johathan Wilk (Darrow) defends two wealthy teenagers who kidnapped and murdered Bobby Franks, a fourteen year-old boy. Both believed that they had committed "the perfect crime." However, when their alibis quickly fall apart under the expert and methodical probing of the prosecutor (Harold Horn / E. G. Marshall), the death sentence seems inevitable. Orson Welles stars as the legendary Clarence Darrow whose history-making defense against capital punishment saves two teenagers from the death penalty. Welles' eloquent and poignant soliloquy during the fifteen-minute summation at the trial is one of the memorable highlights of cinema history. When the movie ends with the closing defense arguments of Darrow and omits the prosecution's rebuttal, it clearly implies that it is against the death penalty. However, when one reads the prosecution's arguments in the novel, it quickly becomes evident that the defense may not have had the last word after all—that another judge could have ruled in favor of execution. Indeed, it raises a basic question: If you had been the judge, would you have been persuaded by the defense of Jonathan Wilk's defense or by the arguments of the District Attorney? If so, why so? If not, why not?

Criteria for Choosing Texts for Socratic Discussion

Vital to the success of the seminar is a careful selection of the readings which are, in the end, the real teachers. According to George Anastaplo of the Chicago Public Schools Socratic Seminar, "The ultimate leaders of the best seminar discussions are the authors of the best books. It is only in the best books that one is likely to encounter the finest examples of minds at work." Indeed, unless the readings are carefully chosen according to the tested and established criteria of the Great Books Foundation (Chicago, IL), there can be no hope of having successful meetings in which there is a mutual increase in understanding and enjoyment. In order of importance, here are four key criteria for choosing good selections.

1. **The readings must be able to support extensive reading and discussion.** The selections must yield multiple interpretations, that is, they must be raise interpretive questions about an author's meaning that is not explicit. Only well-written works that are thematically complete and cohesive suggest real answers—that is, differing interpretations that can be supported with evidence from the text rather than merely being a matter of personal opinion. While every work of literature requires some degree of interpretation, not all works hold up under an extended analysis. This means that not all so-called "classics" qualify for a Socratic Seminar. In other words, if the meaning and intention of a book is transparent to the reader, it cannot sustain a genuine search for meaning because it cannot generate questions that have the vital element of doubt about their answers. For example, as appealing and uplifting as are novels like Wilson's *Where the Red Fern Grows* and Collier's *My Brother Sam is Dead,* they cannot function in Socratic discussion because they are too thin, their meaning obvious, and their intention transparent.
2. **The readings must evoke real questions for adults as well as participants.** This second criterion is but the other side of the coin. Since leaders do not rely on a teacher's manual or refer to an answer key in preparing for Socratic discussion, they must be able to write questions on a selection that are real questions *for them*—that is, questions that raise more than one legitimate answer (at least two) **or** that *seem* to have no answer at all (complete doubt). In other words, leaders do **not** write questions that they believe someone else may have doubt about. They write questions that *they* have doubt about. Because the leaders own questions reflect their personal curiosity about the meaning of a work, and because leaders never give their own personal opinions, participants begin to see their teacher(s) and peers in a new role—as active and involved partners in discussion, as co-learners and not as answer-givers.
3. **The readings must be reasonably self-contained.** The best kind of reading that illustrates this third criteria is the short story. In stories like Saroyan's "Gaston" or Cheever's "Reunion," the reader is given all the information needed to arrive at a good grasp of their overall manning or theme(s). In other words, shorter works are more manageable in discussion and more suited to two readings and intensive analysis. In contrast, works that are not self contained invite numerous questions that cannot be answered on the basis of the text alone and invite mere speculation where one answer begins to sound as plausible as another. The real problem with this criterion is longer works, full-length novels. But this obstacle can be overcome if the reading is carefully divided into chapters that are more or less self-contained. Sometimes, the author makes this

division for us. For example, Camus divides *The Stranger* into two clearly self-contained parts and *The Adventures of Huckleberry Finn* follows an episodic plot that can be easily divided for several discussions.

4. **The readings must be age and grade appropriate.** As Louise Rosenblatt reminds us in her seminal *Literature as Exploration,* reading is an active process, that is, a *transaction* between reader and the story that involves not merely "decoding" the text but, more importantly, a recognition of what the student brings to the text—his or her intellectual grasp, emotional maturity, and life experience. Recognition of these three key elements explains why student interpretations vary, why they ignore or overlook certain elements of the story, and why some interpretations are better (more comprehensive and defendable) than others.

Given this fourth criteria, consider the following examples: *Flowers for Algernon* would not be an appropriate reading for middle school but *Running Loose* or *The Giver* is. Similarly, *Sons and Lovers* of D. H. Lawrence would not be appropriate for high school but *Much Ado About Nothing* would be. Hemingway's "The Killers" (which has a fourth grade readability level) would not be appropriate for middle school but Richard Wilbur's "A Game of Catch," or Shirley Jackson's "Charles," would be well received. *Lady Chatterley's Lover* ought not be in a high school curriculum but Ibsen's *A Doll's House* always evokes strong reactions. *Antigone* is beyond the grasp of middle school students but not a western like *Shane*. *Anna Karenina* is too sophisticated for high school students but not Jane Austen's *Pride and Prejudice*.

In short, teacher's must remember that "in the selection of literary materials to be presented to students, it is NOT enough merely to think of what they OUGHT to read. Choices must also reflect a sense of the possible links between the readings and the present level of a student's emotional maturity" (Rosenblatt, third edition, 42). The implication, then, is that "if the language, the setting, and the theme all are too alien, even a 'great work' [a classic] will fail. Books must be chosen that hold out some link with the student's past and present preoccupation's, anxieties, and ambitions."

CHAPTER

10 Lesson Plan 7

Why Would Someone Choose to Live Without Friends?

1. **Focus:**	*Journal*: Do you agree with Emerson that "The only way to have a friend is to be one"? Illustrate with examples from your personal experience.
2. **Objective:**	To compare and contrast C. S. Lewis' definition of friendship illustrated in "Finding Forrester."
3. **Purpose:**	○ To develop the habit of independent, reflective, and critical thinking. ○ To increase our understanding of the nature of friendship.
4. **Input:**	Readings on friendship, love vs. infatuation, high school romance. *Finding Forrester* DVD (2000, dir. Gus Van Sant, 136 mins)
5. **Modeling:**	Write ten interpretive questions on *Finding Forrester* DVD.
6. **Checking for understanding:**	Co-leaders ask spontaneous follow-up questions of clarification substantiation, more opinion, consistency, implication, resolution.
7. **Guided practice:**	Co-leaders observe the four rules of Socratic Discussion.
8. **Closure and evaluation:**	Essay exam, oral resolution, or written resolution basic question.
Text:	Emerson, "Friendship" (1960, Harcourt Inc., New York, NY)
Film:	*Finding Forrester* DVD (2000, dir. Gus Van Sant, 136 mins)

Finding Forrester

Cast

Screenplay by Mike Rich: His first film script was named after his high school English teacher, Mrs. Forrester, from Enterprise High School, Enterprise Oregon.

Directed by Gus Van Sant: Academy Award winner (*Good Will Hunting*, 1997).

Setting: Mailor-Callow Preparatory HS (Regis HS, Manhattan, the Bronx) NY.

William Forrester (Sean Connery): A reclusive Pulitzer Prize-winning author who is the only white to remain in the Bronx after it became a black ghetto.

Jamal Wallace (Rob Brown): A sixteen-year-old talented black teenager who first encounters Forrester on a dare from his friends to invade his apartment.

Terral Wallace (Busta Rhymes): Jamal's gregarious older brother and rapper who looks out for his younger brother by supporting his decision to go to a prep school.

Clare Spence (Anna Paquin): Jamal's would-be girlfriend who first introduces him to Mailor Academy, an exclusive college preparatory school.

Professor Crawford (F. Murray Abraham): Jamal's English teacher at Mailor whose bias will not allow him to accept Jamal as a serious student.

Lawyer (Matt Damon, cameo appearance).

Finding Forrester

PRE-DISCUSSION EXERCISE AND PLOT REVIEW

Sean Connery as William Forrester and Rob Brown as Jamal Wallace

A Basic Question of Interpretation: Does the title refer *more* to Forrester's helping Jamal to find his future or to Jamal helping Forrester to find his past?

Pre-discussion Exercise

Directions: Mark **A** if the question relates to Forrester helping Jamal, **B** if the question relates to Jamal helping Forrester, **C** if the question relates to both of them helping one another, and **D** if the question relates to neither of them.

Suggestion: When undecided, answer the question first and consider if that answer is related Forrester, Jamal, both, or neither.

1. During an English class on Poe's "The Raven," why does Jamal refuse to recite by saying that he had not read the poem?

2. Why is Mrs. Wallace told by Jamal's English teacher that her son is a C student with an A on the state assessment test?

3. Why did Jamal turn to reading and writing after his father abandoned his family?

4. Does Jamal's peer acceptance depend entirely on basketball?

5. Why does the film contrast the accomplishments of Jamal's gregarious brother, Terral, with Jamal's aspirations?

6. When Jamal finds his backpack in the street, why does he discover comments in red ink in his journals?

7. In a red-ink comment, why does Forrester ask Jamal, "Where are you taking me"?

8. By "constipated thinking," does Forrester mean that Jamal's writing is not clear?

9. When Jamal first knocks on Forrester's door, why does he take up the challenge to write 5000 words on why he should stay away?

10. After professor Crawford tells his students that William Forrester wrote a masterpiece at 23, why is his first assignment to find out why Forrester wrote only one book rather than questions about the book itself?

11. When Jamal asks Forrester why he is a legend at school, why does Forrester shout at him, "The purpose of a question is to obtain information *that matters to you*"?

12. Why does Forrester tell Jamal he will go to Mailor because he wants to answer the question about what he will do with the rest of his life?

13. When Forrester asks Jamal if he had read his only book, *Avalon Landing*, why does Jamal say he couldn't get past the first ten pages?

14. Why does Forrester not want anyone to know about Jamal's visits to his apartment?

15. When Jamal asks if Forrester will keep helping him with his writing, why does Forrester agree only if Jamal asks no questions about him, his family, or why he wrote only one book?

16. What does Forrester mean when he tells Jamal, "People are always *talking* about my book but never *saying* anything about it"?

17. When Jamal tells Forrester that his book means that "Life never works out," why does Forrester reply that he didn't have to read a book to learn that?

18. What does Forrester mean when he says that: "The first step to writing is writing—not thinking about what you are going to write"?

19. What does Forrester mean when he says to "write the first draft with your heart but then to rewrite with your head"?

20. How does Forrester's having Jamal type out a copy of his "A Season of Faith's Perfection" help Jamal to "discover his own words"?

21. Why does Forrester insist that whatever he and Jamal write must stay in his apartment?

22. Why does Forrester warn Jamal that: "Bitterly disappointed teachers [of writing like Robert Crawford] are either very good or very dangerous"?

23. When Jamal gives Clare the unexpected gift of a signed copy of Forrester's book, why does she ask if he had been trying to show her more than how to dribble a basketball?

24. Did Forrester write only one book mostly because he so profoundly resents critics who try to explain what he was "really" trying to say or because of his brother's untimely death?

25. Why does Jamal take Forrester to a stadium on his birthday?

26. After Forrester tells Jamal about his brother's drunk-driving death, why does Jamal quote Forrester's words, "The rest of those who have gone before us cannot study the unrest of those who follow"?

27. What has Jamal learned from Forrester and Forrester from Jamal?

28. When Jamal realizes that Forrester will not defend him publicly, is he serious about giving up writing?

29. Why is Jamal handed the choice of winning a championship to retain his scholarship?

30. Why does Jamal ignore Forrester's question about the missed foul shots?

31. When Jamal goes to the writing contest awards, why does he tell Clare that Mailor will have to kick him out of school—that he will not just walk away?

32. Why does Forrester come out of retirement to defend Jamal?

33. How did Jamal's writing contest entry, "Losing Family," make Forrester realize that "the one wish that [he] was granted so late in life was the gift of friendship"?

34. Even after Forrester convincingly demonstrates that Jamal's "Losing Family" was his own work, why does Professor Crawford still want Jamal disqualified?

35. Why is professor Crawford over ruled and Forrester offered a teaching job?

36. After his death from cancer, why does Forrester want Jamal to have his apartment?

37. In his final letter to Jamal, what does Forrester mean when he says, "I never imagined that I would realize my own dream once again"?

38. Why does Forrester credit Jamal's coming into his life for realizing his dream late in life?

39. Why does Forrester leave to Jamal the manuscript of *Sunset* with "the foreword to be written by Jamal Wallace"?

40. How does the story's resolution imply that Jamal will become one day a successful writer?

Assignment: An **epigram** is a brief, interesting, memorable, and sometimes surprising or satirical statement. Epigrams so dominate Emerson's essays that they are often cited unwittingly by those who readily agree with them. For example, "To be great is to be misunderstood." "Nothing is at last sacred but the integrity of your own mind." In Emerson's essay on friendship (below), how often have you heard someone tell you, "The only way to have a friend is to be one"? Some lesser known epigrams have been italicized in this edited text of Emerson's essay. Have students paraphrase each for discussion.

On Friendship (Essay VI)

Ralph Waldo Emerson (1841)

5 I awoke this morning with devout thanksgiving for my friends, the old and the new. Shall I not call God the Beautiful, who daily showeth himself so to me in his gifts? I chide society, I embrace solitude, and yet I am not so ungrateful as not to see the wise, the lovely, and the noble-minded, as from time to time they pass my gate. *Who hears me, who understands me, becomes mine, — a possession for all time.* Nor is nature so poor but she gives me this joy several times, and thus we weave social threads of our own, a new web of relations; and, as many thoughts in succession substantiate themselves, we shall by and by stand in a new world of our own creation, and no longer strangers and pilgrims in a traditionary globe. My friends have come to me unsought. The great God gave them to me. By oldest right, by the divine affinity of virtue with itself, I find them, or rather not I, but the Deity in me and in them derides and cancels the thick walls of individual character, relation, age, sex, circumstance, at which he usually connives, and now makes many one. High thanks I owe you, excellent lovers, who carry out the world for me to new and noble depths, and enlarge the meaning of all my thoughts. These are new poetry of the first Bard,—poetry without stop,—hymn, ode, and epic, poetry still flowing, Apollo and the Muses chanting still. Will these, too, separate themselves from me again, or some of them? I know not, but I fear it not; for my relation to them is so pure, that we hold by simple affinity, and the Genius of my life being thus social, the same affinity will exert its energy on whomsoever is as noble as these men and women, wherever I may be.

6 I confess to an extreme tenderness of nature on this point. It is almost dangerous to me to "crush the sweet poison of misused wine" of the affections. A new person is to me a great event, and hinders me from

sleep. I have often had fine fancies about persons which have given me delicious hours; but the joy ends in the day; it yields no fruit. Thought is not born of it; my action is very little modified. I must feel pride in my friend's accomplishments as if they were mine,—and a property in his virtues. I feel as warmly when he is praised, as the lover when he hears applause of his engaged maiden. We overestimate the conscience of our friend. His goodness seems better than our goodness, his nature finer, his temptations less. Every thing that is his,—his name, his form, his dress, books, and instruments,—fancy enhances. Our own thought sounds new and larger from his mouth.

7 *Friendship, like the immortality of the soul, is too good to be believed.*

13 *I do not wish to treat friendships daintily, but with roughest courage.* When they are real, they are not glass threads or frost work, but the solidest thing we know. For now, after so many ages of experience, what do we know of nature, or of ourselves? Not one step has man taken toward the solution of the problem of his destiny. In one condemnation of folly stand the whole universe of men. But the sweet sincerity of joy and peace, which I draw from this alliance with my brother's soul, is the nut itself, whereof all nature and all thought is but the husk and shell. *Happy is the house that shelters a friend!* It might well be built, like a festal bower or arch, to entertain him a single day. Happier, if he know the solemnity of that relation, and honor its law! He who offers himself a candidate for that covenant comes up, like an Olympian, to the great games, where the first-born of the world are the competitors. He proposes himself for contests where Time, Want, Danger, are in the lists, and he alone is victor who has truth enough in his constitution to preserve the delicacy of his beauty from the wear and tear of all these. The gifts of fortune may be present or absent, but all the speed in that contest depends on intrinsic nobleness, and the contempt of trifles. *There are two elements that go to the composition of friendship, each so sovereign that I can detect no superiority in either, no reason why either should be first named. One is Truth.* A friend is a person with whom I may be sincere. Before him I may think aloud. I am arrived at last in the presence of a man so real and equal, that I may drop even those under most garments of dissimulation, courtesy, and second thought, which men never put off, and may deal with him with the simplicity and wholeness with which one chemical atom meets another. Sincerity is the luxury allowed, like diadems and authority, only to the highest rank, *that* being permitted to speak truth, as having none above it to court or conform unto. Every man alone is sincere. At the entrance

of a second person, hypocrisy begins. We parry and fend the approach of our fellowman by compliments, by gossip, by amusements, by affairs. We cover up our thought from him under a hundred folds. I knew a man, who, under a certain religious frenzy, cast off this drapery, and, omitting all compliment and commonplace, spoke to the conscience of every person he encountered, and that with great insight and beauty. At first he was resisted, and all men agreed he was mad. But persisting, as indeed he could not help doing, for some time in this course, he attained to the advantage of bringing every man of his acquaintance into true relations with him. No man would think of speaking falsely with him, or of putting him off with any chat of markets or reading-rooms. But every man was constrained by so much sincerity to the like plain dealing, and what love of nature, what poetry, what symbol of truth he had, he did certainly show him. But to most of us society shows not its face and eye, but its side and its back. To stand in true relations with men in a false age is worth a fit of insanity, is it not? We can seldom go erect. Almost every man we meet requires some civility,—requires to be humored; he has some fame, some talent, some whim of religion or philanthropy in his head that is not to be questioned, and which spoils all conversation with him. But a friend is a sane man who exercises not my ingenuity, but me. My friend gives me entertainment without requiring any stipulation on my part. A friend, therefore, is a sort of paradox in nature. I who alone am, I who see nothing in nature whose existence I can affirm with equal evidence to my own, behold now the semblance of my being, in all its height, variety, and curiosity, reiterated in a foreign form; so that a friend may well be reckoned the masterpiece of nature.

14 *The other element of friendship is tenderness.* We are holden to men by every sort of tie, by blood, by pride, by fear, by hope, by lucre, by lust, by hate, by admiration, by every circumstance and badge and trifle, but we can scarce believe that so much character can subsist in another as to draw us by love. Can another be so blessed, and we so pure, that we can offer him tenderness? When a man becomes dear to me, I have touched the goal of fortune. I find very little written directly to the heart of this matter in books. And yet I have one text which I cannot choose but remember. My author says,—"I offer myself faintly and bluntly to those whose I effectually am, and tender myself least to him to whom I am the most devoted." I wish that friendship should have feet, as well as eyes and eloquence. It must plant itself on the ground, before it vaults over the moon. I wish it to be a little of a citizen, before it is quite a cherub. We chide the citizen because he makes love a commodity. It is an exchange

of gifts, of useful loans; it is good neighborhood; it watches with the sick; it holds the pall at the funeral; and quite loses sight of the delicacies and nobility of the relation. But though we cannot find the god under this disguise of a subtler, yet, on the other hand, we cannot forgive the poet if he spins his thread too fine, and does not substantiate his romance by the municipal virtues of justice, punctuality, fidelity, and pity. I hate the prostitution of the name of friendship to signify modish and worldly alliances. I much prefer the company of farm boys and tin-peddlers, to the silken and perfumed amity which celebrates its days of encounter by a frivolous display, by rides in a circle, and dinners at the best taverns. The end of friendship is a commerce the most strict and homely that can be joined; more strict than any of which we have experience. It is for aid and comfort through all the relations and passages of life and death. It is fit for serene days, and graceful gifts, and country rambles, but also for rough roads and hard fare, shipwreck, poverty, and persecution. It keeps company with the sallies of the wit and the trances of religion. We are to dignify to each other the daily needs and offices of man's life, and embellish it by courage, wisdom, and unity. It should never fall into something usual and settled, but should be alert and inventive, and add rhyme and reason to what was drudgery.

17 *Friendship requires that rare mean betwixt likeness and unlikeness, that piques each with the presence of power and of consent in the other party.* Let me be alone to the end of the world, rather than that my friend should overstep, by a word or a look, his real sympathy. I am equally balked by antagonism and by compliance. Let him not cease an instant to be himself. The only joy I have in his being mine, is that the *not mine* is *mine*. I hate, where I looked for a manly furtherance, or at least a manly resistance, to find a mush of concession. Better be a nettle in the side of your friend than his echo. The condition which high friendship demands is ability to do without it. That high office requires great and sublime parts. There must be very two, before there can be very one. Let it be an alliance of two large, formidable natures, mutually beheld, mutually feared, before yet they recognize the deep identity which beneath these disparities unites them.

18 He only is fit for this society who is magnanimous; who is sure that greatness and goodness are always economy; who is not swift to inter meddle with his fortunes. Let him not inter meddle with this. Leave to the diamond its ages to grow, nor expect to accelerate the births of the eternal.

19 Friendship demands a religious treatment. We talk of choosing our friends, but friends are self-elected. Reverence is a great part of it. Treat your friend as a spectacle. Of course he has merits that are not yours, and that you cannot honor, if you must needs hold him close to your person. Stand aside; give those merits room; let them mount and expand. Are you the friend of your friend's buttons, or of his thought? To a great heart he will still be a stranger in a thousand particulars, that he may come near in the holiest ground. Leave it to girls and boys to regard a friend as property, and to suck a short and all-confounding pleasure, instead of the noblest benefit.

20 Let us buy our entrance to this guild by a long probation. Why should we desecrate noble and beautiful souls by intruding on them? Why insist on rash personal relations with your friend? Why go to his house, or know his mother and brother and sisters? Why be visited by him at your own? Are these things material to our covenant? Leave this touching and clawing. Let him be to me a spirit. A message, a thought, a sincerity, a glance from him, I want, but not news, nor pottage. I can get politics, and chat, and neighborly conveniences from cheaper companions. Should not the society of my friend be to me poetic, pure, universal, and great as nature itself? Ought I to feel that our tie is profane in comparison with yonder bar of cloud that sleeps on the horizon, or that clump of waving grass that divides the brook? Let us not vilify, but raise it to that standard. That great, defying eye, that scornful beauty of his mien and action, do not pique yourself on reducing, but rather fortify and enhance. Worship his superiorities; wish him not less by a thought, but hoard and tell them all. Guard him as thy counterpart. Let him be to thee for ever a sort of beautiful enemy, untamable, devoutly revered, and not a trivial conveniency to be soon outgrown and cast aside. The hues of the opal, the light of the diamond, are not to be seen, if the eye is too near. To my friend I write a letter, and from him I receive a letter. That seems to you a little. It suffices me. It is a spiritual gift worthy of him to give, and of me to receive. It profanes nobody. In these warm lines the heart will trust itself, as it will not to the tongue, and pour out the prophecy of a godlier existence than all the annals of heroism have yet made good.

22 What is so great as friendship, let us carry with what grandeur of spirit we can. Let us be silent,—so we may hear the whisper of the gods. Let us not interfere. Who set you to cast about what you should say to the select souls, or how to say any thing to such? No matter how ingenious, no matter how graceful and bland. There are innumerable degrees of

folly and wisdom, and for you to say aught is to be frivolous. Wait, and thy heart shall speak. Wait until the necessary and everlasting overpowers you, until day and night avail themselves of your lips. *The only reward of virtue is virtue; the only way to have a friend is to be one.* You shall not come nearer a man by getting into his house. If unlike, his soul only flees the faster from you, and you shall never catch a true glance of his eye. We see the noble afar off, and they repel us; why should we intrude? Late,—very late,—we perceive that no arrangements, no introductions, no consuetudes or habits of society, would be of any avail to establish us in such relations with them as we desire,—but solely the uprise of nature in us to the same degree it is in them; then shall we meet as water with water; and if we should not meet them then, we shall not want them, for we are already they. In the last analysis, love is only the reflection of a man's own worthiness from other men. Men have sometimes exchanged names with their friends, as if they would signify that in their friend each loved his own soul.

24 *It is foolish to be afraid of making our ties too spiritual, as if so we could lose any genuine love.* Whatever correction of our popular views we make from insight, nature will be sure to bear us out in, and though it seem to rob us of some joy, will repay us with a greater. Let us feel, if we will, the absolute insulation of man. We are sure that we have all in us. We go to Europe, or we pursue persons, or we read books, in the instinctive faith that these will call it out and reveal us to ourselves. Beggars all. The persons are such as we; the Europe an old faded garment of dead persons; the books their ghosts. Let us drop this idolatry. Let us give over this mendicancy. Let us even bid our dearest friends farewell, and defy them, saying, "Who are you? Unhand me: I will be dependent no more." Ah! seest thou not, O brother, that thus we part only to meet again on a higher platform, and only be more each other's, because we are more our own? A friend is Janus-faced: he looks to the past and the future. He is the child of all my foregoing hours, the prophet of those to come, and the harbinger of a greater friend. *I do then with my friends as I do with my books. I would have them where I can find them, but I seldom use them. We must have society on our own terms, and admit or exclude it on the slightest cause.* I cannot afford to speak much with my friend. If he is great, he makes me so great that I cannot descend to converse. In the great days, presentiments hover before me in the firmament. I ought then to dedicate myself to them. I go in that I may seize them, I go out that I may seize them. I fear only that I may lose them receding into the sky in which now they are only a patch of brighter light. Then, though I prize my

friends, I cannot afford to talk with them and study their visions, lest I lose my own. It would indeed give me a certain household joy to quit this lofty seeking, this spiritual astronomy, or search of stars, and come down to warm sympathies with you; but then I know well I shall mourn always the vanishing of my mighty gods. It is true, next week I shall have languid moods, when I can well afford to occupy myself with foreign objects; then I shall regret the lost literature of your mind, and wish you were by my side again. But if you come, perhaps you will fill my mind only with new visions, not with yourself but with your lusters, and I shall not be able any more than now to converse with you. So I will owe to my friends this evanescent intercourse. I will receive from them, not what they have, but what they are. They shall give me that which properly they cannot give, but which emanates from them. But they shall not hold me by any relations less subtle and pure. We will meet as though we met not, and part as though we parted not.

25 True love transcends the unworthy object, and dwells and broods on the eternal, and when the poor interposed mask crumbles, it is not sad, but feels rid of so much earth, and feels its independence the surer. Yet these things may hardly be said without a sort of treachery to the relation. *The essence of friendship is entireness, a total magnanimity and trust. It must not surmise or provide for infirmity. It treats its object as a god, that it may deify both.*

Socratic Seminar: On Friendships

Basic Question: In Emerson's analysis of friendship, what elements are illustrated in the relationship between William Forrester and Jamal Wallace in *Finding Forrester*?

1. What is the common truth and interest that Emerson would likely find in William and Jamal's relationship?
2. How would Emerson explain how the unlikely companionship between Jamal and William developed into genuine friendship?
3. Why would Emerson regard Forrester and Jamal two who became friends by being friends?
4. Would Emerson regard the friendship of Jamal and Forrester as "someone before whom each can think aloud"?
5. According to Emerson, do Jamal and Forrester "see and care about the same truth"?

CHAPTER

11 Lesson Plan 8

How Important is a Brother or Your Country in Your Life?

Two Soldiers

1. **Focus:**	Are you a bumper-sticker patriot? Complete the Exercise after Obama's speech on patriotism and compare your answers with your teacher and your classmates.
2. **Objective:**	To review the Three Kinds of Questions and Qualities of Good Discussion Questions.
3. **Purpose:**	To prepare students for small-group discussion.
4. **Input and modeling:**	Plot-check quiz on Three Kinds of Questions and Exercise on the Qualities of Good Questions on "Gaston" and "Two Soldiers."
5. **Checking for understanding:**	Review the plot-check quiz and the Exercise on Qualities of Good Questions.
6. **Guided practice:**	Discussion of two basic questions of interpretation.
7. **Closure:**	An essay on each individual's resolution of one of the basic questions just discussed.
Text:	William Faulkner, *Collected Stories of William Faulkner* (1950, New York: Random House, "Two Soldiers" (pp. 81–99).
Films:	○ *Two Soldiers* VHS (The American Film Institute, 30 mins; Monterey home video, dir. Christopher Lula) ○ *Two Soldiers* VHS (Shoe Picture Company, 40 mins; dir. Aaron Schneider. Academy Award 2005—Short Subject)

"Two Soldiers"

William Faulkner

ME AND PETE would go down to Old Man Killegrew's and listen to his radio. We would wait until after supper, after dark, and we would stand outside Old Man Killegrew's parlor window, and we could hear it because Old Man Killegrew's wife was deaf, and so he run the radio as loud as it would run, and so me and Pete could hear it plain as Old Man Killegrew's wife could, I reckon, even standing outside with the window closed.

And that night I said, "What? Japanese? What's a pearl harbor?" and Pete said, "Hush."

And so we stood there, it was cold, listening to the fellow in the radio talking, only I couldn't make no heads nor tails neither out of it. Then the fellow said that would be all for a while, and me and Pete walked back up the road to home, and Pete told me what it was. Because he was nigh twenty and he had done finished the Consolidated last June and he knowed a heap: about them Japanese dropping bombs on Pearl Harbor and that Pearl Harbor was across the water.

"Across what water?" I said. "Across that Government reservoy up at Oxford?"

"Naw," Pete said. "Across the big water. The Pacific Ocean."

We went home. Maw and pap was already asleep, and me and Pete laid in the bed, and I still couldn't understand where it was, and Pete told me again the Pacific Ocean.

"What's the matter with you?" Pete said. "You're going on nine years old. You been in school now ever since September. Ain't you learned nothing yet?"

"I reckon we ain't got as fer as the Pacific Ocean yet," I said.

We was still sowing the vetch then that ought to been all finished by the fifteenth of November, because pap was still behind, just like he had been ever since me and Pete had knowed him. And we had firewood to git in, too, but every night me and Pete would go down to Old Man Killegrew's and stand outside his parlor window in the cold and listen to his radio; then we would come back home and lay in the bed and Pete would tell me what it was. That is, he would tell me for a while. Then he wouldn't tell me. It was like he didn't want to talk about it no more. He would tell me to shut up because he wanted to go to sleep, but he never wanted to go to sleep.

He would lay there, a heap stiller than if he was asleep, and it would be something, I could feel it coming out of him, like he was mad at me even, only I knowed he wasn't thinking about me, or like he was worried about something, and it wasn't that neither, because he never had nothing to worry about. He never got behind like pap, let alone stayed behind.

Pap give him ten acres when he graduated from the Consolidated, and me and Pete both reckoned pap was durn glad to get shut of at least ten acres, less to have to worry with himself; and Pete had them ten acres all sowed to vetch and busted out and bedded for the winter, and so it wasn't that.

But it was something. And still we would go down to Old Man Killegrew's every night and listen to his radio, and they was at it in the Philippines now, but General MacArthur was holding um. Then we would come back home and lay in the bed, and Pete wouldn't tell me nothing or talk at all. He would just lay there still as a ambush and when I would touch him, his side or his leg would feel hard and still as iron, until after a while I would go to sleep.

Then one night it was the first time he had said nothing to me except to jump on me about not chopping enough wood at the wood tree where we was cutting he said, "I got to go."

"Go where?" I said.

"To that war," Pete said.

"Before we even finish gettin' in the firewood?"

"Firewood, hell," Pete said.

"All right," I said. "When we going to start?"

But he wasn't even listening. He laid there, hard and still as iron in the dark. "I got to go," he said. "I jest ain't going to put up with no folks treating the Unity States that way."

"Yes," I said. "Firewood or no firewood, I reckon we got to go."

This time he heard me. He laid still again, but it was a different kind of still.

"You?" he said. "To a war?"

"You'll whup the big uns and I'll whup the little uns," I said.

Then he told me I couldn't go. At first I thought he just never wanted me tagging after him, like he wouldn't leave me go with him when he went sparking them girls of Tull's.

Then he told me the Army wouldn't leave me go because I was too little, and then I knowed he really meant it and that I couldn't go nohow noways. And somehow I hadn't believed until then that he was going himself, but now I knowed he was and that he wasn't going to leave me go with him a-tall.

"I'll chop the wood and tote the water for you-all then!" I said. "You got to have wood and water!" Anyway, he was listening to me now. He wasn't like iron now. He turned onto his side and put his hand on my chest because it was me that was laying straight and hard on my back now. "No," he said. "You got to stay here and help pap."

"Help him what?" I said. "He ain't never caught up nohow. He can't get no further behind. He can sholy take care of this little shirttail of a farm while me and you are whupping them Japanese. I got to go too. If you got to go, then so have I."

"No," Pete said. "Hush now. Hush." And he meant it, and I knowed he did. Only I made sho from his own mouth. I quit.

"So I just can't go then," I said.

"No," Pete said. "You just can't go. You're too little, in the first place, and in the second place "

"All right," I said. "Then shut up and leave me go to sleep." So he hushed then and laid back. And I laid there like I was already asleep, and pretty soon he was asleep and I knowed it was the wanting to go to the war that had worried him and kept him awake, and now that he had decided to go, he wasn't worried any more.

The next morning he told maw and pap. Maw was all right. She cried.

"No," she said, crying, "I don't want him to go. I would rather go myself in his place, if I could. I don't want to save the country. Them Japanese could take it and keep it, so long as they left me and my family and my children alone. But I remember my brother Marsh in that other war. He had to go to that one when he wasn't but nineteen, and our mother couldn't understand it then any more than I can now. But she told Marsh if he had to go, he had to go. And so, if Pete's got to go to this one, he's got to go to it. Jest don't ask me to understand why."

But pap was the one. He was the feller. "To the war?" he said. "Why, I just don't see a bit of use in that. You ain't old enough for the draft, and the country ain't being invaded. Our President in Washington, D.C. is watching the conditions and he will notify us. Besides, in that other war your ma just mentioned, I was drafted and sent clean to Texas and was held there nigh eight months until they finally quit fighting. It seems to me that that, along with your Uncle Marsh who received a actual wound on the battlefields of France, is enough for me and mine to have to do to protect the country, at least in my lifetime. Besides, what'll I do for help on the farm with you gone? It seems to me I'll get mighty far behind."

"You been behind as long as I can remember," Pete said. "Anyway, I'm going. I got to."

"Of course he's got to go," I said. "Them Japanese "

"You hush your mouth!" maw said, crying. "Nobody's talking to you! Go and get me a armful of wood! That's what you can do!"

So I got the wood. And all the next day, while me and Pete and pap was getting in as much wood as we could in that time because Pete said how pap's idea of plenty of wood was one more stick laying against the wall that maw ain't put on the fire yet, Maw was getting Pete ready to go. She washed and mended his clothes and cooked him a shoe box of vittles. And that night me and Pete

laid in the bed and listened to her packing his grip and crying, until after a while Pete got up in his nightshirt and went back there, and I could hear them talking, until at last maw said, "You got to go, and so I want you to go. But I don't understand it, and I won't never, and so don't expect me to." And Pete come back and got into the bed again and laid again still and hard as iron on his back, and then he said, and he wasn't talking to me, he wasn't talking to nobody: "I got to go. I just got to."

"Sho you got to," I said. "Them Japanese." He turned over hard, he kind of surged over onto his side, looking at me in the dark.

"Anyway, you're all right," he said. "I expected to have more trouble with you than with all the rest of them put together."

"I reckon I can't help it neither," I said. "But maybe it will run a few years longer and I can get there. Maybe someday I will jest walk in on you."

"I hope not," Pete said. "Folks don't go to wars for fun. A man don't leave his maw crying just for fun."

"Then why are you going?" I said.

"I got to," he said. "I just got to. Now you go on to sleep. I got to ketch that early bus in the morning."

"All right," I said. "I hear tell Memphis is a big place. How will you find where the Army's at?"

"I'll ask somebody where to go to join it," Pete said. "Go on to sleep now."

"Is that what you'll ask for? Where to join the Army?" I said.

"Yes," Pete said. He turned onto his back again. "Shut up and go to sleep."

We went to sleep. The next morning we et breakfast by lamplight because the bus would pass at six o'clock. Maw wasn't crying now. She jest looked grim and busy, putting breakfast on the table while we et it. Then she finished packing Pete's grip, except he never wanted to take no grip to the war, but maw said decent folks never went nowhere, not even to a war, without a change of clothes and something to tote them in. She put in the shoe box of fried chicken and biscuits and she put the Bible in, too, and then it was time to go. We didn't know until then that maw wasn't going to the bus. She jest brought Pete's cap and overcoat, and still she didn't cry no more, she jest stood with her hands on Pete's shoulders and she didn't move, but somehow, and just holding Pete's shoulders, she looked as hard and fierce as when Pete had turned toward me in the bed last night and tole me that anyway I was all right.

"They could take the country and keep the country, so long as they never bothered me and mine," she said. Then she said, "Don't never forget who you are. You ain't rich and the rest of the world outside of Frenchman's Bend never heard of you. But your blood is good as any blood anywhere, and don't you never forget it."

Then she kissed him, and then we was out of the house, with pap toting Pete's grip whether Pete wanted him to or not. There wasn't no dawn even yet, not even after we had stood on the highway by the mailbox, a while. Then we seen the lights of the bus coming and I was watching the bus until it come up and Pete flagged it, and then, sho enough, there was daylight: it had started while I wasn't watching. And now me and Pete expected pap to say something else foolish, like he done before, about how Uncle Marsh getting wounded in France and that trip to Texas pap taken in 1918 ought to be enough to save the Unity States in 1942, but he never. He done all right too. He jest said, "Good-by, son. Always remember what your ma told you and write her when-ever you find the time." Then he shaken Pete's hand, and Pete looked at me a minute and put his hand on my head and rubbed my head durn nigh hard enough to wring my neck off and jumped into the bus, and the feller wound the door shut and the bus began to hum; then it was moving, humming and grinding and whining louder and louder; it was going fast, with two little red lights behind it that never seemed to get no littler, but just seemed to be running together until pretty soon they would touch and jest be one light. But they never did, and then the bus was gone, and even like it was, I could have pretty nigh busted out crying, nigh to nine years old and all.

Me and pap went back to the house. All that day we worked at the wood tree, and so I never had no good chance until about middle of the afternoon. Then I taken my slingshot and I would have liked to took all my bird eggs, too, because Pete had give me his collection and he holp me with mine, and he would like to git the box out and look at them as good as I would, even if he was nigh twenty years old.

But the box was too big to tote a long ways and have to worry with, so I just taken the shike-poke egg, because it was the best un, and wropped it up good into a matchbox and hid it and the slingshot under the corner of the barn.

Then we et supper and went to bed, and I thought then how if I would 'a' had to stayed in that room and that bed like that even for one more night, I jest couldn't 'a' stood it. Then I could hear pap snoring, but I never heard no sound from maw, whether she was asleep or not, and I don't reckon she was. So I taken my shoes and drapped them out the window, and then I clumb out like I used to watch Pete do when he was still jest seventeen and pap held that he was too young yet to be tomcatting around at night, and wouldn't leave him out, and I put on my shoes and went to the barn and got the slingshot and the shikepoke egg and went to the highway.

It wasn't cold, it was jest durn confounded dark, and that highway stretched on in front of me like, without nobody using it, it had stretched out half again as fer just like a man does when he lays down, so that for a time it looked like full sun was going to ketch me before I had finished them twenty-two miles to Jefferson. But it didn't. Daybreak was jest starting when I walked up the hill into town. I could smell breakfast cooking in the cabins and I wished I had thought to brought me a cold biscuit, but that was too late now. And Pete had told me Memphis was a piece beyond Jefferson, but I never knowed it was no eighty miles. So I stood there on that empty square, with daylight coming and coming and the street lights still burning and that Law looking down at me, and me still eighty miles from Memphis, and it had took me all night to walk jest twenty-two miles, and so, by the time I got to Memphis at that rate, Pete would 'a' done already started for Pearl Harbor.

"Where do you come from?" the Law said.

And I told him again. "I got to get to Memphis. My brother's there."

You mean you ain't got any folks around here?" the Law said. "Nobody but that brother? What are you doing way off down here and your brother in Memphis?"

And I told him again, "I got to get to Memphis. I ain't got no time to waste talking about it and I ain't got time to walk it. I got to git there today."

"Come on here," the Law said.

We went down another street. And there was the bus, just like when Pete got into it yestiddy morning, except there wasn't no lights on it now and it was empty. There was a regular bus dee-po like a railroad dee-po, with a ticket counter and a feller behind it, and the Law said, "Set down over there," and I set down on the bench, and the Law said, "I want to use your telephone," and he talked in the telephone a minute and put it down and said to the feller behind the ticket counter, "Keep your eye on him. I'll be back as soon as Mrs. Habersham can arrange to get herself up and dressed." He went out. I got up and went to the ticket counter.

"I want to go to Memphis," I said.

"You bet," the feller said. "You set down on the bench now. Mr. Foote will be back in a minute."

"I don't know no Mr. Foote," I said. "I want to ride that bus to Memphis."

"You got some money?" he said. "It'll cost you seventy-two cents."

I taken out the matchbox and unwropped the shikepoke egg. "I'll swap you this for a ticket to Memphis," I said.

"What's that?" he said.

"It's a shikepoke egg," I said. "You never seen one before. It's worth a dollar. I'll take seventy-two cents fer it."

"No," he said, "the fellers that own that bus insist on a cash basis. If I started swapping tickets for bird eggs and livestock and such, they would fire me. You go and set down on the bench now, like Mr. Foote . . . "

I started for the door, but he caught me, he put one hand on the ticket counter and jumped over it and caught up with me and reached his hand out to ketch my shirt. I whupped out my pocketknife and snapped it open.

"You put a hand on me and I'll cut it off," I said.

I tried to dodge him and run at the door, but he could move quicker than any grown man I ever see, quick as Pete almost. He cut me off and stood with his back against the door and one foot raised a little, and there wasn't no other way to get out. "Get back on that bench and stay there," he said.

And there wasn't no other way out. And he stood there with his back against the door. So I went back to the bench. And then it seemed like to me that dee-po was full of folks.

There was that Law again, and there was two ladies in fur coats and their faces already painted. But they still looked like they had got up in a hurry and they still never liked it, a old one and a young one, looking down at me.

"He hasn't got a overcoat!" the old one said. "How in the world did he ever get down here by himself?"

"I ask you," the Law said. "I couldn't get nothing out of him except his brother is in Memphis and he wants to get back up there."

"That's right," I said. "I got to git to Memphis today."

"Of course you must," the old one said. "Are you sure you can find your brother when you get to Memphis?"

"I reckon I can," I said. "I ain't got but one and I have knowed him all my life. I reckon I will know him again when I see him."

The old one looked at me. "Somehow he doesn't look like he lives in Memphis," she said.

"He probably don't," the Law said. "You can't tell though. He might live anywhere, overhalls or not. This day and time they get scattered overnight from he hope to breakfast; boys and girls, too, almost before they can walk good. He might have been in Missouri or Texas either yestiddy, for all we know. But he don't seem to have any doubt his brother is in Memphis. All I know to do is send him up there and leave him look."

"Yes," the old one said.

The young one set down on the bench by me and opened a hand satchel and taken out a artermatic writing pen and some papers.

"Now, honey," the old one said, "we're going to see that you find your brother, but we must have a case history for our files first. We want to know your name and your brother's name and where you were born and when your parents died."

"I don't need no case history neither," I said. "All I want is to get to Memphis. I got to get there today."

"You see?" the Law said. He said it almost like he enjoyed it. "That's what I told you."

"You're lucky, at that, Mrs. Habersham," the bus feller said. "I don't think he's got a gun on him, but he can open that knife I mean, fast enough to suit any man." But the old one just stood there looking at me. "Well," she said. "Well. I really don't know what to do."

"I do," the bus feller said. "I'm going to give him a ticket out of my own pocket, as a measure of protecting the company against riot and bloodshed. And when Mr. Foote tells the city board about it, it will be a civic matter and they will not only reimburse me, they will give me a medal too. Hey, Mr. Foote?"

But never nobody paid him no mind. The old one still stood looking down at me. She said "Well," again. Then she taken a dollar from her purse and give it to the bus feller.

"I suppose he will travel on a child's ticket, won't he?"

"Wellum," the bus feller said, "I just don't know what the regulations would be. Likely I will be fired for not crating him and marking the crate Poison. But I'll risk it."

Then they were gone. Then the Law come back with a sandwich and give it to me.

"You're sure you can find that brother?" he said.

"I ain't yet convinced why not," I said. "If I don't see Pete first, he'll see me. He knows me too."

Then the Law went out for good, too, and I et the sandwich. Then more folks come in and bought tickets, and then the bus feller said it was time to go, and I got into the bus just like Pete done, and we was gone. I seen all the towns. I seen all of them. When the bus got to going good, I found out I was jest about wore out for sleep.

But there was too much I hadn't never saw before. We run out of Jefferson and run past fields and woods, then we would run into another town and out of that un and past fields and woods again, and then into another town with stores and gins and water tanks, and we run along by the railroad for a spell and I seen the signal arm move, and then I seen the train and then some more towns, and I was jest about plumb wore out for sleep, but I couldn't resk it. Then Memphis begun. It seemed like, to me, it went on for miles.

We would pass a patch of stores and I would think that was sholy it and the bus would even stop. But it wouldn't be Memphis yet and we would go on again past water tanks and smok-estacks on top of the mills, and if they was gins and sawmills, I never knowed there was that many and I never seen any that big, and where they got enough cotton and logs to run um I don't know.

Then I see Memphis. I knowed I was right this time. It was standing up into the air. It looked like about a dozen whole towns bigger than Jefferson was set up on one edge in a field, standing up into the air higher than ara hill in all Yoknapatawpha County. Then we was in it, with the bus stopping ever' few feet, it seemed like to me, and cars rushing past on both sides of it and the street crowded with folks from ever'where in town that day, until I didn't see how there could 'a' been nobody left in Mis'sippi a-tall to even sell me a bus ticket, let alone write out no case histories.

Then the bus stopped. It was another bus dee-po, a heap bigger than the one in Jefferson. And I said, "All right. Where do folks join the Army?"

"What?" the bus feller said.

And I said it again, "Where do folks join the Army?"

"Oh," he said. Then he told me how to get there. I was afraid at first I wouldn't ketch on how to do in a town big as Memphis. But I caught on all right. I never had to ask but twice more. Then I was there, and I was durn glad to git out of all them rushing cars and shoving folks and all that racket for a spell, and I thought, It won't be long now, and I thought how if there was any kind of a crowd there that had done already joined the Army, too, Pete would likely see me before I seen him. And so I walked into the room. And Pete wasn't there.

He wasn't even there. There was a soldier with a big arrer head on his sleeve, writing, and two fellers standing in front of him, and there was some more folks there, I reckon. It seems to me I remember some more folks there. I went to the table where the soldier was writing, and I said,

"Where's Pete?" and he looked up and I said, "My brother. Pete Grier. Where is he?"

"What?" the soldier said. "Who?"

And I told him again. "He joined the Army yestiddy. He's going to Pearl Harbor. So am I. I want to ketch him. Where you all got him?" Now they were all looking at me, but I never paid them no mind. "Come on," I said. "Where is he?"

The soldier had quit writing. He had both hands spraddled out on the table. "Oh," he said. "You're going, too, hah?"

"Yes," I said. "They got to have wood and water. I can chop it and tote it. Come on. Where's Pete?"

The soldier stood up. "Who let you in here?" he said. "Go on. Beat it."

"Durn that," I said. "You tell me where Pete . . . "

I be dog if he couldn't move faster than the bus feller even. He never come over the table, he come around it, he was on me almost before I knowed it, so that I jest had time to jump back and whup out my pocket-knife and snap it open and hit one lick, and he hollered and jumped back and grab-bed one hand with the other and stood there cussing and hollering.

One of the other fellers grabbed me from behind, and I hit at him with the knife, but I couldn't reach him. Then both of the fellers had me from behind, and then another soldier come out of a door at the back. He had on a belt with a britching strop over one shoulder.

"What the hell is this?" he said.

"That little son cut me with a knife!" the first soldier hollered. When he said that I tried to get at him again. but both them fellers was holding me, two against one, and the soldier with the backing strop said, "Here, here. Put your knife up, feller. None of us are armed. A man don't knifefight folks that are barehanded." I could begin to hear him then. He sounded jest like Pete talked to me. "Let him go," he said. They let me go. "Now what's all the trouble about?"

And I told him. "I see," he said. "And you come up to see if he was all right before he left."

"No," I said. "I came to . . . "

But he had already turned to where the first soldier was wropping a handkerchief around his hand.

"Have you got him?" he said. The first soldier went back to the table and looked at some papers.

"Here he is," he said. "He enlisted yestiddy. He's in a detachment leav-ing this morning for Little Rock." He had a watch stropped on his arm. He looked at it. "The train leaves in about fifty minutes. If I know country boys, they're probably all down there at the station right now."

"Get him up here," the one with the backing strop said. "Phone the sta-tion. Tell the porter to get him a cab. And you come with me," he said.

It was another office behind that un, with jest a table and some chairs. We set there while the soldier smoked, and it wasn't long; I knowed Pete's feet soon as I heard them. Then the first soldier opened the door and Pete come in. He never had no soldier clothes on. He looked jest like he did when he got on the bus yestiddy morning, except it seemed to me like it was at least a week, so much had happened, and I had done had to do so much traveling. He come in and there he was, looking at me like he hadn't never left home, except that here we was in Memphis, on the way to Pearl Harbor.

"What in durnation are you doing here?" he said.

And I told him, "You got to have wood and water to cook with. I can chop it and tote it for you-all."

"No," Pete said. "You're going back home."

"No, Pete," I said. "I got to go too. I got to. It hurts my heart, Pete."

"No," Pete said. He looked at the soldier. "I jest don't know what could have happened to him, lootenant," he said. "He never drawed a knife on anybody before in his life."

He looked at me. "What did you do it for?"

"I don't know," I said. "I jest had to. I jest had to git here. I jest had to find you."

"Well, don't you never do it again, you hear?" Pete said.

"You put that knife in your pocket and you keep it there. If I ever again hear of you drawing it on anybody, I'm coming back from wherever I am at and whup the fire out of you. You hear me?"

"I would pure cut a throat if it would bring you back to stay," I said. "Pete," I said. "Pete."

"No," Pete said. Now his voice wasn't hard and quick no more, it was almost quiet, and I knowed now I wouldn't never change him. "You must go home. You must look after maw, and I am depending on you to look after my ten acres. I want you to go back home. Today. Do you hear?"

"I hear," I said.

"Can he get back home by himself?" the soldier said.

"He come up here by himself," Pete said.

"I can get back, I reckon," I said. "I don't live in but one place. I don't reckon it's moved."

Pete taken a dollar out of his pocket and give it to me.

"That'll buy your bus ticket right to our mailbox," he said.

"I want you to mind the lootenant. He'll send you to the bus. And you go back home and you take care of maw and look after my ten acres and keep that durn knife in your pocket. You hear me?"

"Yes, Pete," I said.

"All right," Pete said. "Now I got to go." He put his hand on my head again. But this time he never wrung my neck.

He just laid his hand on my head a minute. And then I be dog if he didn't lean down and kiss me, and I heard his feet and then the door, and I never looked up and that was all, me setting there, rubbing the place where Pete kissed me and the soldier throwed back in his chair, looking out the window and coughing. He reached into his pocket and handed something to me without looking around. It was a piece of chewing gum.

"Much obliged," I said. "Well, I reckon I might as well start back. I got a right fer piece to go."

"Wait," the soldier said. Then he telephoned again and I said again I better start

back, and he said again, "Wait. Remember what Pete told you."

So we waited, and then another lady come in, old, too, in a fur coat, too, but she smelled all right, she never had no artermatic writing pen nor no case history neither. She come in and the soldier got up, and she looked around quick until she saw me, and come and put her hand on my shoulder light and quick and easy as maw herself might 'a' done it.

"Come on," she said. "Let's go home to dinner."

"Nome," I said. "I got to ketch the bus to Jefferson."

"I know. There's plenty of time. We'll go home and eat dinner first."

She had a car. And now we was right down in the middle of all them other cars. We was almost under the busses, and all them crowds of people on the street close enough to where I could have talked to them if I had knowed who they was. After a while she stopped the car. "Here we are," she said, and I looked at it, and if all that was her house, she sho had a big family. But all of it wasn't. We crossed a hall with trees growing in it and went into a little room without nothing in it but a nigger dressed up in a uniform a heap shinier than them soldiers had, and the nigger shut the door, and then I hollered, "Look out!" and grabbed, but it was all right; that whole little room jest went right on up and stopped and the door opened and we was in another hall, and the lady unlocked door and we went in, and there was another soldier, a old feller, with a britching strop, too, and a silver-colored bird on each shoulder.

"Here we are," the lady said. "This is Colonel McKellogg. Now, what would you like for

dinner?"

"I reckon I'll jest have some ham and eggs and coffee," I said. She had done started to pick up the telephone. She stopped, "Coffee?" she said.

"When did you start drinking coffee?"

"I don't know," I said. "I reckon it was before I could remember."

"You're about eight, aren't you?" she said.

"Nome," I said. "I'm eight and ten months. Going on eleven months."

She telephoned then. Then we set there and I told them how Pete had jest left that morning for Pearl Harbor and I had aimed to go with him, but I would have to go back home to take care of maw and look after Pete's ten acres, and she said how they had a little boy about my size, too, in a school in the East. Then a nigger, another one, in a short kind of shirttail coat, rolled a kind of wheelbarrer in. It had my ham and eggs and a glass of milk and a piece of pie, too, and I thought I was hungry But when I taken the first bite I found out I couldn't swallow it, and I got up quick.

"I got to go," I said.

"Wait," she said.

"I got to go," I said.

"Just a minute," she said. "I've already telephoned for the car. It won't be but a minute now. Can't you drink the milk even? Or maybe some of your coffee?"

"Nome," I said. "I ain't hungry. I'll eat when I git home."

Then the telephone rung. She never even answered it.

"There," she said. "There's the car." And we went back down in that 'ere little moving room with the dressed-up nigger. This time it was a big car with a soldier driving it. I got into the front with him. She give the soldier a dollar.

"He might get hungry," she said. "Try to find a decent place for him."

"O. K., Mrs. McKellogg," the soldier said.

Then we was gone again. And now I could see Memphis good, bright in the sunshine, while we was swinging around it. And first thing I knowed, we was back on the same highway the bus run on this morning the patches of stores and them big gins and sawmills, and Memphis running on for miles, it seemed like to me, before it begun to give out. Then we was running again between the fields and woods, running fast now, and except for that soldier, it was like I hadn't never been to Memphis a-tall. We was going fast now.

At this rate, before I knowed it we would be home again, and I thought about me riding up to Frenchman's Bend in this big car with a soldier running it, and all of a sudden I begun to cry. I never knowed I was fixing to, and I couldn't stop it. I set there by that soldier, crying. We was going fast.

"Two Soldiers"

PLOT QUIZ

1. "Me and Pete," the first three words of the story, refers to:

(a) Billy Joe and his brother
(b) The narrator and his cousin
(c) The narrator and brother

2. The narrator of the story is almost ________ years old.

(a) Nine
(b) Ten
(c) Fifteen
(d) Seventeen
(e) Twenty

3. Pete is almost ________ years old.

(a) Nine
(b) Ten
(c) Fifteen
(d) Seventeen
(e) Twenty

4. The story takes place in (two answers):

(a) Memphis
(b) Oxford
(c) Frenchman's Bend
(d) Mississippi
(e) Jefferson

5. The time of the story is during the ________.

(a) Revolutionary War
(b) Civil War
(c) First World War
(d) Second World War

6. Pete goes to the city because he had been drafted.

(a) True
(b) False

7. When Pete left home, he was most concerned about the effect his absence would have on his:

(a) Maw
(b) Pap
(c) Brother
(d) Sister
(e) None of these

8. Pete's mother *<u>is against</u>* his leaving home because she:

(a) Can't think of one good reason
(b) Thinks that her brother did enough in WW I
(c) Knows he will get into trouble
(d) Thinks his brother will want to leave home next

9. Pete's father is *<u>against</u>* his leaving home because:

(a) He had done enough already
(b) He needed Pete's help on the farm
(c) He had gotten into trouble himself
(d) He agreed with Pete's mother's thinking
(e) None of these

10. Pete's brother is both *for and against* his brother's leaving home.

(a) True
(b) False

11. Since Pete felt that he had to leave home, that he's "got to go," his brother assumed that he would have to go with him.

(a) True
(b) False

12. Pete never did give a reason for leaving home.

(a) True
(b) False

13. The author wants us to admire Pete's reason for leaving home.

(a) True
(b) False

14. The author wants us to think that Pete's brother is foolish for wanting to leave home with his brother.

(a) True
(b) False

15. Pete's brother finally gets to the city where Pete had gone by:

(a) Walking
(b) Walking and a bus
(c) Hitchhiking
(d) Bus
(e) Train

16. When the narrator finally gets to Memphis and finds his brother, Pete is:

(a) Curious
(b) Astonished
(c) Disgusted
(d) Angry
(e) Embarrassed

17. Pete immediately reprimands his brother for:

(a) Using profane language
(b) Using his knife
(c) Whining and whimpering
(d) Disobeying him
(e) Not telling his parents he had also left home

18. Peter's brother told him that he had come to Memphis because:

(a) He wanted to say goodbye
(b) His heart hurt
(c) He knew he wanted him to come
(d) He knew he would need wood and water
(e) None of these

19. Pete's brother is astonished when his older brother:

(a) Hits him on the head
(b) Takes away his knife
(c) Kisses him
(d) Shouts angrily at him
(e) Tells him the Army had rejected him

20. When Pete's brother returns home, he:

(a) Tells his parents he is sorry for being so late
(b) Begins crying uncontrollably
(c) Tells his parents he wanted to see Pete
(d) Blames Pete for leaving home
(e) None of these.

Socratic Seminar

1. Why is the story told from the view point of Pete's nine-year-old brother?
2. Why does Faulkner have his narrator speak in dialect?
3. Why does Pete never explain why he *has* to go to war?
4. Why doesn't Pete's mother understand why Pete *has* to go to war?
5. Does Faulkner want us to regard Pete's father as unpatriotic because he can see no use in his son joining the US Army?
6. Why does Pete's brother hold back his tears when Pete gets on the bus to Memphis, but cry uncontrollably when the soldier drives him home to Frenchman's Bend?
7. Why does Faulkner contrast the poverty of the Grier family with the wealth of the Colonel and his wife and son?
8. Why does the movie version omit the scene where Mrs. McKellogg takes Pete's brother to her home for dinner?
9. Why does the movie change Faulkner's ending to the story?
10. Why would Faulkner have rejected the movie's ending of his story?

Two Soldiers

DVD (40 MINS) 2006

Plot Summary

Setting: Mississippi 1941 (story published in 1942)

1. "The Lone Ranger" rides again (background music). Unlike the original story which opens with Pete and his little brother sneaking off to listen to Killegrew's radio, the 2004 version begins with Pete and his nearly nine-year old brother, Willie, examining the nest of a green heron. While looking for a shikepoke egg Pete explains how this bird is special because it returns to the same nest every year. Willie makes a strange offhand comment: "It must be as lazy as Pap."
2. Killegrew's radio: Flash. Flash. Pearl Harbor: "Yesterday, December 7, 1941, a day which will live in infamy . . ." FDR.
3. Pete and Willie try to go to sleep. "Go to sleep. Say your prayers." Pete recalls FDR's memorable words.
4. Pete gives Willie a shikepoke egg and his entire egg collection. "Why don't you want it anymore?" his brother asks.
5. "I don't see a bit of use in this. Who will help me with the plowing? I'll get behind." Pete: "You've been behind as long as I can remember."
6. "You whip the biggins and I'll whip the littens."
7. Maw packs Pete's valise. "You ain't rich and nobody will know where you come from but don't you never forget your heart is as rich as any man's, anywhere."

   Faulkner: "Don't never forget who you are. You ain't rich and the rest of he world outside of Frenchman's Bend never heard of you. But your blood is good as any blood anywhere, and don't you never forget it" (p. 87)
8. Paw puts Pete on the Greyhound to Memphis. "Here's your grandpap's watch . . . When Pete says goodbye to Willie, he rubs his head and then says, "Don't forget your prayers."
9. Before Pete leaves the next morning, Willie stands transfixed by his open pocket knife stuck in a log.
10. Supper at home. Lone Ranger rides again. Willie leaves home at night and walks 30 miles to Jefferson which is 50 miles from Memphis. The Law picks up the boy because he is an evident runaway.

11. The Law (Sheriff Foote) takes Willie to the bus depot. The clerk also wants to swap Willie's egg but he will do so only for a bus ticket to Memphis. When the clerk tries to stop Willie from leaving the room, he threatens him with his pocket knife.
12. While waiting for the social worker to arrive, does Willie understand the sheriff's joke about a skunk? ("The skunk thunk that the stump stunk but the stump thunk the skunk stunk.")
13. After Mrs. Habersham, the social worker arrives, and is repulsed by the "malodorous" boy, she makes a grand display of charity by buying his ticket.
14. On the bus to Memphis, a black guitar player sings "Hold that tiger."
15. In Memphis, after Willie finds the Army registration, he begins calling out Pete's name along a long line of men waiting to sign up. Frustrated, he bursts into the courthouse shouting, "Where's Pete? Pete Grier? He's goin to war in Pearl Harbor and I'm goin too!"
16. An angry sergeant tells Pete the best way he can help Pete is to "GO HOME!" Another sergeant tries to get rid of Willie by telling him that they have no more pint-size uniforms. Finally, when a major tries to grab Willie, he pulls his knife on him, cutting his hand.
17. Colonel McKellogg enters to investigate the ruckus. He tells Willie that we don't attack unarmed men. He hands him his knife. How did you get here? He walked?! How far is Jefferson? How old are you? What do you plan to do in the Army?
18. The Colonel orders the Major to bring Willie's brother to his office. Lone Ranger theme.
19. When Pete enters, the Colonel tells him there's no need for him to apologize for his little brother.
20. Pete asks Willie what he is doing here and then tells the Colonel that he got into his stubborn little head that he was gonna be a soldier. When Pete again asks Willie why he's here, he replies simply, "It hurt my heart."
21. Moved, when Pete makes Willie promise that he will go home, Willie responds, "You ain't comin back, are you?"
22. The Colonel tells Willie that he can watch the big bird (DC 3) that will take Pete to Little Rock.
23. Pete breaks down and kisses Willie. Don't forget the way home. I'll never forget. It's instinct.
24. As a soldier begins driving Willie back to Frenchman's Bend, Willie jumps out of the moving car and begins walking. The Colonel get out of the car, walks quickly after Willie, and asks where he is going. He replies, "I got to get home,

today." When he replies that The Colonel asks if he wants to see his brother leave for Little Rock on the silver bird? When Willie refuses, the Colonel orders the soldier to begin the three-hour drive back to Frenchmen's Bend and then returns his pocket knife.

25. Closing scenes:
    - Pete boards the DC 3 to Little Rock.
    - Willie begins crying uncontrollably on his way back to Frenchmen's Bend.
    - Closing image: Pete hoists Willie on his shoulders and walks down a hill.

Note: For the sequel, "Shall not Perish," published in 1943, Faulkner wrote a TV play for Lux Video Theater in 1954.

Discussion Questions, *Two Soldiers*–DVD (40 mins) 2006

1. Why does the movie open with the Lone Ranger theme music and Pete explaining to his nearly nine-year-old brother, Willie, the significance of the green heron's nest?
2. Why do the boys learn on Killegrew's radio FDR's historic words: "Yesterday, December 7, 1941, a day which will live in infamy, the United States was attacked at Pearl Harbor"?
3. When Pete gives his entire egg collection to his little brother, why is our attention drawn to the shikepoke egg?
4. Is Pete's father or mother more upset about his determination to join the US Army?
5. When Pete's father asks who will help him with the farm when he's away, why does Faulkner have him reply, "You've been behind as long as I can remember"?
6. As he leaves home, why does Faulkner have Maw tell him, "You ain't rich and nobody will know where you come from but your heart is as rich as any man's, anywhere. Don't you ever forget it"?
7. When Paw puts Pete on the Greyhound to Memphis, why doesn't he give him any advice?
8. When Pete says goodbye to his brother, why does he only rub his head and then remind him to say his prayers?
9. When the Law picks up Willie in Jefferson and takes him to his office, why does he offer to swap with him his shikepoke egg?
10. Like the Law, why does the clerk also try to get Willie to swap his shikepoke egg?
11. When the clerk tries to stop Willie from leaving the room, why does he threaten him with his pocket knife?
12. While waiting for the social worker to arrive, does Willie understand the sheriff's joke about a skunk?
13. Why does Faulkner have the social worker make a display of charity when she buys Willie's ticket to Memphis?
14. When the clerk extorts Willie's shikepoke egg, why does Faulkner have him give him an owl's egg?
15. When Willie enters the registration room, how does he attract the attention not only of the staff soldiers but also of strangers?

16. Why does Faulkner again have Willie pull out his knife when a soldier grabs him?
17. Why does Willie give the Colonel his knife?
18. Why does the Colonel order a soldier to bring Pete to his office rather than ordering Willie to go home?
19. When Pete enters, why does the Colonel tells him there's no need to apologize for his brother?
20. When Pete again asks Willie why he came to Memphis, why does he reply only, "My heart hurt?"
21. Unlike the story, when Pete makes Willie promise that he will go home, why does Willie ask, "You ain't comin back, are you?"
22. Why does the Colonel offer to allow Willie to see Pete leave for Little Rock on a plane?
23. Unlike the story when Pete kisses Willie goodbye, why does he tell him he will never forget the way home because "It's instinct"?
24. Why does the movie omit the scene from the story when Willie goes to Mrs. McKellogg home?
25. Why does Willie jump out of the moving car when the soldier begins to take him home?

"Two Soldiers": Then (1942) and Now (2004)

Directions: In a *one-page essay* answer this basic question of interpretation by writing a paragraph on three of the follow up questions. Omit an introduction; begin with a thesis and then conclude with a paraphrase of the thesis.

Basic Question 1: How does the 2004 movie version enhance Faulkner's 1942 story of "Two Soldiers"?

1. Unlike the original story that opens with Killegrew's radio, why does the 2004 version begin with Pete and his little brother, Willie, examining a heron's nest?

2. How does the shikepoke egg become a metaphor for the relationship between the two brothers?

3. At the bus depot in Jefferson, when Willie tries to trade in his shikepoke egg for a ticket to Memphis, why does the agent attempt to cheat him in the movie?

4. In Faulkner's story why does Pete kiss his brother when he promises to return home but kiss him in the movie when Willie says, "You're not coming back, are you?"

5. Why does the movie omit the entire scene where Willie is taken to the home of Mrs. McKellogg?

6. Why does Colonel McKellogg, who is mentioned only in passing in Faulkner's story, become a major character in the 2004 movie?

7. Why does Colonel McKellogg take an immediate liking to Willie?

8. Are Pete and his brother both soldiers in the same way in the movie as they are in Faulkner's story?

Basic Question 2: How does the 2004 movie make the bond between the two brothers more evident than it is in Faulkner's 1942 story?

1. Unlike the original story that opens with Killegrew's radio, why does the 2004 version begin with Pete and his little brother, Willie, examining the nest of a heron?

2. Unlike the original story, how does the shikepoke egg become a metaphor for the relationship between Pete and Willie?

3. What does Faulkner imply by having Willie try to trade his shikepoke egg for a bus ticket to Memphis?

4. Is the movie's scene as poignant as the story when Willie tells Pete, "I would pure cut a throat if it would bring you back to stay"?

5. Unlike the story, when Willie meets Pete in the Colonel's office, why does he suddenly ask him, "You're not coming back, are you?"

6. Why does Pete kiss Willie and tell him "Don't forget the way home"?

7. Unlike the story when Pete kisses Willie goodbye, why does he tell him that instinct will tell him how to return home?

8. Why doesn't the movie version, like the original story, conclude with Pete's brother unable to understand why he begins to cry uncontrollably?

"Two Soldiers" Then (1942) and Now (2004)

How does the 2004 movie version enhance Faulkner's 1942 story of "Two Soldiers"?

1. It makes more evident the depth of the love between the two brothers.
2. The shikepoke egg of the green heron becomes a metaphor for their brotherly love.
   - Opening scene: heron's nest—monogamous / instinct.
   - Pete gives Willie his egg collection as he leaves.
   - The Law tries to swap with Willie for his shikepoke egg.
   - The bus depot clerk tries to extort Willie's egg.
   - The DC 3: "If it laid eggs they'd be as big as you." (Pete) "Don't you want to see your brother leave on the silver bird?" (Col. McKellogg)
3. Willie's knife becomes a major symbol of his desperation and determination to find Pete in Memphis.
   - Knife in log.
   - Willie is transfixed staring at the knife.
4. Willie's visit to Colonel McKellogg's home is omitted.
5. As in the opening scene, the closing scene ends with Willie on Pete's shoulders.

Extra Credit

Read "Shall Not Perish," then answer this basic question of interpretation in an essay:

How does "Shall Not Perish," the sequel to "Two Soldiers," advance and develop the theme of patriotism?

Gary Wills, editor

Note: Gary Wills received the Pulitzer Prize in 1994 for his brilliant rhetorical analysis in *Lincoln at Gettysburg: The Words that Remade America*, Simon & Schuster, 1992. To reach a larger audience, he summarized his book in a lengthy article, "The Words That Remade America," in *The Atlantic Monthly*, June 1992, pp. 57–79.

In his edited version of Lincoln's greatest speech, Wills observes: "Lincoln interlocks his sentences, making of them a constantly self-referential system. This linking up by explicit repetition amounts to a kind of hook-and-eye method for joining the parts of his address. The rhetorical devices are almost invisible, since they use no figurative language. I highlight them topographically here."

The Gettysburg Address

Gary Wills, editor

Four score and seven years ago our fathers brought forth on this continent, *a new nation, conceived* in Liberty, *and dedicated* to the proposition that all men are created equal.

Now we are engaged in A GREAT CIVIL WAR, testing whether *that nation,* or any nation so *conceived and so dedicated,* can long endure.

We are met on a great BATTLEFIELD of THAT WAR.

We have come to *dedicate* a portion of THAT FIELD as a final resting place for those who here gave their lives that *that nation* might live. It is altogether fitting and proper that we should do this.

But in a larger sense, we can not *dedicate*—we can not *consecrate*—we cannot hallow—this ground.

The brave men, living and dead, who struggled here have *consecrated* it, far above our poor power to add or detract. The world will little note, nor long remember what we say here, but it can never forget what they did here.

It is for us the living, rather, to be *dedicated* here to the unfinished work which they who fought here have thus far so nobly advanced. It is rather for us to be here *dedicated* to the great task remaining before us—that from THESE HONORED DEAD we take increased devotion to that cause for which they gave the last full measure of devotion—that we here highly resolve that THESE DEAD shall not have died in vain—that this nation, under God shall have a new birth of freedom—that that government of the people, by the people, for the people, shall not perish from the earth.

Lincoln's Speech Doesn't Compute

March 08, 1990 Mike Royko, Chicago Tribune

The ad caught my eye and intrigued me. It was for a computer program and it said: "Write better in 30 days or your money back!" I'm not a computer nut, but I'm familiar with computer programs that correct spelling and have built-in dictionaries. But the ad for this program said that it would correct "stylistic errors." Style. That's a big part of what writing is about.

So I decided to check it out. I stopped by the computer store to give it a test run. I wanted to see what the program would say about the style of a short piece of writing that has always been one of my favorites. I typed it into the computer just as the author is said to have written and delivered it. Then the computer printed out its critique. Here's the final product, with the computer's comments in parentheses.

Fourscore and seven years ago our fathers brought forth on this continent, a new nation, conceived in Liberty, and dedicated to the proposition that all men are created equal.

> (No. Long sentences can be difficult to read and understand. Consider revising so that no more than one complete thought is expressed in each sentence. No. Passive voice: "are created." Consider revising, using active. See Help for more information. No. Usually a paragraph should have more than one sentence.)

Now we are engaged

> (No. Passive voice: "are engaged." Consider revising using active voice. See Help for more information.)

in a great civil war, testing whether that nation or any nation so conceived and so dedicated can long endure. We are met

> (No. Passive voice: "are met." Consider revising using active voice. See Help for more information.)

on a great battlefield of that war. We have come to dedicate a portion of that field, as a final resting place for those who here gave their lives that that

> (No. Delete doubled word or punctuation mark.)

nation might live. It is altogether fitting and proper that we should do this. But,

(No. Use "But" sparingly to start a sentence.)

in a larger sense, we cannot dedicate-we cannot consecrate-we cannot hallow-this ground. The brave men, living and dead, who struggled here, have consecrated it far above our poor power to add or detract. The world will little note nor long remember

(No. An adjective "long" is usually not followed by a verb "remember."You may need to use an adverbial form of"long" (e.g. "quickly" instead of"quick"), or you may need a comma before "remember.")

what we say here, but it can never forget what they did here. It is for us, the living, rather

(No. This word usually adds little and should be omitted.)

to be dedicated here to the unfinished work which

(No. "That" is almost always preferred to "which" in this situation. If you really mean "which," then it usually needs to be preceded by a comma. See Help key for more help.)

they who fought here have thus far so nobly advanced.

(No. Long sentences can be difficult to read and understand. Consider revising so that no more than one complete thought is expressed in each sentence.)

It is rather

(No. This word usually adds little and should be omitted.)

for us to be here dedicated to the great task remaining before us-that from these honored dead we take increased devotion to that cause for which they gave the last full measure of devotion; that we here highly resolve that these dead

(No. Usually "these" should be followed by a plural noun.)

shall not have died in vain; that this nation, under God, shall have a new birth of freedom; and that government of the people, by the people, for the people, shall not perish from the earth.

(Problems marked/detected: 13/13)

That's something. As often as I've read this speech, getting a lump in my throat every time, I didn't detect even one stylistic problem, much less 13. Shows how little I know.

But I suppose we really shouldn't expect anything better from someone who grew up in a log cabin, hoofed to a one-room schoolhouse, and never made it to college. We might remember, that Abe Lincoln was at a stylistic disadvantage when he wrote what has become known as his Gettysburg Address. The poor guy didn't have a "Help Key" to push.

And even with his 13 stylistic flaws, we can say one thing in Abe's behalf: he sure as hell wasn't a computer nerd. So run that through your program and spit it out.

BARACK OBAMA'S SPEECH ON PATRIOTISM

INDEPENDENCE, MO

JUNE 30, 2008

Precis
Introduction (1–4)

"A shot heard around the world."

In 1775, a band of Lexington and Concord colonists fired "a shot heard 'around the world" that began the American Revolution and America's experiment in democracy. The odds against them were enormous, for ultimate failure would bring charges of treason and death by hanging. And yet they took that chance. They did so not on behalf of a particular tribe or lineage, but on behalf of a larger idea: the idea of liberty, the idea of God-given, inalienable rights.

Those men of Lexington and Concord were among our first patriots. And at the beginning of a week when we celebrate the birth of our nation, I think it's fitting to pause for a moment and reflect on the meaning of patriotism, theirs and ours—about the commitments that bind us together as a nation and that bind us to each other as well.

The meaning of patriotism today (5–7)

How do we keep ourselves safe and secure while preserving our liberties? How do we restore trust in a government that seems increasingly removed from its people and dominated by special interests? How do we ensure that, in an increasingly global economy, the winners maintain allegiance to the less fortunate? How do we resolve our differences at a time of increasing diversity? And finally it's worth considering the meaning of patriotism on this anniversary of the birth of our nation and while we are in the midst of a crucial presidential election, because the question of who is or is not a patriot all too often poisons our political debates in ways that divide us rather than bring us together.

My patriotism now questioned (8–10)

Throughout my life, I've always taken my deep and abiding love for this country as a given. It was how I was raised; it is what propelled me into public service; it is why I am running for president. And yet, during the last sixteen months, for the first time my patriotism has been challenged. So let me say this at the outset of my remarks: I will never question the patriotism of others in this campaign. And I will not stand idly by when I hear others question mine.

Patriotism then and now (11–14)

My concerns here aren't simply personal, however. After all, throughout our history, men and women of far greater significance and stature than me have had their patriotism questioned in the midst of momentous debates.

Thomas Jefferson was accused by the Federalists of selling out to the French; the Anti-Federalists were just as convinced that John Adams was in cahoots with the British, intent on restoring monarchal rule. Likewise, even our wisest presidents have sought sometimes to justify questionable practices on the basis of patriotism: Adams' Alien and Sedition Act, Lincoln's suspension of habeas corpus, Roosevelt's internment of Japanese-Americans during World War II.

All were defended at the time as expressions of patriotism, and those who disagreed with their policies were sometimes labeled as unpatriotic. In other words, the use of patriotism as a political sword or a political shield is as old as the republic.

Still, what's striking about today's patriotism debate is the degree to which it remains rooted in the culture wars of the 1960s, in the arguments that go back 40 years or more.

In the early years of the civil rights movement and the opposition to the Vietnam War, defenders of the status quo often accused anybody who questioned the wisdom of government policies of being unpatriotic. Meanwhile, some of those in the so-called counterculture of the '60s reacted not merely by criticizing particular government policies, but by attacking the symbols, and in extreme cases the very idea of America itself.

Patriotism remains a divisive issue (15–18)

Most Americans never bought into these simplistic world views, these caricatures of left and of right. Most Americans understood that dissent does not make one unpatriotic . . . and most Americans understand that there's nothing smart or sophisticated about a cynical disregard for America's traditions and institutions.

Given the enormous challenges that lie before us, we can no longer afford these sorts of divisions. None of us expect that arguments about patriotism will, or should, vanish entirely. After all, when we argue about patriotism, we're arguing about who we are as a country and, more importantly, who we should be. But surely we can agree that no party or political philosophy has a monopoly on patriotism. And surely we can arrive at a definition of patriotism that, however rough and imperfect, captures the best of America's common spirit.

What is patriotism? (19–20)

What would such a definition look like? For me, as for most Americans, patriotism starts as a gut instinct, a loyalty and love for country that's rooted in some of my earliest memories.

The story of my patriotism (21–24)

I remember listening to my grandmother telling stories about her work on a bomber assembly line during World War II. I remember my grandfather handing me his dog tags from his time in Patton's army and understanding that his defense of this country marked one of his greatest sources of pride. That's my idea of America.

I remember, when living for four years in Indonesia as a child, I listened to my mother reading me the first lines of the Declaration of Independence, "We hold these truths to be self-evident, that all men are created equal, that they're endowed by their creator with certain unalienable rights, that among these are life, liberty and the pursuit of happiness."

I remember her explaining how this declaration applied to every American and how those words and the words of the United States Constitution protected us from the injustices that we witnessed other people suffering during those years abroad.

What my patriotism means to me today (25–29)

As I got older, that gut instinct that so many of us have, that America is the greatest country on Earth, would survive. That instinct that this is the greatest country on Earth survived not only because, in my mind, the joys of American life and culture—its vitality, its variety, its freedom—always outweighed its imperfections, but because I learned that what makes America great has never been its perfection, but the belief that it can be made better.

You know, for a young man like me of mixed race, without firm anchor in any particular community, without even a father's steadying hand, it is this essential American idea—that we are not constrained by the accident of birth, but can make of our lives what we will—that has defined my life, just as it has defined the life of so many other Americans.

And that's why, for me, patriotism is always more than just loyalty to a place on a map or a certain kind of people. Instead, it's also loyalty to America's ideals, ideals for which anyone can sacrifice, or defend, or give their last full measure of devotion.

America's imperfections call for the patriotism of dissent (30–35)

I believe it is this loyalty that allows a country teeming with different races and ethnicities, religions and customs, to come together as one. I believe also that those who attack America's flaws without acknowledging the singular greatness of our ideals, and their proven capacity to inspire a better world, do not truly understand America.

Of course, precisely because America isn't perfect, precisely because our ideals constantly demand more from us, patriotism can never be defined as loyalty to any particular leader, or government, or policy.

Now, we may hope that our leaders and our government stand up for our ideals, stand up for what's right, and there are many times in our history when that's occurred. But when our laws, when our leaders or our government are out of alignment with those ideals, then the dissent of ordinary Americans may prove to be one of the truest expressions of patriotism.

Patriotism also means personal sacrifice and service (36–43)

Beyond a loyalty to America's ideals, beyond a willingness to dissent on behalf of those ideals, I also believe that patriotism must, if it is to mean anything, involve the willingness to sacrifice, to give up something we value on behalf of a larger cause.

Indeed, one of the good things to emerge from the current conflict in Iraq has been the widespread recognition that, whether you support this war or oppose it, the sacrifice of our troops is always worthy of honor. That's a change from the '60s that's been very welcome to many of us.

But for the rest of us, for those of us not in uniform or without loved ones in the military, the call to service for the country's greater good remains an imperative of citizenship. Sadly, in recent years, in the midst of war on two fronts, this call to service never came.

I believe one of the tasks of the next administration is to ensure that this movement towards service grows and sustains itself in the years to come.

We should expand AmeriCorps and grow the Peace Corps. We should encourage national service by making it a part of the requirement for a new college assistance program, even as we strengthen the benefits for those whose sense of duty has already led them to serve in our military.

So government can do its part. We must remember, though, that true patriotism cannot be forced or legislated with a mere set of government programs. Instead, it must reside in the hearts of our people, and cultivated in the heart of our culture, and nurtured in the hearts of our children.

Genuine patriotism is the result of good civic education (44–49)

As we begin our fourth century as a nation, it is easy to take the extraordinary nature of America for granted. But it is our responsibility as Americans and as parents to instill that history in our children, both at home and at school.

The loss of quality civic education from so many of our classrooms has left too many young Americans without the most basic knowledge of who our forefathers are, or what they did, or the significance of the founding documents that bear their names. Too many children are ignorant of the sheer effort, the risks and sacrifices made by previous generations, to ensure that this country survived war and depression, through the great struggles of civil, and social, and worker's rights. It is up to us, then, to teach them.

It is up to us to teach our children a lesson that those of us in politics all too often forget: that patriotism involves not only defending this country against external threat, but also working constantly to make America a better place for future generations.

When we fail to educate effectively millions of our children so that they might compete in a global economy or we fail to invest in the basic scientific research that has driven innovation in this country, we risk leaving behind an America that has fallen in the ranks of the world.

Genuine patriotism also has an eye on posterity (50–53)

Just as patriotism involves each of us making a commitment to this nation that extends beyond our own individual immediate self-interest, so must that commitment extend beyond our own time here on Earth. Our greatest leaders have always understood this. They've defined patriotism with an eye towards posterity.

George Washington is rightly revered for his leadership of the Continental Army, but one of his greatest acts of patriotism was his insistence on stepping down after two terms, reminding future presidents that this is a government of and by and for the people.

Abraham Lincoln did not simply win a war or hold the union together. In his unwillingness to demonize those against whom he fought, in his refusal to succumb to either the hatred or self-righteousness that war can unleash, in his ultimate insistence that in the aftermath of war the nation would no longer remain half-slave and half-free, in his trust in the better angels of our nature, Lincoln displayed the wisdom and courage that sets a standard for patriotism.

And it was the most famous son of Independence, Harry S. Truman, who sat in the White House during his final days in office and said in his farewell address, "When Franklin Roosevelt died, I felt there must be a million men better qualified than I to take up the presidential task. But through all of it, through all the years I have worked here in this room, I have been well aware than I did not really work alone, that you were working with me. No president could ever hope to lead our country or to sustain the burdens of this office, save the people helped with their support."

Patriotism is faith in the American people (54–57)

In the end . . . That's what Truman said. And in the end, it may be this quality that best describes patriotism in my mind, not just a love of America in the abstract, but a very particular love for, and faith in, the American people. For we know that the greatness of this country, all result from the energy and imagination of the American people, their toil, drive, struggle, their restlessness and humor and quiet heroism.

That's the liberty we defend, the liberty of each of us to pursue our own dreams. That's the equality we seek, not an equality of results, but the chance of every single one of us to make it if we try.

That's the community we strive to build, one in which we trust in this sometimes messy democracy of ours, one in which we continue to insist that there is nothing we cannot do when we put our mind to it, one in which we see ourselves as part of a larger story, our own fates wrapped up in the fates of those who share allegiance to America's happy and singular creed.

That's what patriotism means to me. Thank you, Independence. God bless you, and may God bless the United States of America.

Bumper Sticker
Patriotism vs. Memorable Rhetoric

JOURNAL WRITING

Questions: To what historic event do these slogans or quotations refer? To whom have some of the slogans or quotations been attributed? Which of these tone words apply?

insidious	laudatory	simplistic	inspiring
elegiac	false analogy	divisive	bigoted
chauvinistic	either/or fallacy	intolerant	jingoistic

1. "My country, right or wrong."
2. "America—Love it or Leave it!"
3. "I only regret that I have but one life to lose for my country."
4. "No one has a right to desecrate the flag."
5. "Bring 'em on!"
6. "You're with us [America] or against us!"
7. "America's mission today is to spread God's gift of democracy to other nations."
8. "The last full measure of devotion."
9. "We few, we happy few, we band of brothers. For he today that sheds his blood with me shall forever be my brother."
10. "All you have to do [to go to war] is tell the common people that they are being attacked or will be attacked and then denounce the pacifists for lack of patriotism and exposing the country to danger. It works the same in any country."

11. "Never was so much owed by so many to so few."

12. "The only thing we have to fear—is fear itself."

13. "Ask not what your country can do for you. Ask what you can do for your country."

14. "Patriotism is the last refuge of a scoundrel."

15. "Patriotism is not the last resort of a scoundrel but the first."

16. "No soldier *wants* to die for his country. Your job is to make the other bastard die for his."

17. "Love of patriotism becomes a demon when it becomes a god."

18. "We should not ask if God is on our side but whether we are on His side."

19. "God Bless America" vs. "God Save America"

20. "Support our troops!"

CHAPTER

12 Lesson Plan 9

Is Technology as Much a Curse as a Blessing?

"Robbie"

1. **Focus:**	*Journal writing:* Would you like to have a humanoid robot at your beck and call? If so, what services would you expect it to provide? If not, why not?
2. **Objective:**	To resolve a basic question of interpretation about the overall meaning of the story.
3. **Purpose:**	To increase our mutual understanding (comprehension) and, as a result, our enjoyment of the story. To develop the habit of independent and critical thinking.
4. **Input:**	Plot-check quiz on Three Kinds of Questions and Exercise on the Qualities of Good Questions on the story by Asimov.
5. **Modeling, checking, guided practice:**	During discussion the co-leaders *model* the four rules of discussion by asking follow-up questions for clarification, substantiation, consistency, relevance, implication, resolution, and to get more opinion. *Guided practice* **is** the discussion.
6. **Closure:**	Oral or written resolution of one or two basic questions just discussed.
Text:	Asimov, "I, Robot," Ch. 1 "Robbie"
Film:	*I, Robot* DVD 2004 (115 mins).

"Robbie"

Cast of Characters

Setting: A village in upstate New York and New York City. "Robbie" was written in 1939 as the first of nine stories on the history of robotics in *I, Robot*. The story takes place in 1998.

Susan Calvin: She is being interviewed after working for US Robot and Mechanical Men for fifty years.

Robbie: A non-vocal nursemaid robot that was made in 1996. His job was to take care of Gloria Weston.

Gloria Weston: An eight-year-old girl for whom Robbie has become her best friend and playmate.

Grace Weston: Gloria's anxious mother who is entirely worried that Robbie may some day "go berserk" and harm Gloria.

George Weston: In contrast to his wife, George is confident that Robbie has been properly programed "for only one purpose really—to be a companion of a little child . . . He's a machine—made so. That's more than you can say for humans."

The Talking Robot: The First Talking Robot on display in the Museum of Science and Industry in New York City is "a tour de force, a thoroughly impractical device, possessing publicity value only."

Mr. Struthers: General Manager of US Robot and Mechanical Men Inc., gives tour of the factory to the Weston family.

I, Robot

Isaac Asimov

Introduction

I LOOKED AT MY NOTES AND I DIDN'T LIKE THEM. I'd spent three days at U.S. Robots and might as well have spent them at home with the Encyclopedia Tellurica.

Susan Calvin had been born in the year 1982, they said, which made her seventy-five now. Everyone knew that. Appropriately enough, U.S. Robot and Mechanical Men, Inc. was seventy-five also, since it had been in the year of Dr. Calvin's birth that Lawrence Robertson had first taken out incorporation papers for what eventually became the strangest industrial giant in man's history. Well, everyone knew that, too.

At the age of twenty, Susan Calvin had been part of the particular Psycho-Math seminar at which Dr. Alfred Lanning of U.S. Robots had demonstrated the first mobile robot to be equipped with voice. It was a large, clumsy unbeautiful robot, smelling of machine-oil and destined for the projected mines on Mercury. But it could speak and make sense.

Susan said nothing at that seminar; took no part in the hectic discussion period that followed. She was a frosty girl, plain and colorless, who protected herself against a world she disliked by a mask-like expression and a hypertrophy of intellect. But as she watched and listened, she felt the stirrings of a cold enthusiasm.

She obtained her bachelor's degree at Columbia in 2003 and began graduate work in cybernetics.

All that had been done in the mid-twentieth century on "calculating machines" had been upset by Robertson and his positronic brain-paths. The miles of relays and photocells had given way to the spongy globe of plantinumiridium about the size of a human brain.

She learned to calculate the parameters necessary to fix the possible variables within the "positronic brain"; to construct "brains" on paper such that the responses to given stimuli could be accurately predicted.

In 2008, she obtained her Ph.D. and joined United States Robots as a "Robopsychologist," becoming the first great practitioner of a new science. Lawrence Robertson was still president of the corporation; Alfred Lanning had become director of research.

For fifty years, she watched the direction of human progress change and leap ahead.

Now she was retiring—as much as she ever could. At least, she was allowing someone else's name to be inset upon the door of her office.

That, essentially, was what I had. I had a long list of her published papers, of the patents in her name; I had the chronological details of her promotions. In short I had her professional "vita" in full detail.

But that wasn't what I wanted.

I needed more than that for my feature articles for Interplanetary Press. Much more I told her.

"Dr. Calvin," I said, as lushly as possible, "in the mind of the public you and U.S. Robots are identical. Your retirement will end an era and—"

"You want the human-interest angle?" She didn't smile at me. I don't think she ever smiles. But her eyes were sharp, though not angry. I felt her glance slide through me and out my occiput and knew that I was uncommonly transparent to her; that everybody was.

But I said, "That's right."

"Human interest out of robots? A contradiction."

"No, doctor. Out of you."

"Well, I've been called a robot myself. Surely, they've told you I'm not human."They had, but there was no point in saying so. She got up from her chair. She wasn't tall and she looked frail. I followed her to the window and we looked out. The offices and factories of U.S. Robots were a small city; spaced and planned. It was flattened out like an aerial photograph.

"When I first came here," she said, "I had a little room in a building right about there where the fire-house is now." She pointed. "It was torn down before you were born. I shared the room with three others. I had half a desk. We built our robots all in one building. Output—three a week. Now look at us."

"Fifty Years," I hackneyed, "is a long time."

"Not when you're looking back at them," she said. "You wonder how they vanished so quickly."

She went back to her desk and sat down. She didn't need expression on her face to look sad, somehow.

"How old are you?" she wanted to know.

"Thirty-two," I said.

"Then you don't remember a world without robots. There was a time when humanity faced the universe alone and without a friend. Now he has creatures to help him; stronger creatures than himself, more faithful, more useful, and absolutely devoted to him. Mankind is no longer alone. Have you ever thought of it that way?"

"I'm afraid I haven't. May I quote you?"

"You may. To you, a robot is a robot. Gears and metal; electricity and positrons. Mind and iron! Human-made! If necessary, human-destroyed! But you haven't worked with them, so you don't know them. They're a cleaner, better breed than we are."

I tried to nudge her gently with words, "We'd like to hear some of the things you could tell us; get your views on robots. The Interplanetary Press reaches the entire Solar System. Potential audience is three billion, Dr. Calvin. They ought to know what you could tell them on robots.

It wasn't necessary to nudge. She didn't hear me, but she was moving in the right direction.

"They might have known that from the start. We sold robots for Earth-use then—before my time it was, even. Of course, that was when robots could not talk. Afterward, they became more human and opposition began. The labor unions, of course, naturally opposed robot competition for human jobs, and various segments of religious opinion had their superstitious objections. It was all quite ridiculous and quite useless. And yet there it was."

I was taking it down verbatim on my pocket-recorder, trying not to show the knuckle-motions of my hand. If you practice a bit, you can get to the point where you can record accurately without taking the little gadget out of your pocket.

"Take the case of Robbie," she said. "I never knew him. He was dismantled the year before I joined the company—hopelessly out-of-date. But I saw the little girl in the museum—"She stopped, but I didn't say anything I let her eyes mist up and her mind travel back. She had lots of time to cover.

"I heard about it later, and when they called us blasphemers and demon-creators, I always thought of him. Robbie was a non-vocal robot. He couldn't speak. He was made and sold in 1996. Those were the days before extreme specialization, so he was sold as a nursemaid."

"As a what?"

"As a nursemaid."

"Robbie"

"NINETY-EIGHT—NINETY-NINE—ONE HUNDRED." Gloria withdrew her chubby little forearm from before her eyes and stood for a moment, wrinkling her nose and blinking in the sunlight. Then, trying to watch in all directions at once, she withdrew a few cautious steps from the tree against which she had been leaning.

She craned her neck to investigate the possibilities of a clump of bushes to the right and then withdrew farther to obtain a better angle for viewing its dark recesses. The quiet was profound except for the incessant buzzing of insects and the occasional chirrup of some hardy bird, braving the midday sun.

Gloria pouted, "I bet he went inside the house, and I've told him a million times that that's not fair."

With tiny lips pressed together tightly and a severe frown crinkling her forehead, she moved determinedly toward the two-story building up past the driveway.

Too late she heard the rustling sound behind her, followed by the distinctive and rhythmic clump- clump of Robbie's metal feet. She whirled about to see her triumphing companion emerge from hiding and make for the home-tree at full speed.

Gloria shrieked in dismay. "Wait, Robbie! That wasn't fair, Robbie! You promised you wouldn't run until I found you." Her little feet could make no headway at all against Robbie's giant strides. Then, within ten feet of the goal, Robbie's pace slowed suddenly to the merest of crawls and Gloria, with one final burst of wild speed, dashed pantingly past him to touch the welcome bark of home-tree first.

Gleefully, she turned on the faithful Robbie, and with the basest of ingratitude, rewarded him for his sacrifice by taunting him cruelly for a lack of running ability.

"Robbie can't run," she shouted at the top of her eight-year-old voice. "I can beat him any day. I can beat him any day." She chanted the words in a shrill rhythm.

Robbie didn't answer, of course—not in words. He pantomimed running instead, inching away until Gloria found herself running after him as he dodged her narrowly, forcing her to veer in helpless circles, little arms outstretched and fanning at the air.

"Robbie," she squealed, "stand still!"—And the laughter was forced out of her in breathless jerks.

Until he turned suddenly and caught her up, whirling her round, so that for her the world fell away for a moment with a blue emptiness beneath, and green trees stretching hungrily downward toward the void. Then she was down in the grass again, leaning against Robbie's leg and still holding a hard, metal finger.

After a while, her breath returned. She pushed uselessly at her disheveled hair in vague imitation of one of her mother's gestures and twisted to see if her dress were torn.

She slapped her hand against Robbie's torso, "Bad boy! I'll spank you!"

And Robbie cowered, holding his hands over his face so that she had to add, "No, I won't, Robbie. I won't spank you. But anyway, it's my turn to hide now because you've got longer legs and you promised not to run till I found you."

Robbie nodded his head—a small parallelepiped with rounded edges and corners attached to a similar but much larger parallelepiped that served as torso by means of a short, flexible stalk—and obediently faced the tree. A thin, metal film descended over his glowing eyes and from within his body came a steady, resonant ticking.

"Don't peek now—and don't skip any numbers," warned Gloria, and scurried for cover.

With unvarying regularity, seconds were ticked off, and at the hundredth, up went the eyelids, and\the glowing red of Robbie's eyes swept the prospect. They rested for a moment on a bit of colorful gingham that protruded from behind a boulder. He advanced a few steps and convinced himself that it was Gloria who squatted behind it.

Slowly, remaining always between Gloria and home-tree, he advanced on the hiding place, and when Gloria was plainly in sight and could no longer even theorize to herself that she was not seen, he extended one arm toward her, slapping the other against his leg so that it rang again Gloria emerged sulkily.

"You peeked!" she exclaimed, with gross unfairness. "Besides I'm tired of playing hide-and-seek. I want a ride."

But Robbie was hurt at the unjust accusation, so he seated himself carefully and shook his head ponderously from side to side.

Gloria changed her tone to one of gentle coaxing immediately, "Come on, Robbie. I didn't mean it about the peeking. Give me a ride."

Robbie was not to be won over so easily, though. He gazed stubbornly at the sky, and shook his head even more emphatically.

"Please, Robbie, please give me a ride." She encircled his neck with rosy arms and hugged tightly. Then, changing moods in a moment, she moved away. "If you don't, I'm going to cry," and her face twisted appallingly in preparation.

Hard-hearted Robbie paid scant attention to this dreadful possibility, and shook his head a third time. Gloria found it necessary to play her trump card.

"If you don't," she exclaimed warmly, "I won't tell you any more stories, that's all. Not one—"

Robbie gave in immediately and unconditionally before this ultimatum, nodding his head vigorously until the metal of his neck hummed. Carefully, he raised the little girl and placed her on his broad, flat shoulders.

Gloria's threatened tears vanished immediately and she crowed with delight. Robbie's metal skin, kept at a constant temperature of seventy by the high resistance coils within, felt nice and comfort-able, while the beautifully loud sound her heels made as they bumped rhythmically against his chest was enchanting.

"You're an air-coaster, Robbie, you're a big, silver aircoaster. Hold out your arms straight.—You got to, Robbie, if you're going to be an aircoaster."

The logic was irrefutable. Robbie's arms were wings catching the air currents and he was a silver 'coaster.

Gloria twisted the robot's head and leaned to the right. He banked sharply. Gloria equipped the 'coaster with a motor that went "Br-r-r" and then with weapons that went "Powie" and "Sh-sh- shshsh." Pirates were giving chase and the ship's blasters were coming into play. The pirates dropped in a steady rain.

"Got another one. Two more," she cried.

Then "Faster, men," Gloria said pompously, "we're running out of ammunition." She aimed over her shoulder with undaunted courage and Robbie was a blunt-nosed spaceship zooming through the void at maximum acceleration.

Clear across the field he sped, to the patch of tall grass on the other side, where he stopped with a suddenness that evoked a shriek from his flushed rider, and then tumbled her onto the soft, green carpet.

Gloria gasped and panted, and gave voice to intermittent whispered exclamations of "That was nice!"

Robbie waited until she had caught her breath and then pulled gently at a lock of hair.

"You want something?" said Gloria, eyes wide in an apparently artless complexity that fooled her huge "nursemaid" not at all. He pulled the curl harder.

Oh, I know. You want a story."

Robbie nodded rapidly.

"Which one?"

Robbie made a semi-circle in the air with one finger.

The little girl protested, "Again? I've told you Cinderella a million times. Aren't you tired of it?—It's for babies."

Another semi-circle.

"Oh, well," Gloria composed herself, ran over the details of the tale in her mind (together with her own elaborations, of which she had several) and began:

"Are you ready? Well—once upon a time there was a beautiful little girl whose name was Ella. And she had a terribly cruel step-mother and two very ugly and very cruel step-sisters and—"

Gloria was reaching the very climax of the tale—midnight was striking and everything was changing back to the shabby originals lickety-split, while Robbie listened tensely with burning eyes—when the interruption came. "Gloria!"

It was the high-pitched sound of a woman who has been calling not once, but several times; and had the nervous tone of one in whom anxiety was beginning to overcome impatience.

"Mamma's calling me," said Gloria, not quite happily. "You'd better carry me back to the house, Robbie."

Robbie obeyed with alacrity for somehow there was that in him which judged it best to obey Mrs. Weston, without as much as a scrap of hesitation. Gloria's father was rarely home in the daytime except on Sunday—today, for instance—and when he was, he proved a genial and understanding person. Gloria's mother, however, was a source of uneasiness to Robbie and there was always the impulse to sneak away from her sight.

Mrs. Weston caught sight of them the minute they rose above the masking tufts of long grass and retired inside the house to wait.

"I've shouted myself hoarse, Gloria," she said, severely. "Where were you?"

"I was with Robbie," quavered Gloria. "I was telling him Cinderella, and I forgot it was dinner- time."

"Well, it's a pity Robbie forgot, too." Then, as if that reminded her of the robot's presence, she whirled upon him. "You may go, Robbie. She doesn't need you now." Then, brutally, "And don't come back till I call you."

Robbie turned to go, but hesitated as Gloria cried out in his defense, "Wait, Mamma, you got to let him stay. I didn't finish Cinderella for him. I said I would tell him Cinderella and I'm not finished."

"Gloria!"

"Honest and truly, Mamma, he'll stay so quiet, you won't even know he's here. He can sit on the chair in the corner, and he won't say a word, I mean he won't do anything. Will you, Robbie?" Robbie, appealed to, nodded his massive head up and down once.

"Gloria, if you don't stop this at once, you shan't see Robbie for a whole week."

The girl's eyes fell, "All right! But Cinderella is his favorite story and I didn't finish it.—And he likes it so much."

The robot left with a disconsolate step and Gloria choked back a sob.

George Weston was comfortable. It was a habit of his to be comfortable on Sunday afternoons. A good, hearty dinner below the hatches; a nice, soft, dilapidated couch on which to sprawl; a copy of the Times; slippered feet and shirtless chest; how could anyone help but be comfortable?

He wasn't pleased, therefore, when his wife walked in. After ten years of married life, be still was so unutterably foolish as to love her, and there was no question that he was always glad to see her—still Sunday afternoons just after dinner were sacred to him and his idea of solid comfort was to be left in utter solitude for two or three hours. Consequently, he fixed his eye firmly upon the latest reports of the Lefebre-Yoshida expedition to Mars (this one was to take off from Lunar Base and might actually succeed) and pretended she wasn't there.

Mrs. Weston waited patiently for two minutes, then impatiently for two more, and finally broke the silence.

"George!"

"Humph?"

"George, I say! Will you put down that paper and look at me?"

The paper rustled to the floor and Weston turned a weary face toward his wife, "What is it, dear?"

"You know what it is, George. It's Gloria and that terrible machine."

"What terrible machine?"

"Now don't pretend you don't know what I'm talking about. It's that robot Gloria calls Robbie. He doesn't leave her for a moment."

"Well, why should he? He's not supposed to. And he certainly isn't a terrible machine. He's the best darn robot money can buy and I'm damned sure he set me back half a year's income. He's worth it, though—darn sight cleverer than half my office staff."

He made a move to pick up the paper again, but his wife was quicker and snatched it away.

"You listen to me, George. I won't have my daughter entrusted to a machine—and I don't care how clever it is. It has no soul, and no one knows what it may be thinking. A child just isn't made to be guarded by a thing of metal."

Weston frowned, "When did you decide this? He's been with Gloria two years now and I haven't seen you worry till now."

"It was different at first. It was a novelty; it took a load off me, and—and it was a fashionable thing to do. But now I don't know. The neighbors–"

"Well, what have the neighbors to do with it? Now, look. A robot is infinitely more to be trusted than a human nursemaid. Robbie was constructed for only one purpose really—to be the companion of a little child. His entire 'mentality' has been created for the purpose. He just can't help being faithful and loving and kind. He's a machine-made so. That's more than you can say for humans."

"But something might go wrong. Some- some-" Mrs. Weston was a bit hazy about the insides of a robot, "some little jigger will come loose and the awful thing will go berserk and– and–" She couldn't bring herself to complete the quite obvious thought.

"Nonsense," Weston denied, with an involuntary nervous shiver. "That's completely ridiculous. We had a long discussion at the time we bought Robbie about the First Law of Robotics. You know that it is impossible for a robot to harm a human being; that long before enough can go wrong to alter that First Law, a robot would be completely inoperable. It's a mathematical impossibility. Besides I have an engineer from U.S. Robots here twice a year to give the poor gadget a complete overhaul. Why, there's no more chance of anything at all going wrong with Robbie than there is of you or I suddenly going loony—considerably less, in fact. Besides, how are you going to take him away from Gloria?"

He made another futile stab at the paper and his wife tossed it angrily into the next room.

"That's just it, George! She won't play with anyone else. There are dozens of little boys and girls that she should make friends with, but she won't. She won't go near them unless I make her. That's no way for a little girl to grow up. You want her to be normal, don't you? You want her to be able to take her part in society."

"You're jumping at shadows, Grace. Pretend Robbie's a dog. I've seen hundreds of children who would rather have their dog than their father."

"A dog is different, George. We must get rid of that horrible thing. You can sell it back to the company. I've asked, and you can."

"You've asked? Now look here, Grace, let's not go off the deep end. We're keeping the robot until Gloria is older and I don't want the subject brought up again." And with that he walked out of the room in a huff.

Mrs. Weston met her husband at the door two evenings later. "You'll have to listen to this, George. There's bad feeling in the village."

"About what?" asked Weston? He stepped into the washroom and drowned out any possible answer by the splash of water.

Mrs. Weston waited. She said, "About Robbie."

Weston stepped out, towel in hand, face red and angry, "What are you talking about?"

"Oh, it's been building up and building up. I've tried to close my eyes to it, but I'm not going to any more. Most of the villagers consider Robbie dangerous. Children aren't allowed to go near our place in the evenings."

"We trust *our* child with the thing."

"Well, people aren't reasonable about these things."

"Then to hell with them."

"Saying that doesn't solve the problem. I've got to do my shopping down there. I've got to meet them every day. And it's even worse in the city these days when it comes to robots. New York has just passed an ordinance keeping all robots off the streets between sunset and sunrise."

"All right, but they can't stop us from keeping a robot in our home. Grace, this is one of your campaigns.

I recognize it. But it's no use. The answer is still, no! We're keeping Robbie!"

And yet he loved his wife—and what was worse, his wife knew it. George Weston, after all, was only a man—poor thing—and his wife made full use of every device which a clumsier and more scrupulous sex has learned, with reason and futility, to fear.

Ten times in the ensuing week, he cried, "Robbie stays, and that's final!" and each time it was weaker and accompanied by a louder and more agonized groan.

Came the day at last, when Weston approached his daughter guiltily and suggested a "beautiful" visivox show in the village.

Gloria clapped her hands happily, "Can Robbie go?"

"No, dear," he said, and winced at the sound of his voice, "they won't allow robots at the visivox—but you can tell him all about it when you get home." He stumbled all over the last few words and looked away.

Gloria came back from town bubbling over with enthusiasm, for the visivox had been a gorgeous spectacle indeed.

She waited for her father to maneuver the jet-car into the sunken garage, "Wait till I tell Robbie, Daddy. He would have liked it like anything. Especially when Francis Fran was backing away so- o-o quietly, and backed right into one of the Leopard-Men and had to run." She laughed again, "Daddy, are there really Leopard-Men on the Moon?"

"Probably not," said Weston absently. "It's just funny make-believe." He couldn't take much longer with the car. He'd have to face it.

Gloria ran across the lawn. "Robbie.—Robbie!"

Then she stopped suddenly at the sight of a beautiful collie which regarded her out of serious brown eyes as it wagged its tail on the porch.

"Oh, what a nice dog!" Gloria climbed the steps, approached cautiously and patted it. "Is it for me, Daddy?"

Her mother had joined them. "Yes, it is, Gloria. Isn't it nice—soft and furry? It's very gentle. It likes little girls."

"Can he play games?"

"Surely. He can do any number of tricks. Would you like to see some?"

"Right away. I want Robbie to see him, too. Robbie!" She stopped, uncertainly, and frowned, "I'll bet he's just staying in his room because he's mad at me for not taking him to the visivox. You'll have to explain to him, Daddy. He might not believe me, but he knows if you say it, it's so."

Weston's lip grew tighter. He looked toward his wife but could not catch her eye.

Gloria turned precipitously and ran down the basement steps, shouting as she went, "Robbie—Come and see what Daddy and Mamma brought me. They brought me a dog, Robbie."

In a minute she had returned, a frightened little girl. "Mamma, Robbie isn't in his room. Where is he?" There was no answer and George Weston coughed and was suddenly extremely interested in an aimlessly drifting cloud. Gloria's voice quavered on the verge of tears, "Where's Robbie, Mamma?"

Mrs. Weston sat down and drew her daughter gently to her, "Don't feel bad, Gloria. Robbie has gone away, I think."

"Gone away? Where? Where's he gone away, Mamma?"

"No one knows, darling. He just walked away. We've looked and we've looked and we've looked for him, but we can't find him."

"You mean he'll never come back again?" Her eyes were round with horror.

"We may find him soon. We'll keep looking for him. And meanwhile you can play with your nice new doggie. Look at him! His name is Lightning and he can–"

But Gloria's eyelids had overflown, "I don't want the nasty dog—I want Robbie. I want you to find me Robbie." Her feelings became too deep for words, and she spluttered into a shrill wail.

Mrs. Weston glanced at her husband for help, but he merely shuffled his feet morosely and did not withdraw his ardent stare from the heavens, so she bent to the task of consolation, "Why do you cry, Gloria? Robbie was only a machine, just a nasty old machine. He wasn't alive at all."

"He was not no machine!" screamed Gloria, fiercely and ungrammatically. "He was a person just like you and me and he was my friend. I want him back. Oh, Mamma, I want him back."

Her mother groaned in defeat and left Gloria to her sorrow.

"Let her have her cry out," she told her husband. "Childish griefs are never lasting. In a few days, she'll forget that awful robot ever existed."

But time proved Mrs. Weston a bit too optimistic. To be sure, Gloria ceased crying, but she ceased smiling, too, and the passing days found her ever more silent and shadowy. Gradually, her attitude of passive unhappiness wore Mrs. Weston down and all that kept her from yielding was the impossibility of admitting defeat to her husband.

Then, one evening, she flounced into the living room, sat down, folded her arms and looked boiling mad.

Her husband stretched his neck in order to see her over his newspaper, "What now, Grace?" "It's that child, George. I've had to send back the dog today. Gloria positively couldn't stand the sight of him, she said. She's driving me into a nervous breakdown."

Weston laid down the paper and a hopeful gleam entered his eye, "Maybe—Maybe we ought to get Robbie back. It might be done, you know. I can get in touch with—"

"No!" she replied, grimly. "I won't hear of it. We're not giving up that easily. My child shall not be brought up by a robot if it takes years to break her of it."

Weston picked up his paper again with a disappointed air. "A year of this will have me prematurely gray."

"You're a big help, George," was the frigid answer. "What Gloria needs is a change of environment? Of course she can't forget Robbie here. How can she when every tree and rock reminds her of him? It is really the silliest situation I have ever heard of. Imagine a child pining away for the loss of a robot."

"Well, stick to the point. What's the change in environment you're planning?"

"We're going to take her to New York."

"The city! In August! Say, do you know what New York is like in August? It's unbearable."

"Millions do bear it."

"They don't have a place like this to go to. If they didn't have to stay in New York, they wouldn't."

"Well, we have to. I say we're leaving now—or as soon as we can make the arrangements. In the city, Gloria will find sufficient interests and sufficient friends to perk her up and make her forget that machine."

"Oh, Lord," groaned the lesser half, "those frying pavements!"

"We have to," was the unshaken response. "Gloria has lost five pounds in the last month and my little girl's health is more important to me than your comfort."

"It's a pity you didn't think of your little girl's health before you deprived her of her pet robot," he muttered—but to himself.

Gloria displayed immediate signs of improvement when told of the impending trip to the city. She spoke little of it, but when she did, it was always with lively anticipation. Again, she began to smile and to eat with something of her former appetite.

Mrs. Weston hugged herself for joy and lost no opportunity to triumph over her still skeptical husband.

"You see, George, she helps with the packing like a little angel, and chatters away as if she hadn't a care in the world. It's just as I told you—all we need do is substitute other interests."

"Humph," was the skeptical response, "I hope so."

Preliminaries were gone through quickly. Arrangements were made for the preparation of their city home and a couple were engaged as housekeepers for the country home. When the day of the trip finally did come, Gloria was all but her old self again, and no mention of Robbie passed her lips at all.

In high good-humor the family took a taxi-gyro to the airport (Weston would have preferred using his own private 'gyro, but it was only a two-seater with no room for baggage) and entered the waiting liner.

"Come, Gloria," called Mrs. Weston. "I've saved you a seat near the window so you can watch the scenery."

Gloria trotted down the aisle cheerily, flattened her nose into a white oval against the thick clear glass, and watched with an intentness that increased as the sudden coughing of the motor drifted backward into the interior. She was too young to be frightened when the ground dropped away as if let through a trap door and she herself suddenly became twice her usual weight, but not too young to be mightily interested. It wasn't until the ground had changed into a tiny patchwork quilt that she withdrew her nose, and faced her mother again.

"Will we soon be in the city, Mamma?" she asked, rubbing her chilled nose, and watching with interest as the patch of moisture which her breath had formed on the pane shrank slowly and vanished.

"In about half an hour, dear." Then, with just the faintest trace of anxiety, "Aren't you glad we're going? Don't you think you'll be very happy in the city with all the buildings and people and things to see? We'll go to the visivox every day and see shows and go to the circus and the beach and—"

"Yes, Mamma," was Gloria's unenthusiastic rejoinder. The liner passed over a bank of clouds at the moment, and Gloria was instantly absorbed in the usual spectacle of clouds underneath one. Then they were over clear sky again, and she turned to her mother with a sudden mysterious air of secret knowledge.

"I know why we're going to the city, Mamma."

"Do you?" Mrs. Weston was puzzled. "Why, dear?"

"You didn't tell me because you wanted it to be a surprise, but I know." For a moment, she was lost in admiration at her own acute penetration, and then she laughed gaily. "We're going to New York so we can find Robbie, aren't we?—With detectives."

The statement caught George Weston in the middle of a drink of water, with disastrous results. There was a sort of strangled gasp, a geyser of water, and then a bout of choking coughs. When all was over, he stood there, a red-faced, water-drenched and very, very annoyed person.

Mrs. Weston maintained her composure, but when Gloria repeated her question in a more anxious tone of voice, she found her temper rather bent.

"Maybe," she retorted, tartly. "Now sit and be still, for Heaven's sake." New York City, 1998 A.D., was a paradise for the sightseer more than ever in its history. Gloria's parents realized this and made the most of it.

On direct orders from his wife, George Weston arranged to have his business take care of itself for a month or so, in order to be free to spend the time in what he termed, "dissipating Gloria to the verge of ruin." Like everything else Weston did, this was gone about in an efficient, thorough, and business-like way. Before the month had passed, nothing that could be done had not been done.

She was taken to the top of the half-mile tall Roosevelt Building, to gaze down in awe upon the jagged panorama of rooftops that blended far off in the fields of Long Island and the flatlands of New Jersey. They visited the zoos where Gloria stared in delicious fright at the "real live lion" (rather disappointed that the keepers fed him raw steaks, instead of human beings, as she had expected), and asked insistently and peremptorily to see "the whale."

The various museums came in for their share of attention, together with the parks and the beaches and the aquarium. She was taken halfway up the

Hudson in an excursion steamer fitted out in the archaism of the mad Twenties. She traveled into the stratosphere on an exhibition trip, where the sky turned deep purple and the stars came out and the misty earth below looked like a huge concave bowl. Down under the waters of the Long Island Sound she was taken in a glass-walled sub-sea vessel, where in a green and wavering world, quaint and curious sea-things ogled her and wiggled suddenly away.

On a more prosaic level, Mrs. Weston took her to the department stores where she could revel in another type of fairyland. In fact, when the month had nearly sped, the Westons were convinced that everything conceivable had been done to take Gloria's mind once and for all off the departed Robbie—but they were not quite sure they had succeeded.

The fact remained that wherever Gloria went, she displayed the most absorbed and concentrated interest in such robots as happened to be present. No matter how exciting the spectacle before her, nor how novel to her girlish eyes, she turned away instantly if the corner of her eye caught a glimpse of metallic movement.

Mrs. Weston went out of her way to keep Gloria away from all robots.

And the matter was finally climaxed in the episode at the Museum of Science and Industry. The Museum had announced a special "children's program" in which exhibits of scientific witchery scaled down to the child mind were to be shown. The Westons, of course, placed it upon their list of "absolutely."

It was while the Westons were standing totally absorbed in the exploits of a powerful electro-magnet that Mrs. Weston suddenly became aware of the fact that Gloria was no longer with her. Initial panic gave way to calm decision and, enlisting the aid of three attendants, a careful search was begun.

Gloria, of course, was not one to wander aimlessly, however. For her age, she was an unusually determined and purposeful girl, quite full of the maternal genes in that respect. She had seen a huge sign on the third floor, which had said, "This Way to the Talking Robot" Having spelled it out to herself and having noticed that her parents did not seem to wish to move in the proper direction, she did the obvious thing. Waiting for an opportune moment of parental distraction, she calmly disengaged herself and followed the sign.

The Talking Robot was a tour de force, a thoroughly impractical device, possessing publicity value only. Once an hour, an escorted group stood before it and asked questions of the robot engineer in charge in careful whispers. Those the engineer decided were suitable for the robot's circuits were transmitted to the Talking Robot.

It was rather dull. It may be nice to know that the square of fourteen is one hundred ninety-six, that the temperature at the moment is 72 degrees

Fahrenheit, and the air-pressure 30.02 inches of mercury, that the atomic weight of sodium is 23, but one doesn't really need a robot for that. One especially does not need an unwieldy, totally immobile mass of wires and coils spreading over twenty-five square yards.

Few people bothered to return for a second helping, but one girl in her middle teens sat quietly on a bench waiting for a third. She was the only one in the room when Gloria entered.

Gloria did not look at her. To her at the moment, another human being was but an inconsiderable item. She saved her attention for this large thing with the wheels. For a moment, she hesitated in dismay. It didn't look like any robot she had ever seen.

Cautiously and doubtfully she raised her treble voice; "Please, Mr. Robot, sir, are you the Talking Robot, sir?" She wasn't sure, but it seemed to her that a robot that actually talked was worth a great deal of politeness.

(The girl in her mid-teens allowed a look of intense concentration to cross her thin, plain face. She whipped out a small notebook and began writing in rapid pothooks.)

There was an oily whir of gears and a mechanically timbered voice boomed out in words that lacked accent and intonation, "I- am- the- robot- that- talks."

Gloria stared at it ruefully. It did talk, but the sound came from inside somewheres. There was no face to talk to. She said, "Can you help me, Mr. Robot, sir?"

The Talking Robot was designed to answer questions, and only such questions as it could answer had ever been put to it. It was quite confident of its ability, therefore, "I- can- help- you."

"Thank you, Mr. Robot, sir. Have you seen Robbie?"

"Who- is Robbie?"

"He's a robot, Mr. Robot, sir." She stretched to tiptoes. "He's about so high, Mr. Robot, sir, only higher, and he's very nice. He's got a head, you know. I mean you haven't, but he has, Mr. Robot, sir."

The Talking Robot had been left behind, "A—robot?"

"Yes, Mr. Robot, sir. A robot just like you, except he can't talk, of course, and—looks like a real person."

"A- robot- like- me?"

"Yes, Mr. Robot, sir."

To which the Talking Robot's only response was an erratic splutter and an occasional incoherent sound. The radical generalization offered it, i.e., its existence, not as a particular object, but as a member of a general group, was too much for it. Loyally, it tried to encompass the concept and half a dozen coils burnt out. Little warning signals were buzzing.

(The girl in her mid-teens left at that point. She had enough for her Physics-1 paper on "Practical Aspects of Robotics." This paper was Susan Calvin's first of many on the subject.)

Gloria stood waiting, with carefully concealed impatience, for the machine's answer when she heard the cry behind her of "There she is," and recognized that cry as her mother's.

"What are you doing here, you bad girl?" cried Mrs. Weston, anxiety dissolving at once into anger. "Do you know you frightened your mamma and daddy almost to death? Why did you run away?"

The robot engineer had also dashed in, tearing his hair, and demanding who of the gathering crowd had tampered with the machine. "Can't anybody read signs?" he yelled. "You're not allowed in here without an attendant."

Gloria raised her grieved voice over the din, "I only came to see the Talking Robot, Mamma. I thought he might know where Robbie was because they're both robots." And then, as the thought of Robbie was suddenly brought forcefully home to her, she burst into a sudden storm of tears, "And I got to find Robbie, Mamma. I got to."

Mrs. Weston strangled a cry, and said, "Oh, good Heavens. Come home, George. This is more than I can stand."

That evening, George Weston left for several hours, and the next morning, he approached his wife with something that looked suspiciously like smug complacence.

"I've got an idea, Grace."

"About what?" was the gloomy, uninterested query?

"About Gloria."

"You're not going to suggest buying back that robot?"

"No, of course not."

"Then go ahead. I might as well listen to you. Nothing I've done seems to have done any good."

"All right. Here's what I've been thinking. The whole trouble with Gloria is that she thinks of Robbie as a person and not as a machine. Naturally, she can't forget him. Now if we managed to convince her that Robbie was nothing more than a mess of steel and copper in the form of sheets and wires with electricity its juice of life, how long would her longings last? It's the psychological attack, if you see my point."

"How do you plan to do it?"

"Simple. Where do you suppose I went last night? I persuaded Robertson of U.S. Robots and Mechanical Men, Inc. to arrange for a complete tour of his premises tomorrow. The three of us will go, and by the time we're through, Gloria will have it drilled into her that a robot is not alive."

Mrs. Weston's eyes widened gradually and something glinted in her eyes that was quite like sudden admiration, "Why, George, that's a good idea."

And George Weston's vest buttons strained. "Only kind I have," he said.

Mr. Struthers was a conscientious General Manager and naturally inclined to be a bit talkative. The combination, therefore, resulted in a tour that was fully explained, perhaps even over-abundantly explained, at every step. However, Mrs. Weston was not bored. Indeed, she stopped him several times and begged him to repeat his statements in simpler language so that Gloria might understand. Under the influence of this appreciation of his narrative powers, Mr. Struthers expanded genially and became ever more communicative, if possible.

George Weston, himself, showed a gathering impatience.

"Pardon me, Struthers," he said, breaking into the middle of a lecture on the photoelectric cell, "haven't you a section of the factory where only robot labor is employed?"

"Eh? Oh, yes! Yes, indeed!" He smiled at Mrs. Weston. "A vicious circle in a way, robots creating more robots. Of course, we are not making a general practice out of it. For one thing, the unions would never let us. But we can turn out a very few robots using robot labor exclusively, merely as a sort of scientific experiment. You see," he tapped his pince-nez into one palm argumentatively, "what the labor unions don't realize—and I say this as a man who has always been very sympathetic with the labor movement in general—is that the advent of the robot, while involving some dislocation to begin with, will inevitably

"Yes, Struthers," said Weston, "but about that section of the factory you speak of—may we see it? It would be very interesting, I'm sure."

"Yes! Yes, of course!" Mr. Struthers replaced his pince-nez in one convulsive movement and gave vent to a soft cough of discomfiture. "Follow me, please."

He was comparatively quiet while leading the three through a long corridor and down a flight of stairs. Then, when they had entered a large well-lit room that buzzed with metallic activity, the sluices opened and the flood of explanation poured forth again.

"There you are!" he said with pride in his voice. "Robots only! Five men act as overseers and they don't even stay in this room. In five years, that is, since we began this project, not a single accident has occurred. Of course, the robots here assembled are comparatively simple, but . . ."

The General Manager's voice had long died to a rather soothing murmur in Gloria's ears. The whole trip seemed rather dull and pointless to her, though there were many robots in sight. None were even remotely like Robbie, though, and she surveyed them with open contempt.

In this room, there weren't any people at all, she noticed. Then her eyes fell upon six or seven robots busily engaged at a round table halfway across the room. They widened in incredulous surprise. It was a big room. She couldn't see for sure, but one of the robots looked like—looked like—it was!

"Robbie!" Her shriek pierced the air, and one of the robots about the table faltered and dropped the tool he was holding. Gloria went almost mad with joy. Squeezing through the railing before either parent could stop her, she dropped lightly to the floor a few feet below, and ran toward her Robbie, arms waving and hair flying.

And the three horrified adults, as they stood frozen in their tracks, saw what the excited little girl did not see,—a huge, lumbering tractor bearing blindly down upon its appointed track.

It took split-seconds for Weston to come to his senses, and those split-seconds meant everything, for Gloria could not be overtaken. Although Weston vaulted the railing in a wild attempt, it was obviously hopeless. Mr. Struthers signaled wildly to the overseers to stop the tractor, but the overseers were only human and it took time to act.

It was only Robbie that acted immediately and with precision.

With metal legs eating up the space between himself and his little mistress he charged down from the opposite direction. Everything then happened at once. With one sweep of an arm, Robbie snatched up Gloria, slackening his speed not one iota, and, consequently, knocking every breath of air out of her. Weston, not quite comprehending all that was happening, felt, rather than saw, Robbie brush past him, and came to a sudden bewildered halt. The tractor intersected Gloria's path half a second after Robbie had, rolled on ten feet further and came to a grinding, long drawn-out stop.

Gloria regained her breath, submitted to a series of passionate hugs on the part of both her parents and turned eagerly toward Robbie. As far as she was concerned, nothing had happened except that she had found her friend.

But Mrs. Weston's expression had changed from one of relief to one of dark suspicion. She turned to her husband, and, despite her disheveled and undignified appearance, managed to look quite formidable, "You engineered this, didn't you?

George Weston swabbed at a hot forehead with his handkerchief. His hand was unsteady, and his lips could curve only into a tremulous and exceedingly weak smile.

Mrs. Weston pursued the thought, "Robbie wasn't designed for engineering or construction work. He couldn't be of any use to them. You had him placed there deliberately so that Gloria would find him. You know you did."

"Well, I did," said Weston. "But, Grace, how was I to know the reunion would be so violent? And Robbie has saved her life; you'll have to admit that. You can't send him away again."

Grace Weston considered. She turned toward Gloria and Robbie and watched them abstractedly for a moment. Gloria had a grip about the robot's neck that would have asphyxiated any creature but one of metal, and was prattling nonsense in half-hysterical frenzy. Robbie's chrome-steel arms (capable of bending a bar of steel two inches in diameter into a pretzel) wound about the little girl gently and lovingly, and his eyes glowed a deep, deep red.

"Well," said Mrs. Weston, at last, "I guess he can stay with us until he rusts."

Susan Calvin shrugged her shoulders, "Of course, he didn't. That was 1998. By 2002, we had invented the mobile speaking robot which, of course, made all the non-speaking models out of date, and which seemed to be the final straw as far as the non-robot elements were concerned. Most of the world governments banned robot use on Earth for any purpose other than scientific research between 2003 and 2007."

"So that Gloria had to give up Robbie eventually?"

"I'm afraid so. I imagine, however, that it was easier for her at the age of fifteen than at eight. Still, it was a stupid and unnecessary attitude on the part of humanity. U.S. Robots hit its low point, financially; just about the time I joined them in 2007. At first, I thought my job might come to a sudden end in a matter of months, but then we simply developed the extra-Terrestrial market."

"And then you were set, of course."

"Not quite. We began by trying to adapt the models we had on hand. Those first speaking models, for instance. They were about twelve feet high, very clumsy and not much good. We sent them out to Mercury to help build the mining station there, but that failed."

I looked up in surprise, "It did? Why, Mercury Mines is a multi-billion dollar concern."

"It is now, but it was a second attempt that succeeded. It you want to know about that, young man, I'd advise you to look up Gregory Powell. He and Michael Donovan handled our most difficult cases in the teens and twenties I have not heard from Donovan in years, but Powell is living right here in New York. He's a grandfather now, which is a thought difficult to get used to. I can only think of him as a rather young man. Of course, I was younger, too."

I tried to keep her talking, "If you would give me the bare bones, Dr. Calvin, I can have Mr. Powell fill it in afterward." (And this was exactly what I later did.)

"Robbie"

PLOT-CHECK QUIZ

Directions: Answer each question briefly and then identify the type of each question: write FACT for factual, INT for interpretation, and EVAL for evaluation.

1. Unlike George, why does Grace Weston fear Robbie?

2. Why does Asimov give Robbie human emotions and yet remind us that it is a robot?

3. Are people today over dependent on machines?

4. Why does Gloria think her parents are taking her to New York City?

5. How does Grace Weston plan to make Gloria forget Robbie?

6. Why is Gloria portrayed as a spoiled child?

7. How does George Weston plan to make Gloria forget Robbie?

8. Had you been Gloria's mother or father, would you have allowed her to keep Robbie?

9. Unlike Grace, why is George unable to see any harm or danger in Gloria's relationship with Robbie?

10. Why does Gloria fiercely insist that Robbie is not a machine?

11. Does Gloria think "Cinderella" is a story for babies?

12. Do most of the neighbors agree with Grace Weston that Robbie is dangerous?

13. Why does Gloria think she knows why her parents take her to New York City?

14. Why does Asimov have George interrupt Mr. Struthers when he is explaining the future advantages of robots in daily life?

15. While visiting the robot factory in New York, why were the human supervisors unable to save Gloria from being crushed by the tractor?

"Robbie"

REVIEW QUIZ ON QUALITIES OF GOOD QUESTIONS

Directions: On your own paper, mark GOOD if a question would lead to a disagreement based on the story. If the question lacks one of the needed qualities, mark it:
NC if the question is NOT CLEAR and would have to be explained
NS if the question is NOT SPECIFIC and could be asked of any story
LD for LACKS DOUBT since it cannot be answered in more than one way
FACT for FACTUAL and cannot be discussed
EVAL for EVALUATION and not about understanding the story.

1. What kind of relationship does Gloria have with her parents?

2. What's wrong with Robbie?

3. Do Mr. and Mrs. Weston really disagree about robots?

4. What is the biggest reason for George and Grace's disagreement about Robbie's role in their daughter's life?

5. Does George have more trust than Grace in the reliability of robots?

6. How important are robots in our lives today?

7. Why is Mrs. Weston so stupid about robots?

8. What is the point of the story?

9. Why does Gloria go willingly with her parents to New York?

10. What is the role of Mr. Struthers in the story?

11. Why does Asimov begin the story with Gloria playing with Robbie?

12. Why does Gloria keep putting on the way she does?

13. Does Gloria really think that Robbie is not a machine?

14. Why does Grace Weston agree to let Robbie return to Gloria after he saves her life?.

15. With whose attitude towards Robbie does Asimov want us to agree—George or Grace Weston's?

Socratic Seminar: Interpretive Discussion Questions

1. Why does Asimov have George Weston regard Robbie as a great benefit while Grace Weston see it as a threat and potential danger?
2. Why does Asimov give Robbie human emotions?
3. Why does George place more trust in Robbie than in a human nursemaid?
4. Why does Gloria reject a more sophisticated robot for Robbie?
5. Why does Susan Calvin regard robots as a better "breed" than humans?
6. Why does Grace say Robbie has no "soul" when she knows it is a robot?
7. Why is Grace so concerned about her neighbors' opinion of Robbie?
8. Why does Grace think that "something might go wrong" with Robbie when it has never done anything to endanger Gloria?
9. Why does Asimov have Gloria insist that Robbie is not a machine?
10. Does Asimov want us to agree with Grace that Gloria could be harmed psychologically and emotionally by over dependence on Robbie?
11. Why is Gloria unimpressed with the much-publicized Talking Robot that she met in New York City?
12. Why does Asimov end the story by having Robbie save Gloria's life?
13. Why does George Weston admit that he had arranged for Gloria to "find" Robbie working in a factory?
14. Why does Grace Weston agree to let Robbie return to Gloria after he saves her life.
15. With whose attitude towards Robbie does Asimov want us to agree—George or Grace Weston's?

Three Viewpoints on Sputnik

Directions: The three passages that follow are the opening paragraphs of articles dealing with the same event, the launching of the first space satellite by the Soviet Union in 1957. The first two were written at the time of the event while the third was written forty-two years later in 1999 for the millennium issue of the *New York Times Magazine* (April 18, 1999) Make notations on your copies that note differences in the approaches that each author takes on the subject for his audience. Write a well-organized comparison–contrast essay that analyzes the specific stylistic and rhetorical differences among the three essays and then explain why each author approaches the same historic event with entirely different attitudes (tone).

Passage 1: "Sputnik: October 4, 1957"

Hannah Arendt

In 1957, an earth-born object made by man was launched into the universe, where for some weeks it circled the earth according to the same laws of gravitation that swing and keep in motion the celestial bodies—the sun, the moon, and the stars. To be sure, the man-made satellite was no moon or star, no heavenly body which could follow its circling path for a time span that to us mortals, bound by earthly time, lasts form eternity to eternity. Yet, for a time it managed to stay in the skies; it dwelt and moved in the proximity of the heavenly bodies as though it had been admitted tentatively to their sublime company.

This event, second in importance to no other, not even to the splitting of the atom, would have been greeted with unmitigated joy if it had not been for the uncomfortable military and political circumstances attending it. But, curiously enough, this joy was not triumphal; it was not pride or awe at the tremendousness of human power and mastery which filled the hearts of men, who now, when they looked up from the earth toward the skies, could behold there a thing of their own making. The immediate reaction, expressed on the spur of the moment, was relief about the first "step toward escape from men's imprisonment to the earth." And this strange statement, far from being the accidental slip of some American reporter, unwittingly echoed the extraordinary line which, more than twenty years ago, had been carved on the funeral obelisk of one of Russia's great scientists: "Mankind will not remain bound to the earth forever."

Passage 2: "Sputnik: October 4, 1957"

Smithsonian

On October 4, 1957, the Soviet Union launched into orbit a 184-pound sphere carrying a radio transmitter, enough batteries to run it for about two weeks, and four car-radio-style antennas, swept back to conform to the shape of the nose cone in which it rode atop its launch vehicle.

James Van Allen remembers Sputnik differently from most Americans. On a South Pacific expedition aboard the Navy's U.S.S. *Glacier* to study cosmic rays for the International Geophysical Year (IGY) at the time of its launch, he heard the news on the Armed Forces Radio.

"Before I swallowed it, I wanted to personally confirm it," he recalled in an interview at the Smithsonian National Air and Space Museum (NASM). The ship's radioman picked up a signal at the right frequency, and soon Van Allen and his team were listening to Sputnik's steady beeping with astonishment at the strength of the signal. Checking its orbital period, the length of the passes during which the ship's receiver held the signal, and the change in frequency of the signal as it passed like a fast-moving train, they convinced themselves that this was in fact the Russian satellite.

Sputnik demonstrated the muscle of Soviet rocketry, but the satellite was mainly for show: it carried no scientific instruments and took no measurements in space. The launch intensified a scientific and technological competition that continues to this day. The United States was close to launch itself, and had intended all along to orbit apparatus that could measure and record the space environment. Scientists like Van Allen wanted to show, as did the government, that space could be used for peaceful purposes as well as for the missiles of war.

Passage 3: "Sputnik: Dawn of the Space Age"

James Gleick*

It wasn't until the year 4.5 billion or so (reckoning from the birth of the planet) that an earthly life form managed to hurl some stuff into orbit—beyond the atmosphere, to permanent residence in outer space, high enough to look down and see our tiny globe for what it is.

Counted another way, it was October 4, 1957. Russians called the first satellite Sputnik, the American President decided to go golfing and just about everyone else considered the event momentous and scary. *Satellite* was a fancy word. Headline writers called these things *moons.* And why not?

Sputnik was a moon that beeped. That was its entire function, accomplished by a small radio transmitter, four antennas and a few days' worth of batteries. Plenty of scientists and rocket buffs were listening down below and a hatching grander plans. Already, Arthur C. Clarke, the science-fiction writer, had performed one of the millennium's most astounding feats of invention. In 1945, he calculated and published a complete plan for using satellites to relay radio signals. Television had barely arrived, and Clarke announced satellite television—telephone, too. All in all, he imagined a communications system to unite the globe.

And so it is, a whole forty-three years later. Earth, previously naked, has acquired a glittering veil of satellites. They beam our words and pictures hither and yon, and they measure and monitor and spy on the farthest corners of our world, as they forever plunge, in their gravity-defying fashion, past the horizon. Some practically hover, geosynchronously, 23,000 miles high. Others skim past at much lower altitudes.

Here's how crowded the sky has become: the grandly and redundantly named United States Space Command Space Control Center tracks more than 8,000 nontrivial objects, ranging from functional communications satellites to lost gloves (careless astronauts!). Smaller detritus can't even be counted.

We've littered our bit of the cosmos with millions or billions of pea-size or mite-size junk fragments. There is talk of sending up robot satellites to collect the trash.

**New York Times Magazine* (April 18, 1999).

CHAPTER

13 Lesson Plan 10

Can We Forget That We Are Human?

Brave New World

Day 1–2	Plot-check quiz (handout) and discussion of two basic questions.
Day 3–4	Make notations while viewing the film versions of the story.
Day 5	Discussion of major film differences and 'Would Huxley reject the 1980 film but approve the 1998 version of his story?"

1. **Focus:**	*Journal*: Would you want to live in a world without crime, war, or poverty where suffering no longer existed and happiness was universal?
2. **Objective:**	To participate in a comparison-contrast discussion of the film version of the story and to write a follow-up contrast essay.
3. **Purpose:**	To recognize and to explain the differences between film interpretations of two versions of the novel and the original story.
4. **Input:**	○ *Before viewing the film*: Plot-check quiz of the short story followed by discussion of two basic questions of interpretation. ○ Film version of the novel: 1980 (145 mins) and clips of 1998 (85 mins).
5. **Modeling:**	*After viewing the film*: Model some examples of how to write a few differences between the film and the story.
6. **Checking for understanding:**	Review guidelines for writing differences between the film version and the original story.
7. **Guided practice:**	After viewing the film: Discussion of the significance of major differences between the film versions of the novel.

8. **Closure:** Comparison-contrast follow-up essay and/or a movie review of the film (see Lesson 1 for guidelines).

Text: Aldous Huxley, *Brave New World*. Harper & Row, Publishers, New York 1969

Film: Burt Brinckerhoff, *Brave New World* TV (1980) 145 mins and Leslie Libman, *Brave New World* TV (1998) 87 mins

Brave New World by Aldous Huxley (1894–1963)

Characters

Title: "O wonder! How many goodly creatures are there here! How beauteous mankind is! O **brave new world** that has such people in it!" (*The Tempest* 5.1.183) Chapter 8.

Setting: London and New Mexico, 632 A. F. (after Ford—1932)—the 26th century.

Director of Hatcheries and Conditioning (DHC): a bureaucrat who Bernard forces to resign.

Henry Foster: an Alpha who works at the DHC and is, in every way, the ideal citizen of the World State.

Lenina Crowne: a Gamma, Henry's occasional lover. She has a crisis when she cannot understand her feelings for John the Savage.

Fanny Crowne: a Gamma, Lenina's friend who cautions her to be more promiscuous because she sometimes gets too involved with one man.

Mustapha Mond: an Alpha plus, one of Ten World Controllers of the World State Government. As the Resident Controller for Western Europe, he appears early in the story (Ch. 3) and at the conclusion (Ch. 16 and 17).

Bernard Marx: an Alpha who works at the Psychology Bureau and confides his feelings of inadequacy in Helmholtz, his only real friend.

Helmholtz Watson: Like Bernard, he knows that he is different, an individual. Along with Mustapha Mond and later the Savage John, he becomes one of three mouthpieces for the ideas and beliefs of Huxley in the brave new world.

John, the Savage: the only one in the world of 632 A.F. who has a human birth. He never fully assimilates into the Malpais culture because he is white and rejects the filth of civilization in London. He educates himself by reading the *Complete Works of William Shakespeare*.

Linda: a Beta who becomes the mother of John when she is marooned in New Mexico. She finally returns to London when Bernard asks her to come with John as part of an experiment.

Tomakin: John's father who leaves Linda in New Mexico and returns alone to the brave new world and becomes the Director of Hatcheries and Conditioning.

Five castes

Alphas (gray, leadership positions), **Beta** (positions demanding high intelligence), **Gammas** (green), **Deltas** (khaki, positions demanding some intelligence), and **Epsilons**, (black, those who can neither read nor write).

World State's Motto
COMMUNITY, IDENTITY, STABILITY.
"Everyone works for everyone."
"Everyone belongs to everyone."

Brave New World

PLOT QUIZ

Chapter 1

1. What is the motto of the World State Government in the brave new world?

2. How are babies produced in 632 After Ford (A.F.)?

3. What happens to babies in the "Social Predestination Room"?

4. Of the five different types (castes) of people in the brave new world, who are the highest level and who are the lowest?

Chapter 2

5. What is the function or purpose of "Infant Nurseries"?

Chapter 3

6. What does the Director of Hatcheries and Conditioning explain to the new students about sexual activity among children?

7. Why is Mustapha Mond such an important person in the World State Government?

8. What advice does Fanny give Lenina Crowne?

Chapter 4

9. Although he is an Alpha, why does Bernard Marx feel inadequate and different?

10. Why is Helmholtz Watson Bernard's only real friend?

Chapter 5

11. What is "*soma*" and "Orgy-porgy"?

Chapter 6

12. When Bernard gets a permit to visit the Savage Reservation in New Mexico, what does the DHC Director warn him about?

Chapter 7

13. Why is Lenina so upset and disgusted by a Savage ritual dance?

14. Who are John, Linda and Tomakin?

Chapter 8

15. What kind of education does John received on the Reservation?

16. Why is John eager to accept Bernard's offer to leave the Reservation for London?

Chapter 9

17. When John finds Lenina in a *soma* induced sleep, who does he compare her to?

Chapter 10

18. When Bernard returns to London with Linda and John and the Director of Hatcheries and Conditioning exiles him to Iceland, how does Bernard turn the tables against him?

Chapter 11

19. As a result of the Director's resignation, what happens to Bernard and John?

20. When Bernard gives John a tour of life in London, how does he react?

Chapter 12

21. After Bernard has paraded John before many important personages, why does John now refuse to appear?

Chapter 13

22. When Lenina tries to seduce John into having sex with her, why does he refuse?

Chapter 14

23. What are two important things that so upset John when he goes to the hospital to visit his dying mother, Linda?

Chapter 15

24. Enraged, why does John call for the people at the hospital to overthrow the government of the World State?

25. What is the difference between Bernard's and Helmholtz's reaction to John's revolt.

Chapter 16

26. Why have Bernard, Helmholtz, and John been arrested and taken to Mustapha Mond?

27. To defend the government of the World State, why does Mustapha bring up the Cyprus experiment?

Chapter 17

28. What is John's rebuttal to Mustapha's argument that modern man has substituted universal happiness for God and the religious impulse?

Chapter 18

29. When condemned to live in London, how does John try to adapt to society?

30. When forced to choose between conformity or annihilation, what does John do?

31. In his introduction, what third choice does Huxley say he should have given John?

Socratic Seminar

Brave New World

Directions: For your assigned or chosen basic question (1–4) during pre-discussion, write at least eight related interpretive follow-up questions (include a page reference for each). Before discussion, please submit your questions for teacher approval.

Those who will not be co-leading a discussion should write three interpretive follow-up questions for each basic question—a total of twelve questions. Hand in after discussion.

Basic Question 1: Why is science and technology a public danger as well as the foundation of happiness in the brave new world?

Basic Question 2: Why does Mustapha Mond's "experiment" to assimilate John the Savage into the brave new world fail?

Basic Question 3: What is the relevance of Huxley's numerous references to Shakespeare?

Basic Question 4: Why does Huxley have John counter Mustapha Mond's defense of the brave new world with many references to Shakespeare?

Directions: Your teacher will lead your class in a comparison-contrast discussion of the 1980 and 1998 film versions of Huxley's novel. After viewing the films *but before discussion,* jot down a brief answer for as many as you can.

Basic Question 5: Would Huxley reject the 1998 film but approve the 1980 version of his story? Rephrased: Would Huxley reject the 1998 film because it is not as faithful to his original story as the 1980 film?

Basic Question 1: Why is science and technology a public danger as well as the foundation of happiness in the brave new world?

1. What does Huxley mean when he says that "The theme of BNW is not the advancement of science as such; it is the advancement of science as it affects human individuals"? (Foreword, p. ix)
2. Why does Huxley begin his story with a detailed description of cloning? (Ch. 1)
3. How are scientific advances the foundation of happiness in the world of 632 A.F.?

4. Why does the Department of Hatcheries and Conditioning sometimes fail to indoctrinate people like Bernard and Helmholtz?
5. Why do people come to love their oppression and adore the technologies that undo their capacity to think?
6. Why does Mond regard "real" science as an enemy? (p. 153)
7. Does Huxley imply that Mond's choice to give up "pure science" to become a World Controller is a rationalization and a delusion? (p. 154)
8. Why isn't God compatible with "machinery and scientific medicine and universal happiness"? (p. 159)
9. Why does John the Savage regard unhappiness as a right? (p. 163)
10. Why has the Reservation in New Mexico been allowed to continue? (Ch. 6 and 7)

Basic Question 2: Why does Mustapha Mond's "experiment" to assimilate John the Savage into the brave new world fail?

1. Does John feel so guilty because of his unkindness to Linda or because of his lust for Lenina? (pp. 162, 166, 172)
2. Does Mond allow John to escape to an abandoned lighthouse? (p. 166)
3. Why is John allowed to live in solitude? (p. 167)
4. Why does John think he can escape the civilization of London? (p. 167)
5. Why does John's attempt to live alone draw so much public attention? (p. 173)
6. Why do people reject John's plea to be left alone? (p. 174)
7. When Lenina appears with Henry, why does John promptly attack her? (p. 175)
8. Why does the narrator compare Lenina's death to "Orgy-porgy"? (p. 176)
9. After Lenina's death, why does John take *soma*? (p. 176)
10. Why does Huxley have John commit suicide? (p. 177)

Basic Question 3: What is the relevance of Huxley's numerous references to Shakespeare?

1. Why does Huxley have John study Shakespeare, "that old fellow," rather than another author? (pp. 88, 124)
2. Like Miranda in *The Tempest* who exclaims "O brave new world that has such people in it" (5.1.183), why does Huxley have John anxious to embrace a way of life that he neither knows or understands? (p. 94)
3. Why does John recall the title's phrase from *The Tempest* when he observes Deltas working in a factory? (p. 107ff)

4. Why does John again recall the same words of *The Tempest* when he shouts for the overthrow of the World State Government? (pp. 143–5)
5. Why does John compare Lenina to Juliet? (p. 97)
6. Why does John reread Romeo and Juliet after meeting Lenina? (p. 119)
7. Why does Helmholtz find it so hilarious when John reads the lines about Juliet being forced to marry Tybalt? (p. 124)
8. Does Huxley have Lenina see no difference between lust and love because she thinks that sexual fidelity is absurd? (p. 129)
9. Why does Huxley have John recall the caskets of *The Merchant of Venice* when Bernard explains that the day's ration of *soma* is in a casket? (p. 110)
10. Why does John think of Othello after Lenina's first attempt to seduce him? (p. 115)
11. After her second attempt to seduce him, why does John think of Othello's wife, Desdemona? (p. 133)
12. Why does Huxley have John and Helmholtz compare the feelies and advertising to Macbeth's soliloquy about life as a tale told by an idiot? (p. 150)

Basic Question 4: Why does Huxley have John counter Mustapha Mond's defense of the brave new world with many references to Shakespeare?

1. What does Mond mean when he tells John and Helmholtz that "our world is not like Othello's"? (p. 149)
2. Why does John refer to King Lear to assert that God's justice will prevail in the end? (p. 160)
3. Why does John quote Othello ("But tears are necessary") when Mond stresses the importance of *soma* as "Christianity without tears"? (p. 162)
4. Why does Huxley have John recall the words of Hamlet's third soliloquy ("Whether 'tis better to suffer the slings and arrows of outrageous fortune") when he accuses Mustapha of eliminating suffering? (p. 162)
5. Why does Othello's murder of Desdemona occur to John when John protests that he has "the right to be unhappy"? (p. 163)
6. Why does the narrator have John refer to the guilt of Claudius in Hamlet when he begins praying? (p. 166)
7. Why does John refer to Macbeth's final soliloquy when he asks why Linda died? (p. 173)
8. Why does John reflect on Gloucester's charge (King Lear) that the gods seem to kill us for sport? (p. 173)
9. Why does Huxley have John recall Hamlet's debate on suicide after Linda's death? (p. 173)

Basic Question 5: Would Huxley reject the 1998 film but approve the 1980 version of his story? *Rephrased*: Would Huxley reject the 1998 film because it is not as faithful to his original story as the 1980 film?

1998 (90 mins)

Director of Hatcheries and Conditioning	Miguel Ferrer
Lenina Crowne	Rya Kihlstedt
Bernard Marx	Peter Gallagher
Mustapha Mond	Leonard Nimoy
Henry Foster	Patrick Dancy
Fanny Crowne	Wendy Benson
Linda	Sally Kirkland
The Savage	Tim Guinee

1. Why does Bernard ask the Director of Hatcheries and Conditioning if too much time is spent on conditioning?
2. Why does a Delta worker (brown overalls) hold up an assembly line by accepting a live mouse from another worker?
3. Does the DHC require more conditioning for the Delta worker only because he held up production?
4. Why does the DHC later condition the Delta worker to murder Bernard Marx?
5. Does the Delta's failure to kill Bernard lead directly to the DHC's downfall?
6. Unlike the novel, when Bernard and Lenina arrive at the Reservation, why do they crash land?
7. When Henry and Lenina arrive at the Reservation, why are they immediately attacked by the inmates?
8. Why does John have to defend Henry and Lenina?
9. Why does John tell Henry and Lenina that an Alpha seduced his mother?
10. When Linda returns to civilization, why does John remark, "O brave new world that has such people in it"?
11. Why is Mond so concerned that Bernard has brought back John to civilization but later defends his decision?
12. Why does Mond accept Bernard's explanation but order that he report his findings to him first?
13. Why has Bernard's friend and confidant, Helmholtz Watson, been omitted?
14. Does the DHC delete John's file only to conceal his relationship with Linda?

15. Why does Bernard's recovery of John's file lead to the DHC's downfall?
16. Why do both John and Lenina speak to children about love and heroism when they know that they will not be understood?
17. Why does John reject Lenina's attempt to seduce him?
18. When Linda is dying in the hospital, why does Lenina remain with John?
19. Why does Bernard want to know why Lenina is seeing John?
20. Why does the DHC murder Linda when he has already deleted John's file?
21. When John causes a *soma* riot and begs the Deltas to revolt, why is he granted a pardon by the Controller?
22. Why does the Controller maintain that John is "the exception that proves the rule"?
23. When confronted by the reporter's question, "What do you want, John?" why does he quote Thoreau ("I went to the woods to . . .") rather than Shakespeare?
24. Is John's falling off the cliff meant to be a suicide or an accident?
25. Does Lenina intentionally get pregnant with Bernard's baby?
26. Why is Lenina so determined to keep the baby?
27. Why does Bernard banish Lenina to an island to have her baby?
28. After Lenina's banishment, why does the film return to the opening scene with the children in the Hatchery?
29. Why does the Controller laugh when he is told that Bernard Marx is not at the Director's meeting because he took a trip?
30. Why does the film end with Bernard and Lenina embracing their baby on a seashore?

1980 (165 mins)

Director of Hatcheries and Conditioning	Nigel Bullard
Lenina Crowne	Marcia Strassman
Bernard Marx	Bud Cort
Helmholtz Watson	Dick Anthony Williams
Mustapha Mond	Rob O'Neal
Henry Foster	Reb Brown
Fanny Crowne	Jonelle Allen
Linda	Julie Cobb
John Savage	Kristoffer Tabori

31. Why does the film begin with a lecture by Tomakin (DHC) to a group of Alphas rather than a lecture to new students in the Hatcheries and Conditioning Center?

32. Why does Tomakin (DHC) abandon Linda at the Savage Reservation?
33. When Bernard tells two Gammas that he must think and consider certain things, why are they appalled?
34. Why do Bernard and Helmholtz become friends?
35. Why does Lenina think it is so "unnatural" to be alone with Bernard?
36. Why does John tell Bernard and Lenina that Linda is his mother?
37. Why do Linda and John readily agree to return with Bernard and Lenina to civilization?
38. Even before he sees the Other Place, why does John refer to it as a brave new world?
39. When Bernard can have anything that he wants, why does John ask him why he's unhappy?
40. Does Huxley imply that Bernard is not happy because he has not been properly conditioned?
41. During his tour with Bernard, what appalls John most about the brave new world?
42. When he visits the crematorium, why does John refuse to accept death as benign?
43. Why does Mond want to experiment with John, that is, "to determine if the savage can adjust to our higher plane of morality"?
44. At the feelies, why doesn't Lenina question John about his passionate rejection of the parody of Romeo and Juliet?
45. When Helmholtz asks what poetry is, why does John quote Hamlet's paean to mankind, "What a work is man!"?
46. Why does Bernard tell Mond that Helmholtz is to blame for John's rejection of their society?
47. When Lenina tries to seduce John a second time, why does he conclude his angry rejection with a kiss and then tell her: "I did love you once. Love is madness"?
48. When John causes a riot during a *soma* distribution, why does he again quote the title of Huxley's novel?
49. After Mond has John, Helmholtz, and Bernard arrested, why does John refuse to apologize for anything, Helmholtz thank Mond for banishing him to an island but Bernard despair?
50. Why does Mond agree to allow John to live alone "for awhile"?
51. When Mond asks John what he wants most, why does he insist on the right to be unhappy?
52. Why does Mond admit to a technician that the film of John's life in the wild is alluring?
53. Why does Lenina protest the parody ("Darwin Bonapart") of John's life at the feelies?

54. When John is surrounded by crowds, would Huxley approve Lenina's telling John she understands what love is *because she felt it*?
55. After Lenina has been overcome by *soma* gas, why does John kiss his Juliet ("Take your last embrace") and then leave to hang himself?
56. Like Julie, why is Lenina revived from her *soma* sleep?
57. After John's death why does Mond wonder aloud, "Still, I wonder. Was there another way?"
58. Does the film imply that Mond will begin to question his role in the brave new world?
59. Why does the film end with Mond quoting Prospero in *The Tempest*?
    The solemn temples, the great globe itself,
    Yes, like this insubstantial pageant faded,
    Leave not a rack behind. We are such stuff
    As dreams are made of; and our little life
    Is rounded with a sleep.

Basic Question 6: Is Orwell's or Huxley's vision of the future more relevant to our society today? *Rephrased*: Would Orwell agree with those who believe that Huxley's vision of the future is more likely today than the world of 1984?

1. In a personal letter (October 21, 1949) to Orwell, why does Huxley tell his former student that it is more efficient to teach people to love their servitude than to flog and kick them into obedience?
2. In his 1940 review of BNW, why does Orwell argue that "a ruling class that thought principally of a 'good time' would soon lose its vitality and that a ruling class has got to have a strict morality and a quasi-religious belief in itself"?
3. Why is Orwell's world based on punishment and fear of punishment while Huxley's is based on *soma* and nonstop distractions?
4. Why does 1984 end with Winston Smith loving Big Brother while BNW ends with the suicide of John the Savage?
5. Is the caste system of 1984 more like that of 632 A.F.?
6. Why is promiscuity forbidden in 1984 but required of everyone in A.F. 632?
7. Why is Julia a support for Winston while Lenina is John's nemesis?
8. Why is Orwell concerned with lack of information while Huxley feared too much information?
9. Unlike BNW, why is there need for Thought Police to punish thought crime in 1984?
10. Why does Orwell fear the tyranny of Big Brother while Huxley fears that people will be done in by their infinite appetite for distraction?

11. When first written, why did Orwell project his vision only thirty six years in the future while Huxley placed his six hundred years in the future?
12. Have more of Huxley's or Orwell's predictions of the future been realized today?

Socratic Seminar

"*Brave New World*: Virtual Students, Digital Classrooms"

Andrew Postman

1. Why is Postman's title an allusion to *The Tempest* by Shakespeare and the 1932 novel by Aldous Huxley? *Brave New World*'s ironic title derives from Miranda's speech in Shakespeare's last play, *The Tempest:* 5.1:

   O wonder!
   How many goodly creatures are there here! How beauteous mankind is!
   O brave new world! That has such people in it!

   In Shakespeare's *The Tempest* and Huxley's novel, this line itself is ironic; Miranda was raised for most of her life on an isolated island, and the only people she ever knew were her father and his servants, an enslaved savage and a spirit. When she sees other people for the first time, she is understandably overcome with excitement, and utters, among other praise, the famous lines above. However, what she is actually observing is not men acting in a refined or civilized manner, but rather drunken sailors staggering off the wreckage of their ship. Huxley employs the same irony when the "savage" John refers to what he sees as a "brave new world."
2. What does Huxley's novel of 1932 have to do with Postman's thesis that information technology is a false god, an idol?
3. What relevance does his thesis have to Miranda's amazement at people she has never seen before?
4. In addition to socializing students, what is the function of schools?
5. What danger do specialized schools pose for the core curriculum of the liberal arts schools?
6. What should or can schools do for ALL students?
7. Do you agree with Richard Mitchell *(Less Than Words Can Say)* "the school that fails to teach thinking fails in everything"? If so, why so? If not, why not?

8. What does James Howard of the Council for Basic Education mean when he says, "Education is what you have left after you have forgotten everything that you learned in school."
9. How do students learn to think:
   - critically (recognize good and evil, true and false, beauty and vulgarity)
   - reflectively (about a problem about meaning that demands a solution)
   - independently (confidently able to trust one's own judgment).
10. If good teaching is dialogue (a conflict of ideas–thesis, antithesis, synthesis) , why does monologue (telling or "direct teaching") continue to dominate among many teachers?
11. What is the primary distinction between Socratic discussion, casual conversation, and an interview?

Brave New World: Essay Exam 1

Directions: First, identify the speaker (WHO) and the context (WHEN) of each quotation in the space beneath it. Second, in a half-page paragraph write a commentary on FOUR quotations. In each commentary: (1) identify the speaker (who) of the quotation; (2) explain its context (when); and then (3) explain its significance to the play as a whole (theme). Number each commentary.

Example

11. "All men are physico-chemically equal. Besides, even Epsilons perform indispensable services . . . Everybody works for everyone else. We can't do without any one. Even Epsilons are useful. . . . I suppose Epsilons don't really mind being Epsilons. Of course they don't. How can they? We'd mind, of course. But then we've been differently conditioned. I'm glad I'm not an Epsilon. And if you were an Epsilon, your conditioning would have made you no less thankful that you weren't a Beta or an Alpha."

Commentary No. 11

Early in the novel (chapter five) Henry Foster has to remind Lenina Crowne, both Beta technicians in the London Hatchery and Conditioning Center, that "everyone works for every-one" because the World State Government has determined that everyone belong to a specific caste and be conditioned to want to be a member of that caste, and only that caste. As a result, in the brave new world of 632 A.F. (After Ford) "everyone belongs to everyone else." For this reason, the motto of the World State Government is COMMUNITY, IDENTITY, STABILITY.

Quotations

1. "What the two men shared was the knowledge that they were individuals. . . . I'm taking Lenina Crowne to New Mexico with me . . . Did you ever feel as though you had something inside you that was only waiting for you to give it a chance to come out? . . . You mean all the emotions one might feel if things were different? Not quite. I'm thinking of a queer feeling I sometimes get, a feeling that I've got something

important to say and the power to say it—only I don't know what it is, and I can't make any use of the power."

WHO ____________ WHEN ________________________________

2. "It's only about four months since I've been having him . . . Only four months! . . . Seriously, I really do think you ought to be careful. It's horribly bad form to go on and on like this with one man. . . . I haven't been very keen on promiscuity lately. There are times when one doesn't. Haven't you found that too?" She nodded her sympathy and understanding. "But one's got to play the game. After all, everyone belongs to everyone else."

WHO ____________ WHEN ________________________________

3. "I'm not at all pleased with the reports I receive of your behavior outside working hours. You may say this is not my business. But it is. I have the good name of the Center to think of. My workers must be above suspicion, particularly those of the highest castes. Alphas are so conditioned that they do not have to be infantile in their emotional behavior . . .If ever I hear again of any lapse from your proper standard of infantile decorum, I shall ask for your transfer to Iceland."

WHO ____________ WHEN ______________________________

4. "Do you really like me or don't you? I love you more than anything in the world. Then why on earth didn't you say so? . . . Hug me till you drug me, honey. Kiss me till I'm in a coma. Hug me, honey, snuggly . . . He caught her by the wrists, tore her hands from his shoulders, thrust her roughly away at arm's length. . . . What is it? Whore! Impudent strumpet! Get out of my sight or I'll kill you."

WHO ____________ WHEN ______________________________

5. "I'm _____, I'm ______. You made me have a baby. . . . Yes a baby—and I was its mother . . . It wasn't my fault. . . . Because I always did my drill, didn't I? Didn't I? I don't know how . . . If you __________ knew how awful it was . . . But he was a comfort to me, all the same."

WHO _____________ WHEN ________________________________

6. Like maggots they had swarmed defilingly over the mystery of Linda's death . . . "How many goodly creatures are there here! How beauteous mankind is! O brave new world . . ." A jaunty young Alpha entered carrying a black iron cash-box . . . the twins now focused their attention on the box of *soma*. . . . Miranda had proclaimed the possibility of loveliness, the possibility of transforming even the nightmare into something fine and noble. "O brave new world! . . . Stop! Stop! . . . Don't take that horrible stuff. It's poison. Poison to your soul as well as your body."

WHO _____________ WHEN ________________________________

7. "Our world is not the same as Othello's. You can't make flivvers [cheap cars]—and you can't make tragedies without social instability. The world's stable now. People are happy; they get what they want, and they never want what they can't get. They're well off; they're safe; they're never ill; they're not afraid of death; they're blissfully ignorant of passion and old age; they're not plagued with mothers or fathers; they've got no wives, or children or lovers to feel strongly about. . . . And if anything should go wrong, there's *soma*."

WHO ____________ WHEN ______________________________

8. "I was given a choice: to be sent to an island, where I could have got on with my pure science, or to be taken to the Controllers' Council with the prospect of succeeding in due course to an actual Controllership. I chose this and let science go. Sometimes, I rather regret the science. Happiness is a hard master—particularly other people's happiness . . . I am interested in truth, I like science. But truth's a menace, science is a public danger."

WHO ____________ WHEN ______________________________

9. "I'm claiming the right to be unhappy: the right to grow old and ugly and impotent; the right to have syphilis and cancer; the right to have too little to eat; the right to be lousy; the right to live in constant apprehension of what may happen tomorrow; the right to catch typhoid; the right to be tortured by unspeakable pain of every kind."

WHO ____________ WHEN ______________________________

10. "And all our yesterdays have lighted fools the way to dusty death. A convincing thunder rumbled through the words. He lifted another spadeful of earth. Why had Linda died? Why had she been allowed to become gradually less than human and at last . . . He shuddered. He planted his foot on his spade and stamped it fiercely into the tough ground. As flies to wanton boys we are to the gods; they kill us for sport. Thunder again."

WHO ____________ WHEN ______________________________

"Introduction to the Twentieth Anniversary Edition of Amusing Ourselves to Death"

Andrew Postman

Now this?

1 A book of social commentary . . . published 20 years ago? You're not busy enough writing emails, returning calls, downloading tunes, playing games (online, PlayStation, Game Boy), checking out websites, sending text messages, IM'ing, Tivoing, watching what you've Tivoed, browsing through magazines and newspapers, reading new books—now you've got to stop and read a book that first appeared in the last century, not to mention millennium? Come on—like, your outlook on today could seriously be rocked by this plainspoken provocation about The World of 1985, a world yet to be infiltrated by the Internet, cell phones, PDAs, cable channels by the hundreds, DVDs, call-waiting, caller ID, blogs, flat-screens, HDTV and iPods? Is it really plausible that this slim volume, with its once-urgent premonitions about the nuanced and deep-seated perils of television, could feel timely today, in the Age of Computers? Really, could this book about how TV is turning all public life (education, religion, politics, journalism) into entertainment; how the image is undermining other forms of communication, particularly the written word; and how our bottomless appetite for TV will make content so abundantly available, context be damned, that we'll be overwhelmed by "information glut" until what is truly meaningful is lost and we no longer care what we've lost as long as we're being amused . . . Can such a book possibly have relevance to you and The World of 2006 and beyond?

I think you've answered your own question.

2 I, too, think the answer is yes, but as Neil Postman's son, I'm biased. Where are we to find objective corroboration that reading *Amusing Ourselves to Death* in 2006, in a society that worships TV and technology as ours does, is nearly an act of defiance, one of those I-didn't-realize-it-was-dark-until-someone-flipped-the-switch encounters with an illuminating intellect?

Ask the Students

3 Let's not take the word of those who studied under my father at New York University, many of whom have gone on to teach in their own college (and occasionally high school) courses what he argues in these pages. These fine minds are, as my father's was, of a bygone era, a different media environment, and their biases may make them, as they made him, hostage of another time, perhaps incapable of seeing the present world as it is rather than as they'd like it to be. (One man's R-rated is another's PG-13.)

4 And just to make a clean slate of it, let's not rely, either, on the opinions of the numerous readers of the original edition of Amusing Ourselves (translated into a dozen languages, including German, Indonesian, Turkish, Danish and, most recently, Chinese), so many of whom wrote to my father, or buttonholed him at public speaking events, to tell him how dead-on his argument was. Their support, while genuine, was expressed over the last two decades, so some of it might be outdated; we'll disregard the views of these teachers and students, businesspeople and artists, conservatives and liberals, atheists and churchgoers, and all those parents. (We'll also disregard Roger Waters, cofounder of the legendary band Pink Floyd, whose solo album, *Amused to Death*, was inspired by the book. Go, Dad.)

So whose opinion matters?

5 In re-reading this book to figure out what might be said about it twenty years later, I tried to think the way my father would, since he could no longer, nor could I ask him. He died in October 2003, at age 72. Channeling him, I realized immediately who offers the best test of whether **Amusing Ourselves to Death** is still relevant.

College kids.

"Teachers are not considered good if they don't entertain their classes."

6 Today's 18-to-22-year-olds live in a vastly different media environment from the one that existed in 1985. Their relationship to TV differs. Back then, MTV was in its late infancy. Today, news scrolls and corner-of-the-screen promos and "reality" shows and infomercials and 900 channels are the norm. And TV no longer dominates the media landscape. "Screen time" also means hours spent in front of the computer, video monitor, cell phone and handheld. Multitasking is standard.

Communities have been replaced by demographics. Silence has been replaced by background noise. It's a different world. (It's different for all of us, of course—children, young teens, parents, seniors—but college kids form an especially rich grouping, poised between innocence and sophistication, respect and irreverence.)

7 When today's students are assigned *Amusing Ourselves to Death*, almost none of them have heard of Neil Postman or been exposed to his ideas (he wrote over 20 books, on such subjects as education, language, childhood and technology), suggesting that their views, besides being pertinent, are relatively uncorrupted.

8 I called several of my father's former students who are now teachers, and who teach *Amusing Ourselves to Death* in courses that examine some cross-section of ideas about TV, culture, computing, technology, mass media, communications, politics, journalism, education, religion, and language. I asked the teachers what their students thought of the book, particularly its timeliness. The teachers were kind enough to share many of their students' thoughts, from papers and class discussion.

9 "In the book [Postman] makes the point that there is no reflection time in the world anymore," wrote Jonathan. "When I go to a restaurant everyone's on their cell phone, talking or playing games. I have no ability to sit by myself and just think." Said Liz: "It's more relevant now. In class we asked if, now that there's cable, which there really wasn't when the book was written, are there channels that are not just about entertainment? We tried to find one to disprove his theory. One kid said the Weather Channel but another mentioned how they have all those shows on tornadoes and try to make weather fun. The only good example we came up with was C-SPAN, which no one watches."

10 Cara: "Teachers are not considered good if they don't entertain their classes." Ben (whose professor called him the "class skeptic," and who, when the book was assigned, groaned, "Why do we have to read this?"): "Postman says TV makes everything about the present—and there we were, criticizing the book because it wasn't published yesterday." Reginald: "This book is not just about TV." Sandra: "The book was absolutely on-target about the 2004 presidential election campaign and debates." One student pointed out that Arnold Schwarzenegger announced his candidacy for the California governorship on The Tonight Show.

Postman's And Now This . . .

11 Maria noted that the oversimplification and thinking "fragmentation" promoted by TV-watching may contribute to our Red State/Blue State polarization. Another noted the emergence of a new series of 'bible magazines,' whose cover format is modeled on teen magazines, with cover lines like 'Top 10 Trips to Getting Closer to God'—"it's religion mimicking an MTV kind of world," said the student. Others wondered if the recent surge in children diagnosed with Attention Deficit Disorder was an indication of a need to be constantly stimulated.

12 Kaitlin switched her major to print journalism after reading the book. Andrea would recommend it to anyone concerned with media ethics. Mike said even those who won't agree with the book's arguments—as he did not—should still read it, to be provoked. Many students ("left wingers and right wingers both," said the professor) were especially taken with my father's "Now . . . this" idea: the phenomenon whereby the reporting of a horrific event—a rape or a 5-alarm fire or global warming, say—is followed immediately by the anchor's cheerfully exclaiming "Now . . . this," which segues into a story about Janet Jackson's exposed nipple, or a commercial for lite beer, creating a sequencing of information so random, so disparate in scale and value, as to be incoherent, even psychotic.

13 Another teacher remarked that students love how the book is told—by a writer who's at heart a storyteller. "And they love that he refers to books and people they've heard of," she said. Alison: "He doesn't dumb it down—he makes allusions to great art and poetry. Yet it's impossible to lose track of his argument." Matt said that, ironically, "Postman proves you can be entertaining—and without a single picture."

14 Of her students' impressions, one teacher said, "He speaks to them without jargon, in a way in which they feel respected. They feel he's just having a conversation with them, but inspiring them to think at the same time." Another professor noted that "kids come to the conclusion that TV is almost exclusively interested in presenting show business and sensationalism and in making money. Amazing as it seems, they had never realized that before."

15 It no doubt appears to you that, after all my grand talk of objectivity, I've stacked the deck in favor of the book's virtue. But that's honestly the overwhelming reaction– at least among a slice of Generation Y, a population segment that one can imagine has as many reasons not to

like the book as to like it. One professor said that in a typical class of 25 students who read the book, 23 will write papers that either praise, or are animated by, its ideas; two will say the book was a stupid waste of time. A 92% rating? There's no one who expresses an idea—certainly no politician—who wouldn't take that number.

"A common critique was that he should have offered solutions."

16 Of course, students had criticisms of the book, too. Many didn't appreciate the assault on television—a companion to them, a source of pleasure and comfort—and felt as if they had to defend their culture. Some considered TV their parents' culture, not theirs—they are of the Internet—so the book's theses were less relevant. Some thought my father was anti-change, that he so exalted the virtues fostered by the written word and its culture, he was not open to acknowledging many of the positive social improvements TV had brought about, and what a democratic and leveling force it could be. Some disagreed with his assessment that TV is in complete charge: remote control, an abundance of channels, and VCRs and DVRs all enable you to "customize" your programming, even to skip commercials. A common critique was that he should have offered solutions; you can't put the toothpaste back in the tube, after all, so what now?

And there was this: Yeah, what he said in 1985 had come startlingly true, we had amused ourselves to death . . . so why read it?

17 One professor uses the book in conjunction with an experiment she calls an "e-media fast." For 24 hours, each student must refrain from electronic media. When she announces the assignment, she told me, 90% of the students shrug, thinking it's no big deal. But when they realize all the things they must give up for a whole day—cell phone, computer, Internet, TV, car radio, etc.—"they start to moan and groan." She tells them they can still read books. She acknowledges it will be a tough day, though for roughly 8 of the 24 hours they'll be asleep. She says if they break the fast—if they answer the phone, say, or simply have to check email—they must begin from scratch.

They actually walk down the street to visit their friend.

18 "The papers I get back are amazing," says the professor. "They have titles like 'The Worst Day of My Life' or 'The Best Experience I Ever Had,' always extreme. I thought I was going to die, they'll write. I went to turn on the TV but if I did I realized, my God, I'd have to start all over again.

Each student has his or her own weakness—for some it's TV, some the cell phone, some the Internet or their PDA. But no matter how much they hate abstaining, or how hard it is to hear the phone ring and not answer it, they take time to do things they haven't done in years.

19 They actually walk down the street to visit their friend. They have extended conversations. One wrote, I thought to do things I hadn't thought to do ever. The experience changes them. Some are so affected that they determine to fast on their own, one day a month. In that course I take them through the classics—from Plato and Aristotle through today—and years later when former students write or call to say hello the thing they remember is the media fast."

20 Like the media fast, *Amusing Ourselves* is a call to action. It is, in my father's words, "an inquiry . . . and a lamentation," yes, but it aspires to greater things. It is an exhortation to do something. It's a counter punch to what my father thought daily TV news was: "inert, consisting of information that gives us something to talk about but cannot lead to any meaningful action." Dad was a lover of history, a champion for collective memory and what we now quaintly refer to as "civilizing influences," but he did not live in the past. His book urges us to claim a way to be more alert and engaged. My father's ideas are still here, he isn't, and it's time for those of a new generation to take the reins, natives of this brave new world who understand it better.

"'Change changed,' my father wrote."

21 Twenty years isn't what it used to be. Where once it stood for a single generation, now it seems to stand for three. Everything moves faster. "Change changed," my father wrote in another book. A lot has changed since this book appeared. News consumption among the young is way down. Network news and entertainment divisions are far more entwined, despite protests by the news divisions (mostly for their own benefit).

22 When Jon Stewart, host of Comedy Central's The Daily Show, goes on CNN's Crossfire to make this very point—that serious news and show business ought to be distinguishable, for the sake of public discourse and the republic—the hosts seem incapable even of understanding the words coming out of his mouth.

23 The sound bite is now more like a sound nibble, and it's rare, even petulant, to hear someone challenge its absurd insubstantiality; the

question of how television affects us has receded into the background (Dad's words, not mine, from 1985). Fox News has established itself, and thrived. Corporate conglomeration is up, particularly among media companies. Our own media companies don't provide truly gruesome war images as part of the daily news, but then they didn't do so 20 years ago either (though 40 years ago they did). The quality of graphics (i.e., the reality quotient) of computer and video games is way up.

24 Communities exist that didn't, thanks to the Internet, particularly to peer-to-peer computing. A new kind of collaborative creativity abounds, thanks to the "open source" movement, which gave us the Linux operating system. However, other communities are collapsing: far fewer people join clubs that meet regularly, fewer families eat dinner together, and people don't have friends over or know their neighbors the way they used to. More school administrators and politicians and business executives hanker to wire schools for computers, as if that is the key to improving American education.

Huxley, not Orwell

25 The number of hours the average American watches TV has remained steady, at about 4? hours a day, every day (by age 65, a person will have spent 12 uninterrupted years in front of the TV). Childhood obesity is way up. Some things concern our children more than they used to, some not at all. Maybe there's more hope than there was, maybe less. Maybe the amount is a constant.

26 Substantive as this book is, it was predicated on a "hook": that one British writer (George Orwell) with a frightening vision of the future, a vision that many feared would come true, was mostly off-base, while another British writer (Aldous Huxley) with a frightening vision of the future, a vision less well-known and feared, was scarily on target. My father argued his point, persuasively, but it was a point for another time—the Age of Television. New technologies and media are in the ascendancy.

27 Fortunately—and this, more than anything, is what I think makes *Amusing Ourselves to Death* so emphatically relevant—my father asked such good questions that they can be asked of non-television things, of all sorts of transforming developments and events that have happened since 1985, and since his death, and of things still unformed, for generations to come (though "generations to come" may someday mean a span of three years). His questions can be asked about all technologies and media.

28 What happens to us when we become infatuated with and then seduced by them? Do they free us or imprison us? Do they improve or degrade democracy? Do they make our leaders more accountable or less so? Our system more transparent or less so? Do they make us better citizens or better consumers? Are the tradeoffs worth it? If they're not worth it, yet we still can't stop ourselves from embracing the next new thing because that's just how we're wired, then what strategies can we devise to maintain control? Dignity? Meaning?

"It's a twenty-first century book published in the twentieth century."

29 My father was not a curmudgeon about all this, as some thought. It was never optimism he lacked; it was certainty. "We must be careful in praising or condemning because the future may hold surprises for us," he wrote. Nor did he fear TV (as some thought) across the board. Junk television was fine. "The A-Team and Cheers are no threat to our public health," he wrote. "60 Minutes, Eyewitness News and Sesame Street are."

30 A student of Dad's, a teacher himself, says his own students are more responsive, not less, to Amusing Ourselves than they were five or ten years ago. "When the book first came out, it was ahead of its time, and some people didn't understand its reach," he says. "It's a twenty-first century book published in the twentieth century." In 1986, soon after the book was published and started to make ripples, Dad was on ABC's Nightline, discussing with Ted Koppel the effect TV can have on society if we let it control us, rather than vice versa. As I recall, at one juncture, to illustrate his point that our brief attention span and our appetite for feel-good content can short-circuit any meaningful discourse, Dad said, "For example, Ted, we're having an important discussion about the culture but in thirty seconds we'll have to break for a commercial to sell cars or toothpaste."

Mr. Koppel, one of the rare serious figures on network television, smiled wryly—or was it fatigue? "Actually, Dr. Postman," he said, "it's more like ten seconds."

There's still time—[to get your mind back to read, to write, to love, to pray, to be still and see that God is God (Ps 45) always aware of us even when we are unaware of Him. Editor's note]

Brooklyn, New York
November 2005

Brave New World: Essay Exam 2

Directions: In the following passage, contemporary social and education critic, Neil Postman, contrasts George Orwell's vision of the future, as found in his *1984* (written in 1948), with Aldous Huxley's world of 2600 A.F. (after Ford) in *Brave New World* (written in 1931). After reading the passage carefully and making notations (on what you think important, do not understand, agree or disagree with, or find related—connections), consider Postman's interpretation that Huxley's vision is more relevant today than Orwell's. Then, using your critical understanding of contemporary society as evidence, write a carefully argued and clearly organized essay that agrees or disagrees with Postman's assertion. Include a counter argument and a rebuttal.

> We are keeping our eye on 1984. When the year came and the prophecy didn't, thoughtful Americans sang softly in praise of themselves. The roots of liberal democracy had held. Wherever else the terror had happened, we, at least, had not been visited by Orwellian nightmares.
>
> But we had forgotten that alongside Orwell's dark vision, there was another—slightly older, slightly less well-known, equally chilling: Aldous Huxley's *Brave New World*. Contrary to common belief even among the educated, Huxley and Orwell did not prophesy the same thing. Orwell warns that we will be overcome by an externally imposed oppression. But in Huxley's vision, no Big Brother is required to deprive people of their autonomy, maturity and history. As he saw it, people will come to love their oppression, to adore the technologies that undo their capacities to think.
>
> What Orwell feared were those who would ban books. What Huxley feared was that there would be no reason to ban a book, for there would be no one who wanted to read one. Orwell feared those who would deprive us of information. Huxley feared those who would give us so much that we would be reduced to passivity and egoism. Orwell feared that the truth would be concealed from us. Huxley feared the truth would be drowned in a sea of irrelevance. Orwell feared we would become a captive culture. Huxley feared we would become a trivial culture, preoccupied with some

equivalent of the feelies, the orgy porgy, and the centrifugal bumble puppy. As Huxley remarked in *Brave New World Revisited,* the civil libertarians and rationalists who are ever on the alert to oppose tyranny "failed to take into account man's almost infinite appetite for distractions." In *1984*, Huxley added, people are controlled by inflicting pain. In *Brave New World*, they are controlled by inflicting pleasure. In short, Orwell feared that what we hate will ruin us. Huxley feared that what we love will ruin us.

CHAPTER

14 Lesson Plan 11

How Important is God in Your Life?

Pigeon Feathers

1. **Focus:**	*Journal*: How important is God in your life?
2. **Objective:**	To develop the habit of independent, reflective, and critical thinking.
3. **Purpose:**	To compare and contrast the movie version of John Updike's short story.
4. **Input:**	Reading and discussion of basic questions of interpretation. Why David Kern is obsessed with death?
5. **Modeling:**	Co-leaders observe the Four Rules of Socratic Discussion (p. 16).
6. **Checking for understanding:**	Co-leaders ask spontaneous follow-up questions for clarification, substantiation, more opinion, consistency, implication, and resolution.
7. **Guided practice:**	Co-leaders observe the four rules of Socratic discussion.
8. **Closure:**	Essay Exam, oral resolution, written resolution to one of the basic questions.
Readings:	**To download an 18-page copy of the text of "Pigeon Feathers" go to:** http://www.berean9-10english.com/uploads/7/3/3/1/7331350/pigeon_feathers_text.pdf
Film:	*Pigeon Feathers,* VHR (45 mins) Monterey home video (The American Short Story) 1989

Pigeon Feathers

PLOT-CHECK QUIZ

Directions: Answer each question in complete sentences on your own paper. Do not repeat the question.

1. Why is David so upset by what H. G. Wells says about Jesus in his *Outline of History*?
2. Why does David find the dictionary definition of the soul unsatisfying?
3. When his mother asks David what seems to be troubling him, why doesn't he confide in her?
4. While at Sunday school ("catechetical class") what so upsets David about Reverend Dobson's lesson?
5. When David's mother again asks to tell her what is bothering him, what is his complaint?
6. Why does David reject his mother's argument that the beauty of nature is good evidence of the reality of God?
7. When Elsie (David's mother) tells George (his father) that David is worried about death, what does he say?
8. How does David accept his fifteenth birthday gift?
9. After David gets a rifle, what "job" does his mother ask him to do?
10. Why doesn't David really want to do the "job"?
11. What were some of David's feelings as he killed the pigeons?
12. When his mother comes to the barn to ask David how many birds he has killed, what is David's emotional response?
13. How does David's mother feel about his killing the pigeons?
14. After his mother orders David to bury the pigeons, what does he discover as he looks closely at each dead bird?
15. What sudden, profound insight (epiphany) does David have after he buries the birds?

Socratic Seminar

Basic Question of Interpretation: Is David Kern so obsessed with death because he fears his own extinction or because belief in an after life is not enough for him?

If he is more concerned with his own death, then:

1. Why is David horrified by the "blasphemy" of H. G. Wells who does not think Jesus was divine? (p. 118)
2. Was David's prayer at night to be reassured by the touch of Christ answered? (128)
3. Why is David so angered by Reverend Dobson's explanation of Heaven? (133)
4. Why does David think Reverend Dobson's concept of Heaven is a betrayal of Christianity? (134)
5. When David reads his grandfather's Bible, why does he try to find the passage about the good thief being promised Heaven by Jesus on the cross? (135)
6. When David's mother asks him what he wants Heaven to be, why does he say only, "I want it to be *something*"? (136)
7. Is David reassured about Heaven when his mother tells him later, "There will be something "for us"? (138)
8. Why is David so disgusted when his mother says that Man made God? (137)
9. Why does David so strongly reject his mother's argument that the beauty of nature is evidence of God? (137–83)
10. Why is David so depressed when his mother tells him that the big questions of life will matter much less as he gets older? (138–9)
11. As David buries the dead pigeons, why is he so taken with their beauty?
12. Has David come to accept his mother's view that the beauty of nature is evidence of God? (149)
13. How do the dead pigeons give David the certainty that "God would not destroy His whole Creation by refusing to let him live forever"? (149)

If it is more a matter of faith not being enough for him, then:

14. Why doesn't David participate in his parent's argument about whether the land has a soul? (121)
15. Why does David's vision of death so disturb him when he is in the outhouse? (123)
16. Why does the dictionary definition of the soul satisfy David only temporarily? (126)

17. Although David is familiar with the phrase, "This reminds me of death," why does the narrator say that he had never considered its meaning? (127)
18. Why is David so frightened of "his own dying, in a specific bed in a specific room"?
19. Does David think his father is mocking him or being flippant when he claims to look forward to death?
20. Of David, why does the narrator say "we cannot, *cannot,* submit to death"? (140)
21. As he kills the pigeons, why does David feel like "a beautiful avenger and creator"

Nonfiction Readings

Introduction

Why should anyone care about or have any interest in a speech **Bertrand Russell** gave eighty years ago? Eighty years ago Bertrand Russell, although an academic, was as much of a political lightning rod in England as Clarence Darrow was in America. British philosopher, mathematician, social reformer, and zealous rationalist, Russell's radicalism kept him from a conventional academic career and put him in the public spotlight. His views on marriage, sex, adultery, homosexuality, and religion made him so controversial in the 1930s that he was often censured or denied a public platform. On March 6, 1927, Russell delivered one of his best-known lectures, "Why I am Not a Christian," to the National Secular Society, South London Branch, at Battersea Town Hall. Published in pamphlet form in that same year, the essay subsequently achieved new fame with Paul Edwards' collection of Russell's essays, *Why I am Not a Christian and Other Essays* (1957). In 1950, Russell was awarded the Nobel Prize for literature. He died in 1970.

This abridged speech raises two basic questions of interpretation: (1) Are Bertrand Russell's three reasons for rejecting Christianity equally important?; and (2) Why does Russell think that Christians must believe in God and immortality but not in the divinity of Christ?

WHY I AM NOT A CHRISTIAN

BERTRAND RUSSELL

As your Chairman has told you, the subject about which I am going to speak to you tonight is "Why I am Not a Christian." Perhaps it would be as well, first of all, to try to make out what one means by the word *Christian*. It is used these days in a very loose sense by a great many people. Some people mean no more by it than a person who attempts to live a good life. In that sense I suppose there would be Christians in all sects and creeds; but I do not think that that is the proper sense of the word, if only because it would imply that all the people who are not Christians—all the Buddhists, Confucians, Mohammedans, and so on—are not trying to live a good life. I do not mean by a Christian any person who tries to live decently according to his lights. I think that you must have a certain amount of definite belief before you have a right to call yourself a Christian.

What Is a Christian?

Nowadays it is not quite that. We have to be a little more vague in our meaning of Christianity. I think, however, that there are two different items which are quite essential to anybody calling himself a Christian. The first is one of a dogmatic nature—namely, that you must believe in God and immortality. If you do not believe in those two things, I do not think that you can properly call yourself a Christian. Then, further than that, as the name implies, you must have some kind of belief about Christ. The Mohammedans, for instance, also believe in God and in immortality, and yet they would not call themselves Christians. I think you must have at the very lowest the belief that Christ was, if not divine, at least the best and wisest of men. If you are not going to believe that much about Christ, I do not think you have any right to call yourself a Christian. Of course, there is another sense, which you find in *Whitaker's Almanac* and in geography books, where the population of the world is said to be divided into Christians, Mohammedans, Buddhists, fetish worshipers, and so on; and in that sense we are all Christians. The geography books count us all in, but that is a purely geographical sense, which I suppose we can ignore. Therefore I take it that when I tell you why I am not a Christian I have to tell you two different things: first, why I do not believe in God and in immortality; and, secondly, why I do not think that Christ was the best and wisest of men, although I grant him a very high degree of moral goodness.

That is a very curious argument. If you looked at the matter from a scientific point of view, you would say, "After all, I only know this world. I do not know about the rest of the universe, but so far as one can argue at all on probabilities one would say that probably this world is a fair sample, and if there is injustice here the odds are that there is injustice elsewhere also." Supposing you got a crate of oranges that you opened, and you found all the top layer of oranges bad, you would not argue, "The underneath ones must be good, so as to redress the balance." You would say, "Probably the whole lot is a bad consignment"; and that is really what a scientific person would argue about the universe. He would say, "Here we find in this world a great deal of injustice, and so far as that goes that is a reason for supposing that justice does not rule in the world; and therefore so far as it goes it affords a moral argument against deity and not in favor of one." Of course I know that the sort of intellectual arguments that I have been talking to you about are not what really moves people. What really moves people to believe in God is not any intellectual argument at all. Most people believe in God because they have been taught from early infancy to do it, and that is the main reason.

The Character of Christ

I now want to say a few words upon a topic which I often think is not quite sufficiently dealt with by Rationalists, and that is the question whether Christ was the best and the wisest of men. It is generally taken for granted that we should all agree that that was so. I do not myself. I think that there are a good many points upon which I agree with Christ a great deal more than the professing Christians do. I do not know that I could go with Him all the way, but I could go with Him much further than most professing Christians can. You will remember that He said, "Resist not evil: but whosoever shall smite thee on thy right cheek, turn to him the other also." That is not a new precept or a new principle. It was used by Lao-tse and Buddha some 500 or 600 years before Christ, but it is not a principle which as a matter of fact Christians accept. I have no doubt that the present prime minister [Stanley Baldwin], for instance, is a most sincere Christian, but I should not advise any of you to go and smite him on one cheek. I think you might find that he thought this text was intended in a figurative sense.

The Moral Problem

Then you come to moral questions. There is one very serious defect to my mind in Christ's moral character, and that is that He believed in hell. I do not myself feel that any person who is really profoundly humane can believe in everlasting punishment. Christ certainly as depicted in the Gospels did believe in everlasting punishment, and one does find repeatedly a vindictive fury against those people who would not listen to His preaching—an attitude which is not uncommon with preachers, but which does somewhat detract from superlative excellence. You do not, for instance find that attitude in Socrates. You find him quite bland and urbane toward the people who would not listen to him; and it is, to my mind, far more worthy of a sage to take that line than to take the line of indignation. You probably all remember the sorts of things that Socrates was saying when he was dying, and the sort of things that he generally did say to people who did not agree with him.

You will find that in the Gospels Christ said, "Ye serpents, ye generation of vipers, how can ye escape the damnation of Hell." That was said to people who did not like His preaching. It is not really to my mind quite the best tone, and there are a great many of these things about Hell. There is, of course, the familiar text about the sin against the Holy Ghost: "Whosoever speaketh against the Holy Ghost it shall not be forgiven him neither in this World nor in the world to come." That text has caused an unspeakable amount of misery in the world, for all sorts of people have imagined that they have committed the sin against the Holy Ghost, and thought that it would not be forgiven them either in this world or in the world to come. I really do not think that a person with a proper degree of kindliness in his nature would have put fears and terrors of that sort into the world.

Then Christ says, "The Son of Man shall send forth his His angels, and they shall gather out of His kingdom all things that offend, and them which do iniquity, and shall cast them into a furnace of fire; there shall be wailing and gnashing of teeth"; and He goes on about the wailing and gnashing of teeth. It comes in one verse after another, and it is quite manifest to the reader that there is a certain pleasure in contemplating wailing and gnashing of teeth, or else it would not occur so often. Then you all, of course, remember about the sheep and the goats; how at the second coming He is going to divide the sheep from the goats, and He is going to say to the goats, "Depart from me, ye cursed, into everlasting fire." He continues, "And these shall go away into everlasting fire." Then He says again, "If thy hand offend thee, cut it off; it is better for thee to enter into life maimed, than having two hands to go into Hell, into the fire that never shall be quenched; where the worm dieth not and the fire is not quenched." He repeats that again and again also. I must say that I think all this doctrine, that hellfire is a punishment for sin, is a doctrine of cruelty. It is a doctrine that put cruelty into the world and gave the world generations of cruel torture; and the Christ of the Gospels, if you could take Him as His chroniclers represent Him, would certainly have to be considered partly responsible for that.

The Emotional Factor

As I said before, I do not think that the real reason why people accept religion has anything to do with argumentation. They accept religion on emotional grounds. One is often told that it is a very wrong thing to attack religion, because religion makes men virtuous. So I am told; I have not noticed it. You know, of course, the parody of that argument in Samuel Butler's book, *Erewhon Revisited*. You will remember that in *Erewhon* there is a certain Higgs who arrives in a remote country, and after spending some time there he escapes from that country in a balloon. Twenty years later he comes back to that country and finds a new religion in which he is worshipped under the name of the "Sun Child," and it is said that he ascended into heaven. He finds that the Feast of the Ascension is about to be celebrated, and he hears Professors Hanky and Panky say to each other that they never set eyes on the man Higgs, and they hope they never will; but they are the high priests of the religion of the Sun Child. He is very indignant, and he comes up to them, and he says, "I am going to expose all this humbug and tell the people of Erewhon that it was only I, the man Higgs, and I went up in a balloon." He was told, "You must not do that, because all the morals of this country are bound round this myth, and if they once know that you did not ascend into Heaven they will all become wicked"; and so he is persuaded of that and he goes quietly away.

That is the idea—that we should all be wicked if we did not hold to the Christian religion. It seems to me that the people who have held to it have been for the most part extremely wicked. You find this curious fact, that the more intense has been the religion of any period and the more profound has been the dogmatic belief, the greater has been the cruelty and the worse has been the state of affairs. In the so-called ages of faith, when men really did believe the Christian religion in all its completeness, there was the Inquisition, with all its tortures; there were millions of unfortunate women burned as witches; and there was every kind of cruelty practiced upon all sorts of people in the name of religion.

You find as you look around the world that every single bit of progress in humane feeling, every improvement in the criminal law, every step toward the diminution of war, every step toward better treatment of the colored races, or every mitigation of slavery, every moral progress that there has been in the world, has been consistently opposed by the organized churches of the world. I say quite deliberately that the Christian religion, as organized in its churches, has been and still is the principal enemy of moral progress in the world.

WHY I AM STILL A CHRISTIAN

HANS KUNG

> "Always be ready to give an explanation to anyone who asks for the reason for your hope."
>
> 1 Peter 3:15

Where do I get my Christian commitment from? I get my essential values from Jesus of Nazareth, who is a historical figure not a myth, and who is for that very reason the Christ who is authoritative in all things for Christians of all times. He proclaimed the one and only God, his God and our Father (Abba) who had already spoken and been addressed in the history of the people of Israel, in the experiences of men and women; he proclaimed this God with a human face, as living and close. In his whole life and in everything he did he made this face of God shine out. When Jesus spoke of this God and acted in his name, he made clear what was vague in the Old Testament, made what seemed ambiguous there unambiguous. The one true God of Israel is now understood in a new way. We can sum it up by saying that he is understood as the "running Father" (Luke 15:20) of the Prodigal Son, indeed as the Father of all the lost, not simply as the Father of the devout and those who were righteous from the very beginning.

This God as Jesus proclaimed him, is not—as has often be taught to children—an all too masculine, arbitrary, legal-minded God, a kind of martinet, a God without features. He is not a God created in the images of kings, tyrants, an dictators. This God really is—not in its superficial meaning, but in its deepest sense—the loving God who is my Mother too: that is, he is the God of love who for all his justice, commits himself unreservedly to all human beings, in all their needs and hopes.

He is a God who does not always merely demand, but gives; who does not oppress, but liberates; who does not make people ill or poison their lives, but heals them. He is a God who spares those who fall—and who does not fall? A God who forgives instead of condemning, liberates instead of punishing, makes grace rule instead of law; who rejoices more over the repentance of one sinner than over ninety-nine just people. He is therefore a God who prefers the Prodigal Son to the one who stayed home, the tax collector to the Pharisee, the Samaritan heretic to the orthodox, the prostitutes and adulterers to their self-righteous judges. As you see, this preaching of Jesus was offensive and scandalous, not only for that time in history but for today as well, particularly since it was accompanied by an equally offensive and scandalous practice: not excommunication but communication—even communion! He sat down—he even sat down at table—with the despised and the failures, "sinners" of every kind.

Yes, this God is a different God: a God who sets himself above the formal, logical, merciless correctness of the law and proclaims a "better" righteousness, and may even justify a transgressor of the law; a God for whom the commandments and the Sabbath exist for the sake of the human person, and not the human person for the sake of the commandments and the Sabbath.

It was for this God and his wonderful kindness that Jesus pleaded. For him he spoke, fought, suffered, and was executed. And at this point, of course, the question always arises: did it not all end with his death? The cautious answer can at first be one that even the non-Christian can accept. It is a fact of world history that Jesus' death was not the end of everything but only the beginning; that his first community, in a truly reckless fashion, proclaimed him—the heretical teacher, false prophet, seducer of the people, blasphemer, allegedly condemned by God—to be God's Messiah, the Christ, Lord, Son of man, Son of God. And why? According to the New Testament sources, they were convinced—and only this conviction explains the emergence of Christianity at all—that Jesus had died, not into nothingness, but into God. That means that Jesus is living: living through, with and in God. What for? For us: as hope, as obligation, for our essential values.

Even since then both Christians and non-Christians have been faced with a clear alternative in the direction they lead their lives.

There is the possibility that we die into nothingness. I would not deny my respect for anyone who adopts this position. This is the view which sometimes demands heroism, and can certainly not be refuted. Of course no one has proved it positively either. There has never yet been anyone who could prove that we die into nothingness, that all our living, laboring, loving and suffering ends in nothingness and was ultimately for nothing. And to me this possibility does not seem reasonable; under no circumstances does it seem reasonable.

This is the other possibility: that we die into an absolute reality which we call God, because we still have no better name for it. This alternative too cannot be proved; nor of course can it be refuted. Here every human being is faced with a decision that no one can take away. We have no rational proof for eternal life. But we do have reasonable grounds. We can commit ourselves to this in enlightened, reasonable trust. Truly, not to console ourselves with the promise of a hereafter, but to set ourselves all the more decisively in the here and now, in this life, in this present-day society. And that we do not die into nothingness but into God seems to me more reasonable. Think: if God really exists and if he really is God, he cannot be merely the god of the beginning, but must also be the God of the end. Then he is our Finisher as well as our Creator. And it is he alone, the Creator and Preserver of the cosmos and of human beings, who can be expected to have one more word to say, even in dying at death, beyond the frontiers of all that has hitherto been experienced: to have the last word, just as he had the first. If I seriously believe in an eternal living God, I believe also in God's eternal life, in my own eternal life. So if I begin my profession of faith in the Creed with belief in God the almighty, the creator I may very well finish it with belief in "life everlasting."

A firm faith of this kind changes even this present life completely. It enables us to live quite differently, with more meaning, more responsibility, with greater involvement. In fact it enables us to life in accordance with the standard of this Christ. With his proclamation, the way he lived, and his fate. He became the standard for those who believe in him: the standard for their relations with their fellow human beings, with society, and above all with God. To put it briefly, for believers the true man Jesus of Nazareth has therefore always been the real and clear revelation of the one God: his Messiah, his Christ, his image and his son.

But it is in this very way that he is truly a human being, *the* true human being. Through his proclamation, his behavior, his whole destiny, he provided *a model of being human* which, if we commit ourselves trustingly to it, enables us again and again to discover and to realize the meaning of our own being human, of our freedom, of our life: in our own existence and in living with our fellow human beings. Confirmed by God in the resurrection, he thus represents for us the enduring, reliable, ultimate standard of what being human means. What has surely become plain in recent theological disputes is that Christology, or a theory about Christ, may be important, particularly for theologians and bishops, but faith in Christ and discipleship are the essentials. Being a Christian is the important thing. And it is he who makes that possible for me—he the Christ of God, who is identical with the historical human being who lived, died, and rose again—the Jesus of Nazareth, the devout Galilean Jew of the first third of the first century. So that is how I answer the question of why I am still a Christian and where I get my Christian commitment from.

CHAPTER

15 Lesson Plan 12

How Does Someone Cope with the Death of a Child?

The Stone Boy

Lesson 1: Plot-check quiz and discussion of a basic question
Lesson 2: The movie version of "The Stone Boy" (90 minutes).
Lesson 3: Background on the movie with Gina Berriault and discussion of Gene Siskel's movie review.

1. **Focus:**	Journal writing: Have you ever been disappointed with a film version of a novel or short story or novel that you liked? If so, why so? If not, why?
2. **Objective:**	To resolve a basic question of interpretation on the short story.
3. **Purpose:**	To increase our mutual understanding and enjoyment of the original story.
4. **Input:**	Begin with a factual plot quiz to check that everyone has read the story. A basic question of interpretation.
5. **Modeling, checking for understanding, guided practice:**	During discussion, the teacher (or student co-leaders) *model* the four rules of Socratic discussion and *check for understanding* by asking follow-up questions for clarification, substantiation, consistency, relevance, implication, resolution and to get more opinion. *Guided practice is* the discussion.
6. **Closure:**	Oral or written resolution (in the journal) of the basic question discussed.
Text:	Gina Berriault (1972). "The Stone Boy" *Mademoiselle Magazine*, 1957; Judith Guest, *Ordinary People* (Lesson Plan 12 alternative)
Film:	*The Stone Boy* DVD (91 mins) 1984

"The Stone Boy"

Gina Berriault

Arnold drew his overalls and raveling gray sweater over his naked body. In the other narrow bed his brother Eugene went on sleeping, undisturbed by the alarm clock's rusty ring. Arnold, watching his brother sleeping, felt a peculiar dismay; he was nine, six years younger that Eugie, and in their waking hours it was he who was subordinate. To dispel emphatically his uneasy advantage over his sleeping brother, he threw himself on the hump of Eugie's body.

"Get up! Get up!" he cried.

Arnold felt his brother twist away and saw the blankets lifted in a great wing, and, all in an instant, he was lying on his back under the covers with only his face showing, like a baby and Eugie was sprawled on top of him.

"Whassa matter with you?" asked Eugie in sleepy anger, his face hanging close.

"Get up," Arnold repeated. "You said you'd pick peas with me."

Stupidly, Eugie gazed around the room to see if morning had come into it yet. Arnold began to laugh derisively, making soft, snorting noises, and was thrown off the bed. He got up from the floor and went down the stairs, the laughter continuing like hiccups, against his will. But when he opened the staircase door and entered the parlor, he hunched up his shoulders and was quiet because his parents slept in the bedroom downstairs.

Arnold lifted his .22-caliber rifle from the rack on the kitchen wall. It was an old lever-action that his father had given him because nobody else used it anymore. On their way down to the garden he and Eugie would go by the lake, and if there were any ducks on it he'd take a shot at them. Standing on the stool before the cupboard, he searched on the top shelf in the confusion of medicines and ointments for man and beast and found a small yellow box of .22 cartridges. Then he sat down on the stool and began to load his gun.

It was cold in the kitchen so early, but later in the day, when his mother canned the peas, the heat from the wood stove would be almost unbearable. Yesterday she had finished preserving the huckleberries that the family had picked along the mountain, and before that she had canned all the cherries his father had brought from the warehouse in Corinth. Sometimes, on these summer days, Arnold would deliberately come out from the shade where he was playing and make himself as uncomfortable as his mother was in the kitchen by standing in the sun until the sweat ran down his body.

Eugie came clomping down the stairs and into the kitchen, his head drooping with sleepiness. From his perch on the stool Arnold watched

Eugie slip on his green knit cap. Eugie didn't really need a cap; he hadn't had a haircut in a long time and his brown curls grew thick and matted, close around his ears and down his neck, tapering there to a small whorl. Eugie passed his left hand through his hair before he set his cap down with his right. The very way he slipped his cap on was an announcement of his status; almost everything he did was a reminder that he was eldest—first he, then Nora, then Arnold—and called attention to how tall he was, almost as tall as his father, how long his legs were, how small he was in the hips, and what a neat dip above his buttocks his thick-soled logger's boots gave him. Arnold never tired of watching Eugie offer silent praise to himself. He wondered, as he sat enthralled, if when he got to be Eugie's age he would still be undersized and his hair still straight.

Eugie eyed the gun. "Don't you know this ain't duck season?" he asked gruffly, as if he were the sheriff.

"No, I don't know," Arnold said with a snigger.

Eugie picked up the tin washtub for the peas, unbolted the door with his free hand and kicked it open. then, lifting the tub to his head, he went clomping down the back steps. Arnold followed, closing the door behind him.

The sky was faintly gray, almost white. The mountains behind the farm made the sun climb a long way to show itself. Several miles to the south, where the range opened up, hung an orange mist, but the valley in which the farm lay was still cold and colorless.

Eugie opened the gate to the yard and the boys passed between the barn and the row of chicken houses, their feet stirring up the carpet of brown feathers dropped by the molting chickens. They paused before going down the slope to the lake. A fluky morning wind ran among the shocks of wheat that covered the slope. It sent a shimmer northward across the lake, gently moving the rushes that formed an island in the center. Killdeer, their white markings flashing, skimmed the water, crying their shrill sweet cry. And there at the south end of the lake were four wild ducks, swimming out from the willows into open water.

Arnold followed Eugie down the slope, stealing, as his brother did, from one shock of wheat to another. Eugie paused before climbing through the wire fence that divided the wheat field from the marshy pasture around the lake. They were screened from the ducks by the willows along the lake's edge.

"If you hit your duck, you want me to go in after it?" Eugie said.

"If you want," Arnold said.

Eugie lowered his eyelids, leaving slits of mocking blue. "You'd drown 'fore you got to it, them legs of yours so puny," he said.

He shoved the tub under the fence and, pressing down the center wire, climbed through into the pasture.

Arnold pressed down the bottom wire, thrust a leg through and leaned forward to bring the other leg after. His rifle caught on the wire and he jerked at it. The air was rocked by the sound of a shot. Feeling foolish, he lifted his face, baring it to an expected shower of derision from his brother. But Eugie did not turn around. Instead, from his crouching position, he fell to his knees and then pitched forward onto his face. The ducks rose up crying from the lake, cleared the mountain background and beat away northward across the pale sky.

Arnold squatted beside his brother. Eugie seemed to be climbing the earth, as if the earth ran up and down, and when he found he couldn't scale it he lay still.

"Eugie?"

Then Arnold saw it, under the tendril of hair at the nape of the neck—a slow rising of bright blood. It had an obnoxious movement, like that of a parasite.

"Hey, Eugie," he said again. He was feeling the same discomfort he had felt when he had watched Eugie sleeping; his brother didn't know that he was lying face down in the pasture. Again he said, "Hey, Eugie," an anxious nudge in his voice. But Eugie was still as the morning around them.

Arnold set his rifle on the ground and stood up. He picked up the tub and, dragging it behind him, walked along by the willows to the garden fence and climbed through. He went down on his knees among the tangled vines. The pods were cold with the night, but his hands were strange to him, and not until some time had passed did he realize that the pods were numbing his fingers. He picked from the top of the vine first, then lifted the vine to look underneath for pods, and moved on to the next.

It was a warmth on his back, like a large hand laid firmly there, that made him raise his head. Way up the slope the gray farmhouse was struck by the sun. While his head had been bent the land had grown bright around him.

When he got up his legs were so stiff that he had to go down on his knees again to ease the pain. Then, walking sideways, he dragged the tub, half full of peas, up the slope.

The kitchen was warm now; a fire was roaring in the stove with a closed-up, rushing sound. His mother was spooning eggs from a pot of boiling water and putting them into a bowl. Her short brown hair was uncombed and fell forward across her eyes as she bent her head. Nora was lifting a frying pan full of trout from the stove, holding the handle with a dish towel. His father had just come in from bringing the cows from the north pasture to the barn, and was sitting on the stool, unbuttoning his red plaid Mackinaw.

"Did you boys fill the tub?" his mother asked.

"They ought of by now," his father said. "They went out of the house and hour ago. Eugie woke me up comin' downstairs. I heard you shootin'—did you get a duck?"

"No," Arnold said. They would want to know why Eugie wasn't coming in for breakfast, he thought. "Eugie's dead," he told them.

They stared at him. The pitch crackled in the stove.

"You kids plain' a joke?" his father asked.

"Where's Eugene?" his mother asked scoldingly. She wanted, Arnold knew, to see his eyes, and when he had glanced at her she put the bowl and spoon down on the stove and walked past him. His father stood up and went out the door after her. Nora followed them with little skipping steps, as if afraid to be alone.

Arnold went into the barn, down the foddering passage past the cows waiting to be milked, and climbed into the loft. After a few minutes he heard a terrifying sound coming toward the house. His parents and Nora were returning from the willows, and sounds sharp as knives were rising from his mother's breast and carrying over the sloping fields. In a short while he heard his father go down the back steps, slam the car door and drive away.

Arnold lay still as a fugitive, listening to the cows eating close by. If his parents never called him, he thought he would stay up in the loft forever, out of the way. In the night he would sneak down for a drink of water from the faucet over the trough and for whatever food they left him by the barn.

The rattle of his father's car as it turned down the lane recalled him to the present. He heard the voices of his Uncle Andy and Aunt Alice and they and his father went past the barn to the lake. He could feel the morning growing heavier with sun. Someone, probably Nora, had let the chickens out of their coops and they were cackling in the yard.

After a while another car turned down the road off the highway. The car drew to a stop and he heard the voices of strange men. The men also went past the barn and down to the lake. The undertakers, whom his father must have phoned from Uncle Andy's house, had arrived from Corinth. And then he heard everyone come back and heard the car turn around and leave.

"Arnold!" It was his father calling from the yard.

He climbed down the ladder and went out into the sun, picking wisps of hay from his overalls.

Corinth, nine miles away, was the county seat. Arnold sat in the front of the old Ford between his father, who was driving, and Uncle Andy; no one spoke. Uncle Andy was his mother's brother, and he had been fond of Eugie because Eugie had resembled him. Andy had taken Eugie hunting and had given him a knife and a lot of things, and now Andy, his eyes narrowed, sat tall and stiff beside Arnold.

Arnold's father parked the car before the courthouse. It was a two-story brick building with a lamp on both sides of the bottom step. They went up the wide stone steps, Arnold and his father going first, and entered the darkly paneled hallway. The shirt-sleeved man in the sheriff's office said the sheriff was at Carlson's Parlor examining the Curwing boy.

Andy went off to get the sheriff while Arnold and his father waited on a bench in the corridor. Arnold felt his father watching him, and he lifted his eyes with painful casualness to the announcement, on the opposite wall, of the Corinth County Annual Rodeo, and then to the clock with its loudly clucking pendulum. After he had come down from the loft his father and Uncle Andy had stood in the yard with him and asked him to tell them everything, and he had explained to them how the gun had caught on the wire. But when they had asked him why he hadn't run back to the house to tell his parents, he had had no answer—all he could say was that he had gone down into the garden to pick the peas. His father had stared at him in a pale, puzzled way, and it was then that he had felt his father and the others set their cold, turbulent silence against him. Arnold shifted on the bench, his only feeling a small one of compunction imposed by his father's eyes.

At a quarter past nine Andy and the sheriff came in. They all went into the sheriff's private office, and Arnold was sent forward to sit in the chair by the sheriff's desk; his father and Andy sat down on the bench against the wall.

The sheriff lumped down into his swivel chair and swung toward Arnold. He was an old man with white hair like wheat stubble. His restless green eyes made him seem not to be in his office but to be hurrying and bobbing around somewhere else.

"What did you say your name was?" the sheriff asked.

"Arnold," he replied, but he could not remember telling the sheriff his name before.

"Curwing?"

"Yes."

"What were you doing with a .22, Arnold?"

"It's mine," he said.

"Okay. What were you going to shoot?"

"Some ducks," he replied.

"Out of season?"

He nodded.

"That's bad," said the sheriff. "Were you and your brother good friends?"

What did he mean—good friends? Eugie was his brother. That was different from a friend, Arnold thought. A best friend was your own age, but

Eugie was almost a man. Eugie had had a way of looking at him, slyly and mockingly and yet confidentially, that had summed up how they both felt about being brothers. Arnold had wanted to be with Eugie more than with anybody else but he couldn't say that they had been good friends.

"Did they ever quarrel?" the sheriff asked his father.

"Not that I know," his father replied. "It seemed to me that Arnold cared a lot for Eugie."

"Did you?" the sheriff asked Arnold.

If it seemed so to his father, then it was so. Arnold nodded.

"Were you mad at him this morning?"

"No."

"How did you happen to shoot him?"

"We was crawlin' through the fence."

"Yes?"

"An' the gun got caught on the wire."

"Seems the hammer must of caught," his father put in.

"All right, that's what happened," said the sheriff. "But what I want you to tell me is this. Why didn't you go back to the house and tell your father right away? Why did you go and pick peas for an hour?"

Arnold gazed over his shoulder at his father, expecting his father to have an answer for this also. But his father's eyes, larger and even lighter blue than usual, were fixed upon him curiously. Arnold picked at a callus in his right palm. It seemed odd now that he had not run back to the house and wakened his father, but he could not remember why he had not. They were all waiting for him to answer.

"I come down to pick peas," he said.

"Didn't you think," asked the sheriff stepping carefully from word to word, "that it was more important for you to go tell your parents what had happened?"

"The sun was gonna come up," Arnold said.

"What's that got to do with it?"

"It's better to pick peas while they're cool."

The sheriff swung away from him, laid both hands flat on his desk. "Well, all I can say is," he said across to Arnold's father and Uncle Andy, "he's either a moron or he's so reasonable that he's way ahead of us." He gave a challenging snort. "It's come to my notice that the most reasonable guys are mean ones. They don't feel nothing."

For a moment the three men sat still. Then the sheriff lifted his hand like a man taking an oath. "Take him home," he said.

Andy uncrossed his legs. "You don't want him?"?

"Not now," replied the sheriff. "Maybe in a few years."

Arnold's father stood up. He held his hat against his chest. "The gun ain't his no more," he said wanly.

Arnold went first through the hallway, hearing behind him the heels of his father and Uncle Andy striking the floorboards. He went down the steps ahead of them and climbed into the back seat of the car. Andy paused as he was getting into the front seat and gazed back at Arnold, and Arnold saw that his uncle's eyes had absorbed the knowingness from the sheriff's eyes. Andy and his father and the sheriff had discovered what made him go down into the grain. It was because he was cruel, the sheriff had said, and didn't care about his brother. Arnold lowered his eyelids meekly against his uncle's stare.

The rest of the day he did his tasks around the farm, keeping apart from the family. At evening, when he saw his father stomp tiredly into the house, Arnold did not put down his hammer and leave the chicken coop he was repairing. He was afraid that they did not want him to eat supper with them. But in a few minutes another fear that they would go to the trouble of calling him and that he would be made conspicuous by his tardiness made him follow his father into the house. As he went through the kitchen, he saw the jars of peas standing in rows on the workbench, a reproach to him.

No one spoke at supper, and his mother, who sat next to him, leaned her head in her hand all throughout he meal, curving her fingers over her eyes so as not to see him. They were finishing their small, silent supper when the visitors began to arrive, knocking hard on the back door. The men were coming from their farms now that it was growing dark and they could not work anymore.

Old Man Matthews, gray and stocky, came first, with his two sons, Orion, the elder, and Clint, who was Eugie's age. As the callers entered the parlor where the family ate, Arnold sat down in a rocking chair. Even as he had been undecided before supper whether to remain outside or take his place at the table, he now thought that he should go upstairs, and yet he stayed to avoid being conspicuous by his absence. If he stayed, he thought, as he always stayed and listened when visitors came, they would see that he was only Arnold and not the person the sheriff thought he was. He sat with his arms crossed and his hands tucked into his armpits and did not lift his eyes.

The Matthews men had hardly settled down around the table, after Arnold's mother and Nora had cleared away the dishes, when another car rattled down the road and someone else rapped on the back door. This time it was Sullivan, a spare and sandy man, so nimble of gesture and expression that Arnold had never been able to catch more than a few of his meanings. Sullivan, in dusty jeans, sat down in another rocker, shot out his skinny legs and began to talk in his fast way, recalling everything that Eugene had ever said to him. The other men interrupted to tell of occasions they remembered, and after a time Clint's young voice, hoarse like Eugene's had been, broke in to tell about the time Eugene had beat him in a wrestling match.

Out of the kitchen the voices of Orion's wife and of Mrs. Sullivan mingled with Nora's voice but not, Arnold noticed, with his mother's. Then dry little Mr. Cram came, leaving large Mrs. Cram in the kitchen, and there was no chair left for Mr. Cram to sit in. No one asked Arnold to get up and he was unable to rise. He knew that the story had got around to them during the day about how he had gone and picked peas after he had shot his brother, and he knew that although they were talking only about Eugie they were thinking about him and if he got up, if he moved even his foot, they would all be alerted. Then Uncle Andy arrived and leaned his tall, lanky body against the doorjamb and there were two men standing.

Presently Arnold was aware that the talk had stopped. He knew without looking up that the men were watching him.

"Not a tear in his eye," said Andy, and Arnold knew that it was his uncle who had gestured the men to attention.

"He don't give a hoot, is that how it goes?" asked Sullivan, trippingly.

"He's a reasonable fellow," Andy explained. "That's what the sheriff said. It's us who ain't reasonable. If we'd of shot our brother, we'd of come runnin' back to the house, cryin' like a baby. Well, we'd of been unreasonable. What would of been the use of actin' like that? If your brother is shot dead, he's shot dead. What's the use of getting' emotional about it? The thing to do is go down to the garden to pick peas. Am I right?"

The men around the room shifted their heavy, satisfying weight of unreasonableness.

Matthew's son Orion said: "If I'd of done what he done, Pa would've hung my pelt by the side of the big coyote's in the barn."

Arnold sat in the rocker until the last man filed out. While his family was out in the kitchen bidding the callers good night and the cars were driving away down the dirt lane to the highway, he picked up one of the kerosene lamps and slipped quickly up the stairs. In his room he undressed by lamplight, although he and Eugie had always undressed in the dark, and not until he was lying in his bed did he blow out the flame. He felt nothing, not any grief. There was only the same immense silence and crawling inside of him; it was the way the house and fields felt under a merciless man.

He awoke suddenly. He knew that his father was out in the yard, closing the doors of the chicken houses. The sound that had wakened him was the step of his father as he got up from the rocker and went down the back steps. And he knew that his mother was awake in her bed.

Throwing off the covers, he rose swiftly, went down the stairs and across the dark parlor to his parent's room. He rapped on the door.

"Mother?"

From the closed room her voice rose to him, a seeking and retreating voice. "Yes?"

"Mother?" he asked insistently. He had expected her to realize that he wanted to go down on his knees by her bed and tell her that Eugie was dead. She did not know it yet, nobody knew it, and yet she was sitting up in bed, waiting to be told, waiting for him to confirm her dread. He had expected her to tell him to come in, to allow him to dig his head into her blankets and tell her about the terror he had felt when he had knelt beside Eugie. He had come to clasp her in his arms and, in his terror, to pommel her breasts with his head. He put his hand upon the knob.

"Go back to bed, Arnold," she called sharply.

But he waited.

"Go back! Is night when you get afraid?"

At first he did not understand. Then, silently, he left the door and for a stricken moment stood by the rocker. Outside everything was still. The fences, the shocks of wheat seen through the window before him were so still it was as if they moved and breathed in the daytime and had fallen silent with the lateness of the hour. It was a silence that seemed to observe his father, a figure moving alone around the yard, his lantern casting a circle of light by his feet. In a few minutes his father would enter the dark house, the lantern still lighting his way.

Arnold was suddenly aware that he was naked. He had thrown off his blankets and come down the stairs to tell his mother how he felt about Eugie, but she had refused to listen to him and his nakedness had become unpardonable. At once he went back up the stairs, fleeing from his father's lantern.

At breakfast he kept his eyelids lowered as if to deny the humiliating nights. Nora, sitting at his left, did not pass the pitcher of milk to him and he did not ask for it. He would never again, he vowed, ask them for anything, and he ate his fried eggs and potatoes only because everybody ate meals—the cattle ate, and the cats; if was customary for everybody to eat.

"Nora, you gonna keep that pitcher for yourself?" his father asked.

Nora lowered her head unsurely.

"Pass it on to Arnold," his father said.

Nora put her hands in her lap.

His father picked up the metal pitcher and set it down at Arnold's plate.

Arnold, pretending to be deaf to the discord, did not glance up, but relief rained over his shoulders at the thought that his parents recognized him again. They must have lain awake after his father had come in from the yard: had they realized together why he had come down the stairs and knocked on their door?

"Bessie's missin' this morning," his father called out to his mother, who had gone into the kitchen. "She went up the mountain last night and had her calf, most likely. Somebody's got to go up and find her 'fore the coyotes get the calf."

That had been Eugie's job, Arnold thought. Eugie would climb the cattle trails in search of a newborn calf and come down the mountain carrying the calf across his back, with the cow running behind him, mooing in alarm.

Arnold ate the few more forkfuls of his breakfast, put his hands on the edge of the table and pushed back his chair. If he went for the calf he'd be away from the farm all morning. He could switch the cow down the mountain slowly, and the calf would run along at its mother's side.

When he passed through the kitchen his mother was setting a kettle of water on the stove.

"Where you going?" she asked awkwardly.

"Up to get the calf," he replied, averting his face.

"Arnold?"

At the door he paused reluctantly, his back to her, knowing that she was seeking him out, as his father was doing, and he called upon his pride to protect him from them.

"Was you knocking at my door last night?"

He looked over his shoulder at her, his eyes narrow and dry.

"What'd you want?" she asked humbly.

"I didn't want nothing," he said flatly.

Then he went out the door and down the back steps, his legs trembling from the fright his answer gave him.

"The Stone Boy" by Gina Berriault

PLOT QUIZ

Directions: On your own paper, next to each number, write a short answer to complete this plot summary of the story.

As the story begins, the Curwing brothers, Arnold and Eugene set out in early morning to (1) ____________________. Arnold, who is (2) ________________ years old, idolizes his older brother who is (3) __________________ years old. Arnold wonders if when he reached Eugene's age he would still be (4) ________________. As the boys leave the farmhouse, (5) ________________ brings along his (6) ______________ in hopes that he might (7) ___________________________. But before they can get to work, a terrible accident (8) ________________________________ ____________ occurs. Strangely, after the accident, Arnold does not (9) ____________________________ but rather (10) ____________.

When Arnold returns to the farmhouse, he says only that (11) ____________________. At first, his parents think he is (12) ______________. Soon, however, they discover the awful truth that (13) ________________. Because of Arnold's behavior—(14) ______ ________________________________—many problems arise for him. For example, he becomes (15) ________________________; as a result, he becomes the film's title character.

Arnold's father and (16) ________________________, who favors Eugene because (17) ____________________, take Arnold to Corinth to be questioned by the sheriff. After the sheriff asks if Arnold had been friends with Eugene or if he had been (18) ____________ with him, he then asks the all-important question about (19) ____________________________ In reply, Arnold says only that (20) ____________________. The sheriff then comments that Arnold is "either a (21) ________________ or he's so (22) ________________ that he's way ahead of us."

After Arnold returns to the farmhouse, visitors arrive who begin to (23) ______________________________ for his behavior after Eugene's death. That night Arnold wants to speak with his mother but she turns him away because she is too (24) ____________________ to hear his confession of grief. In the morning after she realizes what she has done to hurt her son, she asks Arnold what he wanted the night before. He replies flatly, "I didn't want (25) __________________." Then he walks out the door and down the back steps. He legs tremble from the (26) _________________ his answer gave him.

Socratic Seminar

Basic Question of Interpretation: Why do none of the adults in the story understand what Arnold has gone through in killing his brother?

1. Why is Uncle Andy surprised that the sheriff lets Arnold return home after questioning him?
2. What does the sheriff mean when he says in Arnold's presence, "he's either a moron or he's so reasonable that he's way ahead of us"?
3. Why does Arnold's mother refuse to let him come into her bedroom on the night of Eugene's death?
4. Does Arnold's father fail to understand Arnold's grief because his son can offer no reasonable explanation for not running back to the house for help?
5. Why does Berriault reveal to readers the depth of Arnold's grief while none of the adults are able to perceive it?
6. Does Arnold become a stone boy chiefly because none of the adults were able to understand his lack of evident emotion at the loss of his brother?
7. After Uncle Andy's comment during the wake shaming Arnold for his lack of a show of emotion, why does the narrator say, "The men around the room shifted their heavy, satisfying weight of unreasonableness"?
8. When the author ends her story with Arnold's reply to his mother's question that he didn't want anything, is Berriault implying that his parents have lost two sons?

Ordinary People: Lesson Plan 12A

Lesson 1: Plot-check quiz on entire novel or sections as assigned. Begin movie version. Make notations on ten important differences.
Lesson 2: Movie version concluded. Discussion of major differences.
Lesson 3: Exercise 1 on film version of the novel.
Lesson 4: Seminar discussions—Exercise 2
Lesson 5: Exercise 3 on the grieving process (Kubler-Ross).
Lesson 6: Exercise 4 on Essay Exam questions.

1. **Focus:** Review
   What questions do you have?
2. **Objective:** To solve several questions of interpretation about the overall meaning of the novel.

3. Purpose:	◦ To increase our mutual understanding (comprehension) and, as a result, our enjoyment of the story. ◦ To develop the habit of independent and critical thinking.
4. Input:	Begin with a factual plot quiz to check that everyone has read the novel. (Rule 1: No one may participate who has not read the selection). Seminar: Two or four basic questions.
5. Modeling, checking and guided practice:	During discussion the co-leaders *model* the four rules of discussion, *check for understanding* by asking follow-up questions for clarification, substantiation, consistency, relevance, implication, resolution, and to get more opinion. *Guided practice* **is** the discussion.
6. Closure:	Oral or written resolution of one or two basic questions.
Text:	Judith Guest, *Ordinary People,* New York: Penguin Books, 1976
Film:	*Ordinary People* DVD (125 mins) 1980, dir. Robert Redford

ORDINARY PEOPLE

JUDITH GUEST

Exercise 1: Film version

A. Are there any significant plot changes that Judith Guest would have rejected? For example, why does Calvin leave Beth in the film while Beth leaves Calvin in the novel?

B. Read several student reviews of the novel on **Amazon.com.** Select one with which you particularly disagree and *write a personal letter of rebuttal* (one page). Select one with which you entirely agree and explain why you agree in your own movie review.

C. Think about previous work you have undertaken on conducting a comparison-contrast discussion, then undertake one on the film version of the original story.

Exercise 2: Seminar Discussions

The novel raises several basic questions of interpretation. *Write at least eight specific follow-up questions* for one question (1 OR 2) and give a page reference for each. For example: Why is Lazenby the only one who wrote Conrad during his hospital confinement (96). Or: At the end of the novel when Conrad is finally reconciled with his father, why does he make no mention of his brother? (259)

1. Has Conrad finally learned to cope with the death of Jordan (Buck)?
2. How has Conrad finally learned to cope with the death of his brother?

Exercise 3: The Grieving Process

Review Kubler-Ross's description of the stages of the grieving process: denial, anger, bargaining, resignation, and acceptance. Note: these five stages are not linear and they can and do overlap. Indeed, at times a person may get stuck at one stage and skip or never experience a stage at all.

A. *Define and illustrate each stage from common experience.* (The topic of your example need not be about the death of a loved one but about any major crisis. For example, the news that you are going to have to have a leg amputated or that you will be paralyzed for life.)

B. How does each stage of the grieving process apply *or not* apply to Conrad, to Calvin, and to Beth? For each character cite an apt passage from the novel that illustrates the state a character reveals in that scene.

Exercise 4. Essay questions

In a well organized reply to ONE of these questions; be sure to include specific supporting evidence from the novel. Begin with a thesis statement; omit an introduction.

A. What is the relevance of the poem by Edna St.Vincent Millay (fore piece) to the theme of the novel?

B. Conrad says he is an atheist (251) while his father, Calvin, asks: "How does a Christian deal with grief?" (51) Does Christian faith (belief in God's provident love for each of us) help Calvin in his struggle to cope with his son's death?

C. What (or how) does each major character contribute to Conrad's healing? (Beth, Calvin, Karen (Chapter 7 and p. 210 ff), Jeannie (Chapter 30, and p. 100 ff), Dr. Berger)

Socratic Seminar

Basic Question 1: Does the author want her readers to conclude that Conrad has finally learned how to cope with the death of his brother?

If YES, then:

1. Why did Conrad attempt to kill himself? (pp. 41, 44, 70, 119, 213)
2. At what point does Conrad decide that life is worth living?
3. Did Jordan want life to go on *as if* his brother had not died? (43, 94, 127)
4. Does the author want us to agree with Karen's approval of Dr. Crawford's statement that "the only one who can help you is you"? (55)
5. In what sense are the Jarrett family "ordinary people"? (94, 161, 216)
6. Why does Dr. Berger place so much importance on Conrad's feelings? (98, 136, 225)
7. Who is "the guy in the closet" that Dr. Berger wants Conrad to release? (100, 138)
8. Did Conrad ever release "the guy in the closet"? (100, 138)
9. At the end of the story when Conrad is finally reconciled with his father, why does he make no mention of his brother? (59)

If NO, then:

1. Why does Edna St. Vincent Millay speak of man as "a shining animal"? (Fore piece)
2. Who or what did Conrad hold responsible for the death of his brother, Jordan? (120) (Why does Dr. Berger ask, "Who is it who can't forgive who"?)
3. Why did Karen's suicide have such a devastating effect on Conrad? (210–214)
4. Did Conrad believe for a time that Jordan let go of the overturned boat on purpose?
5. Why did Conrad believe that it had to be somebody's fault that Jordan died? (224)
6. At the end of the story why does Conrad try to console his father that Beth will eventually return? (259, 263)
7. Why does the story end with Conrad telling his father that he loves him? (259)
8. Why does Conrad want to play golf with Lazenby? (Epilogue) (262)
9. What is Conrad thanking Dr. Berger for at the end of the story? (260)
10. Why does Dr. Berger regard Conrad as his "prize pupil"? (260)

Alternative Basic Questions

Here are three more basic questions that you can qualify for discussion if you can come up with at least eight related interpretive follow-up questions for each. When students are struggling to write their own basic questions, I sometimes "give" them a basic question as an intermediate step to writing their own clusters. They then have to develop at least eight of their own related interpretive follow-up questions.

Basic Question 2: Who or what was most instrumental in Conrad's learning how to cope with his brother's death?

1. Why is Lazenby the only one who visits Conrad in the hospital after his attempted suicide? (p. 96)
2. When Dr. Burger says Beth loves Conrad "as much as she is able," does he mean that Conrad is wrong to fault her for not helping him to cope with Jordan's death? (120)
3. Why does the author want us to know that Conrad regards himself as an atheist? (251)
4. Does Beth leave Calvin primarily because she disagrees with the way that her husband treats Conrad after his attempted suicide? (252)
5. Is Beth unable to help Conrad because she herself had not accepted Jordan's death?
6. After Conrad's conversation with Jeannie, why does the narrator say "He is in touch for good, with hope, with himself... Berger is right, the body never lies." (251)
7. Why couldn't Dr. Crawford help Conrad during his eight months in the hospital? (41, 43, 55)
8. Why does Calvin refer to his son as "this mysterious stranger"? (61)
9. Why does the story end with Conrad telling his father that he loves him? (259)
10. What does Calvin mean when he says that "Grief is ugly. It is isolating"? (127)
11. Why does Dr. Berger place so much importance on Conrad's feelings? (98,136)
12. Does Calvin conclude that Jordan's death is also nobody's fault but just "the way things are"? (258)
13. Unlike Dr. Crawford at the hospital who had Conrad speak of Jordan's death "every day," why does Dr. Berger speak so little about it? (77, 97, 117, 135, 221)

Basic Question 3: Why does Judith Guest have Calvin ask the question, "How does a Christian deal with grief?" (51)

1. What does Calvin mean when he says "there is no dealing" with grief? (51)
2. What does Calvin mean when he says "the old definitions, the neat, knowing pigeonholes have disappeared or no longer apply" after his son's death? (51)
3. What "unanswered questions" does the reminder of Jordan's death raise in Calvin's mind? (51)
4. What does Calvin mean when he says that "Grief is ugly. It is isolating"? (127)
5. When Calvin visits Dr. Berger, why does he tell him that all of life's events are "accidents"? (146)

An Interview with Gina Berriault

When asked about her inspiration for the film version of "The Stone Boy," Gina Berriault replied "The idea for the story came from a news item about a hunting accident; and at the time I read it, I was living for the summer on a farm in Montana, and that is where I set the story . . . But I make up all the persons in the story . . . It is an original idea."

Was she pleased with her screenplay? "Not really. I was ultimately disappointed in the way that the film turned out." She explained that the screenplay was her attempt to answer the question that students most frequently asked her, "What's going to happen to Arnold?"

1. Given this background information, what do you think it was that made Berriault dissatisfied with her screenplay? [The interviewer did not follow up to ask her to explain her dissapointment.]
2. **How** does the movie try to link to two plots—the plot of the original short story (Arnold's rejection by adults) and the plot of the screenplay (the demise of Uncle Andy and Lucille's marriage)?
3. Which, if any, of the connections between the two plots are plausible? For example, why did Arnold go to Reno to apologize to his aunt Lucille?

"Sympathetic Relationship Heals 'Stone Boy' Wounds": Mini-Review

Gene Siskel Chicago Tribune, Thursday, April 26, 1984

"Silence is not always golden"

The cast

Joe Hillerman	Robert Duvall
Andy Jensen	Frederic Forrest
Ruth Hillerman	Glenn Close
George Jensen	Wilford Brimley
Arnold Hillerman	Jason Presson
Lu Jensen	Gail Youngs
Amalie	Cindy Fisher
Nora Hillerman	Susan Blackstone
Eugene Hillerman	Dean Cain

1. If you are excited at the prospect of seeing another Robert Duvall film, you probably will be disappointed with "The Stone Boy." It's not anything that Duvall does; it's what he doesn't do. Even though he receives top billing, his role is one of the smallest in the film. He spends most of his time staring off into the darkness, his back to the camera. Making a similarly limited impression is Glen Close, playing his wife. Indeed, theirs is not the central relationship in this purposefully noncommercial movie.
2. Rather, at the center of "The Stone Boy" is the relationship between a traumatized child and his sensitive, loving grandfather, played by Wilford Brimley, a superb character actor who has his best role in this film. "The Stone Boy" is a drama of silence and communication built upon a tragedy. Set in the big sky country of Montana, "The Stone Boy" opens with two boys, one 12 years old, the other a few years older, leaving their farmhouse to go pick peas.
3. The younger brother has brought along his gun, hoping to bag a wild duck, but before they get to work, a terrible accident occurs. As the boys climb through a fence, the gun gets caught on a wire. Trying to free it, the younger brother accidentally causes the gun to fire, killing his older brother.

4. It's one of those moments that seems both small and monumental. A bullet passes through a body and snuffs out a life. It doesn't seem right that something that small can do so much damage. Those, though are the thoughts of an adult. No one knows what goes through the mind of twelve year-old Arnold Hillerman [played by Jason Presson] as he stands in the field, feeling responsible for his brother's death. Instead of running to tell his parents, Arnold stays in the field for some time and in some kind of twisted way to deny what's happened, he begins to pick peas.
5. The delay means nothing, because his brother is dead. But later that delay, that denial, will cause more problems for Arnold, who in silent suffering becomes the film's title character. The rest of "The Stone Boy" follows the forces that keep Arnold in his shell and those that work to free him and his family of their curse of resentment and silence. It's a journey in search of a way to come back from being dead while alive, and the character of the grandfather holds the key. The boy's father and mother [Duvall and Close] are too distraught to heal their own son.
6. "The Stone Boy" would be a more commercial film if it narrowed its focus to these four characters: the father, mother, son, and grandfather. But in what may turn out to be a fatal box-office decision, the story has been enlarged to include sizable roles for Close's philandering brother [Frederic Forrest] and his put-upon wife. These two characters rail at each other throughout the movie to no great purpose.
7. The Academy Award-winning Duvall has already received ample praise for his past many achievements. So let us now praise Wilford Brimley. There is a quiet power within Brimley that results from his just being there. He comes across as a person who has lived a lot of years and seen a lot of things and probably knows a things or two about life. That describes every character Brimley has played, and those qualities are desperately needed by his grandson in "The Stone Boy." Someone in this family has to reach out and make a connection to this hurting boy.
8. "The Stone Boy" tells the story at a labored pace, not giving in to easy, cathartic drama. That makes it less commercial and a bit frustrating at times to sit through. Nevertheless, "The Stone Boy" reveals in detail the work that goes into the art of healing, and that is a subject foreign to most American movies. For that reason, "The Stone Boy" is recommended.

"Sympathetic Relationship Heals 'Stone Boy' Wounds"

Gene Siskel

Directions: As you read Siskel's movie review make notations and then answer these questions in complete sentences in your journal.

***Before** viewing the movie version*:

1. Why does Siskel think we will be disappointed with the movie version of Gina Berriault's story?
2. Why does Siskel think that Arnold picked peas after his brother's death?
3. Based on your reading of the original story, do you agree with Siskel's interpretation of Arnold's behavior after Eugene's death? If so, why so? If not, why not?
4. In the original story, why does no one reach out to help Arnold cope with the loss of his brother?
5. What is Siskel's chief objection to the movie?
6. In spite of his objections, why does Siskel still recommend the movie?
7. Explain how, specifically, Siskel's movie review is a model of good writing.

***After** viewing the movie version*:

8. Unlike the short story, why does the movie concentrate not on Arnold's growing isolation but on the sympathetic relationship between Arnold and his loving grandfather?
9. Do you agree with Siskel that "the philandering brother" [uncle Andy] of Arnold's mother [Ruth] and his "put-upon wife" [Lucille] rail at each other for no dramatic purpose? If so, why so? If not, why not?
10. Unlike the movie, does the short story imply that the Curwings have lost two sons? If so, why so? If not, why not?
11. List three specific changes *that you liked* in the movie.
12. List three specific changes *that you disliked* in the movie.

Nonfiction Reading

The following is the unabridged transcript of President Obama's speech at the Sandy Hook Interfaith Prayer Vigil in Newtown, Connecticut, on December 16, 2012

In the Face of Unconscionable Evil

Thank you. Thank you, Governor. To all the families, first responders, to the community of Newtown, clergy, guests—Scripture tells us: ". . .do not lose heart. Though outwardly we are wasting away . . . inwardly we are being renewed day by day. For our light and momentary troubles are achieving for us an eternal glory that far outweighs them all. So we fix our eyes not on what is seen, but on what is unseen, since what is seen is temporary, but what is unseen is eternal. For we know that if the earthly tent we live in is destroyed, we have a building from God, an eternal house in heaven, not built by human hands." (2 Cor 4:16–5:1)

We gather here in memory of twenty beautiful children and six remarkable adults. They lost their lives in a school that could have been any school; in a quiet town full of good and decent people that could be any town in America.

Here in Newtown, I come to offer the love and prayers of a nation. I am very mindful that mere words cannot match the depths of your sorrow, nor can they heal your wounded hearts. I can only hope it helps *for you to know that you're not alone in your grief*; that our world too has been torn apart; that all across this land of ours, we have wept with you, we've pulled our children tight. And you must know that whatever measure of comfort we can provide, we will provide; whatever portion of sadness that we can share with you to ease this heavy load, we will gladly bear it. Newtown—you are not alone.

As these difficult days have unfolded, you've also inspired us with stories of strength and resolve and sacrifice. We know that when danger arrived in the halls of Sandy Hook Elementary, the school's staff did not flinch, they did not hesitate. Dawn Hochsprung and Mary Sherlach, Vicki Soto, Lauren Rousseau, Rachel Davino and Anne Marie Murphy—they responded as we all hope we might respond in such terrifying circumstances—with courage and with love, *giving their lives to protect the children in their care.*

We know that there were *other teachers* who barricaded themselves inside classrooms, and kept steady through it all, and reassured their students by saying "wait for the good guys, they're coming"; "show me your smile."

And we know that good guys came. The first responders who raced to the scene, helping to guide those in harm's way to safety, and comfort those in need, *holding at bay their own shock and trauma* because they had a job to do, and others needed them more.

And then there were the scenes of the schoolchildren, helping one another, holding each other, dutifully following instructions in the way that young children sometimes do; one child even trying to encourage a grown-up by saying, "I know karate. So it's okay. I'll lead the way out." (Laughter.). As a community, you've inspired us, Newtown. In the face of indescribable violence, *in the face of unconscionable evil*, you've looked out for each other, and *you've cared for one another* and you've loved one another. This is how Newtown will be remembered. And with time, and God's grace, that love will see you through.

But we, as a nation, we are left with some hard questions. Someone once described the joy and anxiety of parenthood as the equivalent of having your heart outside of your body all the time, walking around. With their very first cry, this most precious, vital part of ourselves—our child—is suddenly exposed to the world, to possible mishap or malice. *And every parent knows* there is nothing we will not do to shield our children from harm. *And yet,* we also know that with that child's very first step, and each step after that, they are separating from us; that we won't—that we can't always be there for them. They'll suffer sickness and setbacks and broken hearts and disappointments. And we learn that our most important job is to give them what they need to become self-reliant and capable and resilient, ready to face the world without fear.

And we know we can't do this by ourselves. It comes as a shock at a certain point where you realize, no matter how much you love these kids, *you can't do it by yourself.* That this job of keeping our children safe, and teaching them well, is something we can only do together, with the help of friends and neighbors, the help of a community, and the help of a nation. And in that way, we come to realize that we bear a responsibility for every child because we're counting on everybody else to help look after ours; that we're all parents; that they're all our children.

This is our first task—caring for our children. It's our first job. If we don't get that right, we don't get anything right. That's how, as a society, we will be judged.

And by that measure, can we truly say, as a nation, that we are meeting our obligations? Can we honestly say that we're doing enough to keep our children—all of them—safe from harm? Can we claim, as a nation, that we're all together there, letting them know that they are loved, and teaching them to love in return? Can we say that we're truly doing enough to give all the children of this country the chance they deserve to live out their lives in happiness and with purpose?

I've been reflecting on this the last few days, and if we're honest with ourselves, the answer is no. *We're not doing enough. And we will have to change.*

Since I've been President, this is the fourth time we have come together to comfort a grieving community torn apart by a mass shooting. The fourth time we've hugged survivors. The fourth time we've consoled the families of victims. And in between, there have been an endless series of deadly shootings across the country, almost daily reports of victims, many of them children, in small towns and big cities all across America—victims whose—much of the time, their only fault was being in the wrong place at the wrong time.

We can't tolerate this anymore. These tragedies must end. And to end them, we must change. We will be told that the causes of such violence are complex, and that is true. No single law—no set of laws can eliminate evil from the world, or prevent every senseless act of violence in our society.

But that can't be an excuse for inaction. Surely, we can do better than this. If there is even one step we can take to save another child, or another parent, or another town, from the grief that has visited Tucson, and Aurora, and Oak Creek, and Newtown, and communities from Columbine to Blacksburg before that—then surely we have an obligation to try.

In the coming weeks, I will use whatever power this office holds to engage my fellow citizens—from law enforcement to mental health professionals to parents and educators—in an effort aimed at preventing more tragedies like this. Because what choice do we have? We can't accept events like this as routine. Are we really prepared to say that we're powerless in the face of such carnage, that the politics are too hard? Are we prepared to say that such violence visited on our children year after year after year is somehow the price of our freedom?

All the world's religions—so many of them represented here today—start with a simple question: Why are we here? What gives our life meaning? What gives our acts purpose? We know our time on this Earth is fleeting. We know that we will each have our share of pleasure and pain; that even after we chase after some earthly goal, whether it's wealth or power or fame, or just simple comfort, we will, in some fashion, fall short of what we had hoped. We know that no matter how good our intentions, we will all stumble sometimes, in some way. We will make mistakes, we will experience hardships. And even when we're trying to do the right thing, we know that much of our time will be spent groping through the darkness, so often unable to discern God's heavenly plans.

There's only one thing we can be sure of, and that is the love that we have—for our children, for our families, for each other. The warmth of a small child's embrace—that is true. The memories we have of them, the joy that they bring, the wonder we see through their eyes, that fierce and boundless love we feel for them, a love that takes us out of ourselves, and binds us to something larger—we know that's what matters. We know we're always doing right when we're taking care of them, when we're teaching them well, when we're showing acts of kindness. We don't go wrong when we do that.

That's what we can be sure of. And that's what you, the people of Newtown, have reminded us. That's how you've inspired us. You remind us what matters. And that's what should drive us forward in everything we do, for as long as God sees fit to keep us on this Earth.

"Let the little children come to me," Jesus said, "and do not hinder them—for to such belongs the kingdom of heaven." (Lk 18:16, Mt 19:14, Mk 19:14)

"It is impossible that scandals should not come; but woe to him by whom they come. It would be better for him that a millstone were hanged about his neck, and cast into the sea than that he should scandalize one of these little children." (Lk 17:2)

"Unless you become as little children, you shall not enter the Kingdom of Heaven." Mt 18:3 Charlotte. Daniel. Olivia. Josephine. Ana. Dylan. Madeleine. Catherine. Chase. Jesse. James. Grace, Emilie. Jack. Noah. Caroline. Jessica. Benjamin. Avielle. Allison.

God has called them all home.* For those of us who remain, let us find the strength to carry on, and make our country worthy of their memory.

May God bless and keep those we've lost in His heavenly place.

May He grace those we still have with His holy comfort.

And may He bless and watch over this community, and the United States of America.

*Editorial note: To hold God responsible is bad theology. God did not call these children Home. On the contrary, a madman sent them Home.

CHAPTER

16 Lesson Plan 13

Do We all Have the Same Unconditional Right to Life?

Day 1 Journal	Death Penalty Information Center Quiz; Scenario of a dilemma; Quiz on "The Bet" and discussion: "Does Chekhov want us to agree with the banker that capital punishment is more humane than life in prison"
Day 2	*Dead Man Walking* DVD part one (90 mins). Notations: pros and cons.
Day 3	*Dead Man Walking* DVD concluded (50 mins) and discussion: Is the film as balanced pro and con the death penalty as director Tim Robbins claims? Journal: your resolution to the basic question.
Day 4	*Compulsion* DVD Clarence Darrow's defense scene (30 mins). Journal: "Had you been the judge, would you have voted for the prosecution or the defense?"

1. **Focus:**	Journal: Scenario of a dilemma—death penalty vs. life imprisonment without parole and "Purgatorio," *Harpers* (p. 234).
2. **Objective:**	Persuasive essay: The death penalty should [not] be abolished.
3. **Purpose:**	To develop habits of independent, critical, and reflective thinking.
4. **Input:**	Three movies, three basic interpretive questions, research articles.
5. **Modeling:**	Co-leaders observe the four rules of Socratic discussion.
6. **Checking for understanding, and guided practice:**	Co-leaders ask spontaneous follow-up questions for clarification and substantiation, more opinion, consistency, implication, relevance, and resolution.

7. Closure:	Review Guidelines for persuasive essay on the death penalty.
Text:	Anton Chekhov, "The Bet", trans. Constance Garnett in *The Schoolmistress and Other Stories*, 1921

Death Penalty Quiz

> "The question with which we must deal is **not** whether a substantial proportion of American citizens would today, if polled, opine that capital punishment is barbarously cruel, **but** whether they would find it to be so in light of all the information presently available."
>
> Chief Justice Thurgood Marshall

TRUE or FALSE:

1. The death penalty saves taxpayers' money because execution is cheaper than keeping someone in prison for life.
2. In 1976, the Supreme Court allowed individual states to restore the death penalty to avoid ruling whether or not capital punishment violates the Eighth Amendment which forbids "cruel and unusual punishment."
3. Since the death penalty was reinstated in 1976, more blacks than whites have been executed.
4. Since the death penalty was reinstated in the US, more than a dozen prisoners have been released from death row because they were found innocent.
5. In some states with the death penalty, even the mentally retarded can be executed.
6. Someone who commits murder in Wisconsin or Massachusetts cannot be given the death penalty.
7. Hanging has not been used as a method of execution in the US for over thirty years.
8. When US police chiefs were polled on their views on ways to lower the crime rate, only 1% placed the death penalty as their top priority.
9. No woman has been executed in the US since the Civil War.
10. The Supreme Court has ruled that teenage defendants who were seventeen at the time of their crime could be executed.

Death Penalty Journal

PRE-WRITING EXERCISE: SCENARIO OF A DILEMMA

You have been convicted of a capital crime and await execution on death row within a month. However, Governor George Ryan has placed a moratorium on the death penalty because its implementation in Illinois has been capricious, arbitrary, and beyond reform in the near future. Since 1985, eleven men on death row in Illinois were found innocent because of DNA testing. Nationwide, more than a hundred (119) sentenced to death have been exonerated!

Like Ohio (and fourteen other states) which allows convicted felons sentenced to death to choose their method of execution, you have the choice of accepting life imprisonment with no chance of parole OR you may choose your method of execution within the month (hanging, firing squad, electrocution, gas chamber, or lethal injection). If you refuse to participate in this experiment, you will remain in prison for life. What is your decision? Why? How will you decide?

Note: Before writing this journal, read first "The Bet." Would Chekhov agree with the lawyer: "Capital punishment and life-imprisonment are equally immoral; *but if I were offered a choice between them,* I would certainly choose the second. It's better to live somehow than not to live at all"? Then read the letter to Italian President Napolitano, "Purgatorio," in *Harpers*, August 2007.

Purgatorio

From a May letter to Italian President Giorgio Napolitano, signed by 310 prisoners serving life sentences for murder, the only crime that carries a life sentence in Italy, which banned the death penalty for all crimes in 1994. Translated from the Italian by Stefania Heim

> **Dear Mr. President of the Republic,**
> We are tired of dying a little bit each day. We have decided to die once and for all, and we ask that our penalties of life imprisonment be converted to penalties of death. To be not dead but not alive either, life imprisonment turns light into shadow, it kills you inside, bit by bit: death in small doses. It renders life useless, makes the future seem the same as the past. It crushes the present and takes away hope. To a life prisoner, only life remains. But life without a future is less than nothing. It is flat and everlasting. Life imprisonment is the invention of Antichrist with a malice that transcends the imagination. It is a victory over death, stronger than death itself.

"The Bet"

Anton Chekhov

Part I

1 IT WAS a dark autumn night. The old banker was walking up and down his study and remembering how, fifteen years before, he had given a party one autumn evening. There had been many clever men there, and there had been interesting conversations. Among other things they had talked of capital punishment. The majority of the guests, among whom were many journalists and intellectual men, disapproved of the death penalty. They considered that form of punishment out of date, immoral, and unsuitable for Christian States. In the opinion of some of them the death penalty ought to be replaced everywhere by imprisonment for life.

2 "I don't agree with you," said their host the banker. "I have not tried either the death penalty or imprisonment for life, but if one may judge *à priori*, the death penalty is more moral and more humane than imprisonment for life. Capital punishment kills a man at once, but lifelong imprisonment kills him slowly. Which executioner is the more humane, he who kills you in a few minutes or he who drags the life out of you in the course of many years?"

3 "Both are equally immoral," observed one of the guests, "for they both have the same object—to take away life. The State is not God. It has not the right to take away what it cannot restore when it wants to." Among the guests was a young lawyer, a young man of five-and-twenty. When he was asked his opinion, he said: "The death sentence and the life sentence are equally immoral, but if I had to choose between the death penalty and imprisonment for life, I would certainly choose the second. To live anyhow is better than not at all."

4 A lively discussion arose. The banker, who was younger and more nervous in those days, was suddenly carried away by excitement; he struck the table with his fist and shouted at the young man: "It's not true! I'll bet you two million you wouldn't stay in solitary confinement for five years."

"If you mean that in earnest," said the young man, "I'll take the bet, but I would stay not five but fifteen years."

"Fifteen? Done!" cried the banker. "Gentlemen, I stake two millions!"

"Agreed! You stake your millions and I stake my freedom!" said the young man.

5 And this wild, senseless bet was carried out! The banker, spoilt and frivolous, with millions beyond his reckoning, was delighted at the bet. At supper he made fun of the young man, and said: "Think better of it,

young man, while there is still time. To me two millions are a trifle, but you are losing three or four of the best years of your life. I say three or four, because you won't stay longer. Don't forget either, you unhappy man, that voluntary confinement is a great deal harder to bear than compulsory. The thought that you have the right to step out in liberty at any moment will poison your whole existence in prison. I am sorry for you."

6 And now the banker, walking to and fro, remembered all this, and asked himself: "What was the object of that bet? What is the good of that man's losing fifteen years of his life and my throwing away two millions? Can it prove that the death penalty is better or worse than imprisonment for life? No, no. It was all nonsensical and meaningless. On my part it was the caprice of a pampered man, and on his part simple greed for money . . ." Then he remembered what followed that evening. It was decided that the young man should spend the years of his captivity under the strictest supervision in one of the lodges in the banker's garden. It was agreed that for fifteen years he should not be free to cross the threshold of the lodge, to see human beings, to hear the human voice, or to receive letters and newspapers. He was allowed to have a musical instrument and books, and was allowed to write letters, to drink wine, and to smoke. By the terms of the agreement, the only relations he could have with the outer world were by a little window made purposely for that object. He might have anything he wanted—books, music, wine, and so on—in any quantity he desired by writing an order, but could only receive them through the window. The agreement provided for every detail and every trifle that would make his imprisonment strictly solitary, and bound the young man to stay there *exactly* fifteen years, beginning from twelve o'clock of November 14, 1870, and ending at twelve o'clock of November 14, 1885. The slightest attempt on his part to break the conditions, if only two minutes before the end, released the banker from the obligation to pay him two millions.

7 For the first year of his confinement, as far as one could judge from his brief notes, the prisoner suffered severely from loneliness and depression. The sounds of the piano could be heard continually day and night from his lodge. He refused wine and tobacco. Wine, he wrote, excites the desires, and desires are the worst foes of the prisoner; and besides, nothing could be more dreary than drinking good wine and seeing no one. And tobacco spoilt the air of his room. In the first year the books he sent for were principally of a light character; novels with a complicated love plot, sensational and fantastic stories, and so on.

8 In the second year the piano was silent in the lodge, and the prisoner asked only for the classics. In the fifth year music was audible again,

and the prisoner asked for wine. Those who watched him through the window said that all that year he spent doing nothing but eating and drinking and lying on his bed, frequently yawning and angrily talking to himself. He did not read books. Sometimes at night he would sit down to write; he would spend hours writing, and in the morning tear up all that he had written. More than once he could be heard crying.

9 In the second half of the sixth year the prisoner began zealously studying languages, philosophy, and history. He threw himself eagerly into these studies—so much so that the banker had enough to do to get him the books he ordered. In the course of four years some six hundred volumes were procured at his request. It was during this period that the banker received the following letter from his prisoner:

> **"My dear Jailer,**
> I write you these lines in six languages. Show them to people who know the languages. Let them read them. If they find not one mistake I implore you to fire a shot in the garden. That shot will show me that my efforts have not been thrown away. The geniuses of all ages and of all lands speak different languages, but the same flame burns in them all. Oh, if you only knew what unearthly happiness my soul feels now from being able to understand them!"

10 The prisoner's desire was fulfilled. The banker ordered two shots to be fired in the garden. Then after the tenth year, the prisoner sat immovably at the table and read nothing but the Gospel. It seemed strange to the banker that a man who in four years had mastered six hundred learned volumes should waste nearly a year over one thin book easy of comprehension. Theology and histories of religion followed the Gospels.

11 In the last two years of his confinement the prisoner read an immense quantity of books quite indiscriminately. At one time he was busy with the natural sciences, then he would ask for Byron or Shakespeare. There were notes in which he demanded at the same time books on chemistry, and a manual of medicine, and a novel, and some treatise on philosophy or theology. His reading suggested a man swimming in the sea among the wreckage of his ship, and trying to save his life by greedily clutching first at one spar and then at another.

Part II

12 The old banker remembered all this, and thought: "Tomorrow at twelve o'clock he will regain his freedom. By our agreement I ought to pay

him two millions. If I do pay him, it is all over with me: I shall be utterly ruined."

13 Fifteen years before, his millions had been beyond his reckoning; now he was afraid to ask himself which were greater, his debts or his assets. Desperate gambling on the Stock Exchange, wild speculation and the excitability which he could not get over even in advancing years, had by degrees led to the decline of his fortune and the proud, fearless, self-confident millionaire had become a banker of middling rank, trembling at every rise and fall in his investments. "Cursed bet!" muttered the old man, clutching his head in despair "Why didn't the man die? He is only forty now. He will take my last penny from me, he will marry, will enjoy life, will gamble on the Exchange; while I shall look at him with envy like a beggar, and hear from him every day the same sentence: 'I am indebted to you for the happiness of my life, let me help you!' No, it is too much! The one means of being saved from bankruptcy and disgrace is the death of that man!"

14 It struck three o'clock, the banker listened; everyone was asleep in the house and nothing could be heard outside but the rustling of the chilled trees. Trying to make no noise, he took from a fireproof safe the key of the door which had not been opened for fifteen years, put on his overcoat, and went out of the house.

15 It was dark and cold in the garden. Rain was falling. A damp cutting wind was racing about the garden, howling and giving the trees no rest. The banker strained his eyes, but could see neither the earth nor the white statues, nor the lodge, nor the trees. Going to the spot where the lodge stood, he twice called the watchman. No answer followed. Evidently the watchman had sought shelter from the weather, and was now asleep somewhere either in the kitchen or in the greenhouse.

16 "If I had the pluck to carry out my intention," thought the old man, "Suspicion would fall first upon the watchman." He felt in the darkness for the steps and the door, and went into the entry of the lodge. Then he groped his way into a little passage and lighted a match. There was not a soul there. There was a bedstead with no bedding on it, and in the corner there was a dark cast-iron stove. The seals on the door leading to the prisoner's rooms were intact.

17 When the match went out the old man, trembling with emotion, peeped through the little window. A candle was burning dimly in the prisoner's room. He was sitting at the table. Nothing could be seen but his back, the hair on his head, and his hands. Open books were lying on the table, on the two easy-chairs, and on the carpet near the table.

18 Five minutes passed and the prisoner did not once stir. Fifteen years' imprisonment had taught him to sit still. The banker tapped at the window with his finger, and the prisoner made no movement whatever in response. Then the banker cautiously broke the seals off the door and put the key in the keyhole. The rusty lock gave a grating sound and the door creaked. The banker expected to hear at once footsteps and a cry of astonishment, but three minutes passed and it was as quiet as ever in the room. He made up his mind to go in.

19 At the table a man unlike ordinary people was sitting motionless. He was a skeleton with the skin drawn tight over his bones, with long curls like a woman's and a shaggy beard. His face was yellow with an earthy tint in it, his cheeks were hollow, his back long and narrow, and the hand on which his shaggy head was propped was so thin and delicate that it was dreadful to look at it. His hair was already streaked with silver, and seeing his emaciated, aged-looking face, no one would have believed that he was only forty. He was asleep. In front of his bowed head there lay on the table a sheet of paper on which there was something written in fine handwriting.

20 "Poor creature!" thought the banker, "he is asleep and most likely dreaming of the millions. And I have only to take this half-dead man, throw him on the bed, stifle him a little with the pillow, and the most conscientious expert would find no sign of a violent death. But let us first read what he has written here. The banker took the page from the table and read as follows:

21 "Tomorrow at twelve o'clock I regain my freedom and the right to associate with other men, but before I leave this room and see the sunshine, I think it necessary to say a few words to you. With a clear conscience I tell you, as before God, who beholds me, that I despise freedom and life and health, and all that in your books is called the good things of the world.

22 "For fifteen years I have been intently studying earthly life. It is true I have not seen the earth nor men, but in your books I have drunk fragrant wine, I have sung songs, I have hunted stags and wild boars in the forests, have loved women . . . Beauties as ethereal as clouds, created by the magic of your poets and geniuses, have visited me at night, and have whispered in my ears wonderful tales that have set my brain in a whirl. In your books I have climbed to the peaks of Elburz and Mont Blanc, and from there I have seen the sun rise and have watched it at evening flood the sky, the ocean, and the mountaintops with gold and crimson. I have watched from there the lightning flashing over my head and cleaving the storm clouds. I have seen green forests, fields, rivers, lakes, towns. I have heard the singing of the sirens, and the strains of the shepherds' pipes; I have touched the wings of comely devils who flew down to converse with me of God . . . In your

books I have flung myself into the bottomless pit, performed miracles, slain, burned towns, preached new religions, conquered whole kingdoms.

23 "Your books have given me wisdom. All that the unresting thought of man has created in the ages is compressed into a small compass in my brain. I know that I am wiser than all of you.

24 "And I despise your books, I despise wisdom and the blessings of this world. It is all worthless, fleeting, illusory, and deceptive, like a mirage. You may be proud, wise, and fine, but death will wipe you off the face of the earth as though you were no more than mice burrowing under the floor, and your posterity, your history, your immortal geniuses will burn or freeze together with the earthly globe.

25 "You have lost your reason and taken the wrong path. You have taken lies for truth, and hideousness for beauty. You would marvel if, owing to strange events of some sorts, frogs and lizards suddenly grew on apple and orange trees instead of fruit or if roses began to smell like a sweating horse; so I marvel at you who exchange heaven for earth. I don't want to understand you.

26 "To prove to you in action how I despise all that you live by, I renounce the two millions of which I once dreamed as of paradise and which now I despise. To deprive myself of the right to the money I shall go out from here five hours before the time fixed, and so break the compact."

27 When the banker had read this he laid the page on the table, kissed the strange man on the head, and went out of the lodge, weeping. At no other time, even when he had lost heavily on the Stock Exchange, had he felt so great a contempt for himself. When he got home he lay on his bed, but his tears and emotion kept him for hours from sleeping.

28 Next morning the watchmen ran in with pale faces, and told him they had seen the man who lived in the lodge climb out of the window into the garden, go to the gate, and disappear. The banker went at once with the servants to the lodge and made sure of the flight of his prisoner. To avoid arousing unnecessary talk, he took from the table the writing in which the millions were renounced, and when he got home locked it up in the fireproof safe.

"The Bet"

PLOT QUIZ

1. What are two of the four conditions of the bet about capital punishment?

2. Why does the banker think capital punishment more humane than life imprisonment?

3. Why does the lawyer think *both* capital punishment and life imprisonment are wrong?

4. How does the lawyer reply to the banker's challenge of five years in jail?

5. In what situation does the banker find himself fifteen years later?

6. How does the banker plan to resolve his situation?

7. What conclusion about life does the lawyer arrive at as his confinement ends?

8. How old is the lawyer at the end of the story?

9. Why does the banker weep when he finished reading the prisoner-lawyer's exit letter?

10. Why does the banker lock the lawyer's letter in his safe "to avoid rumors"?

Socratic Seminar

Basic Question 1: Does Chekhov want us to agree with the banker that capital punishment is more humane than life imprisonment?

If YES, then:

1. Is the banker speaking for Chekhov when he says that their bet will do nothing to convince anyone that capital punishment is better than life imprisonment?
2. Why does the banker give no consideration to the morality of the death penalty?
3. In his letter of renunciation, why does the lawyer make no mention of their bet about capital punishment?
4. Does Chekhov want us to agree with the banker that the lawyer has ruined his life after fifteen years of voluntary confinement?
5. Why does the narrator make no comment at the end of the story about the argument that had provoked the bet?

If NO, then:

6. Why is the bet between the lawyer and the banker about the death penalty?
7. Why does the lawyer believe that both capital punishment and life imprisonment are immoral because they both take away human life?
8. Does the lawyer refuse to listen to the banker's plea not to ruin his life because he is arrogant or to prove that the banker is wrong about the death penalty being more humane?
9. Why does the banker argue that capital punishment, which takes away life instantly, is more humane than life imprisonment which takes life away day by day?
10. Why does Chekhov emphasize the physical and mental breakdown that fifteen years of voluntary confinement had made in the lawyer's life?

A Short Film About Killing, by Krzysztof Kieslowski

Cast of Characters

Setting: 1988, a modern Warsaw apartment complex during the collapse of the old Soviet bloc.

Jack Lazar: a young twenty-year-old psychopath and misanthrope who seems to have never gotten over the death of his young sister.

Marysia: Jack's deceased little sister whose death still plagues him.

Cab driver: Jack's random, anonymous victim.
Piotr Balicki: a young, idealistic defense lawyer whose first case is to defend Jack Lazar.

Prologue

The film opens with a voice-over stating eight propositions about the relationship between law and justice in society. Paraphrase four propositions and explain the relevance of each to the movie.

1. "The law should not imitate nature; the law should improve nature."
2. "People invented the law to govern their relationships."
3. "The law determines who we are and how we live."
4. "We either observe it or break it."
5. "People are free. Their freedom is limited only by the freedom of others."
6. "Punishment means revenge. In particular when it comes to harm, but it does not prevent crime."
7. "For whom does the law avenge?"
8. "In the name of the innocent? Do the innocent make the rules?"

Basic Question 2: Is a *A Short Film about Killing* meant to be as much an argument for as well as against the death penalty?

"Not since Krzysztof Kieslowski's *A Short Film About Killing* has a motion picture about capital punishment been so disturbing as *Dead Man Walking* which gives pain and personality to both sides of the issue." *New York Times* review.

Basic Question 3: Is *A Short Film About Killing* as balanced pro and con the death penalty as *Dead Man Walking*?

1. Why does the film begin with eight propositions about law in society?
2. Why does the film end with the defense lawyer screaming, "The horror of it"?
3. Why does Jacek murder the cab driver without any apparent motive?
4. Why does Jacek never display any remorse for murdering the cab driver?
5. Does Kieslowski intend to portray Jacek as a monster?
6. If so, why is Jacek as still grieving over the death of his young sister, Marysia?
7. Why does Jacek want Marysia's picture returned to her mother?
8. Why are the entire proceedings of Jacek's trial omitted even though the judge tells Piotr that he gave the best speech against the death penalty that he had ever heard?

9. What does the judge mean when he tells Piotr that "the verdict was inevitable"?
10. Why does the murder take as much screen time as the execution?
11. Is the murder or the execution meant to be more brutal?

Dead Man Walking, by Tim Robbins, Director (130 mins)

Cast of Characters

Setting: St.Thomas Housing Project and Angola State Prison, New Orleans, LA 1995.

Matthew Poncelet (Sean Penn): A dirt-poor and manipulative prisoner who has been convicted of first degree murder of two teenagers but adamantly maintains his innocence.

Sister Helen Prejean, CSJ (Susan Sarandon): As Sister of St. Joseph who reluctantly answers a letter for help from Matthew. This is but the first step to her weeks of involvement with Poncelet's case that would lead to a life-ministry that she continues to pursue today.

Hilton Barber: Matthew Poncelet's pro bono defense lawyer and long-time activist against the death penalty. He warns Sister Prejean to be realistic about his chances of getting life imprisonment for Matthew.

Mr. and Mrs. Percy: Bitter and revengeful parents of their daughter, Hope, one of Matthew's victims. Mr. Percy sincerely regrets that he did not kill Matthew with a policeman's gun when he had the opportunity.

Hope Percy: Eighteen-year-old daughter of the Percys who was raped and stabbed seventeen times.

Mr. and Mrs. Delacroix: Distraught parents of Walter who are so upset that Mrs. Delacroix leaves her husband.

Walter DeLacroix: Seventeen-year-old son of the Delacroix's, also murdered by Matthew. Mr. Delacroix angrily tells Sister Prejean: "This is an evil man. This scum robbed me of my only son, my family name dies with me."

Basic Question 4: Is *Dead Man Walking* as balanced pro and con the death penalty as director Tim Robbins claims?

1. Why does the prison chaplain defend the death penalty by citing the OT (Genesis 6) while Sister Prejean replies by citing Jesus' rejection of violence in the NT?
2. Why does Robbins have a guard refer to the Bible's statement of an "eye for an eye"?

3. Is Sister Prejean's chief opposition to the death penalty based on her statement, "I don't see why we kill people to tell other people that killing is wrong"?
4. Why does Sister Prejean believe that capital punishment dehumanizes everyone who is in any way involved in its implementation?
5. Does Robbins portray Matthew Poncelet as so repulsive a man to make him unworthy of anyone's sympathy?
6. Why does Sister Prejean help Matthew during his last days on death row?
7. What does Sister Prejean mean when she says, "Everyone is worth more than his own worst act"?
8. Throughout the film, why does Robbins reveal increasingly more details of the violent murders of Hope Percy and Walter Delacroix?
9. Were you surprised to find out that Poncelet was in fact guilty of rape and murder?
10. Does Robbins want us to agree with Matthew's final words, "Killing is wrong. No matter who does it. Whether it's me, y'all, or your government"?
11. Does Robbins portray Poncelet's execution as well as the deaths of his victims as crucifixions?
12. Do you agree with a movie critic who argues that whether we view this film as for or against the death penalty depends on our personal views of the issue?
13. Do you agree with the film critic who sees the movie's conclusion in a positive light—as the redemption of Poncelet?
14. Why does Walter's father, Mr. Delacroix, but not the parents of Hope Percy, attend Poncelet's funeral?

Nonfiction Reading

Compulsion: Edited Closing Arguments

Meyer Levin, *Compulsion,* 1956, pp. 377–391.

Prosecutor
Harold Horn (E. G. Marshall)

1. You have no right to forgive personally, but sitting here as Chief Justice of this great court, your honor, you have no right to forgive anybody who violates the law!
2. Your Honor, in this case, with the mass of evidence presented by the State, to grant life imprisonment would mean "the verdict was founded on corruption!"

3. Illinois law says in extreme cases death shall be the penalty. As a judge, you have no right to set aside the law. You have no right to defeat the will of the people of Illinois.
4. Mr. Wilk says that hanging does not stop murder. More murders take place in Chicago than in all of Great Britain where justice is handed out swiftly and surely.
5. The psychological-thrill motive is baloney and even if it were true, it is no reason at all for these two unrepentant murderers to avoid death. Their real motive was money.

Defense Counsel
Jonathan Wilk (Clarence Darrow/Orson Welles)

1. I am accused of having my clients plead guilty out of fear. That's right. I want a judge to decide this case not diluted among a jury of twelve people. Yes, your honor, I asked for a judge. If these boys are to hang, you must do it.
2. Crime and punishment. Yes the long history of crime and punishment is marked by a catalogue of methods of execution—one more gruesome than another. However, it has been proven that where the punishments for crimes are less barbarous, crimes are less frequent. Throughout the centuries, our laws have been modified. Cruelty breeds only more cruelty. If there's anyway to kill hatred and evil, it's not by killing men. It's through charity, love, and understanding. We say ours is a Christian community. Can there be any doubt what the fate of these boys would be safe in the hands of the Founder of the Christian religion?
3. I am asking for life imprisonment. Any cry for more goes back to the beasts of the jungle. Some say the state should show these boys the same mercy that they gave their victim. If the state cannot be kinder and more humane than these two sick boys, I am sorry that I have lived so long.
4. I am profoundly sorry about the cruel death of the victim, Bobby Franks. They bludgeoned him to death, threw acid on him to disfigure him and then threw his body in a ditch. If killing these boys would bring Bobby Franks back to life, then let it done. Since the State cannot give life it has no moral right to take it. The death penalty is legalized murder.
5. If these boys are executed, will it be done in the name of justice? Who knows what justice is? Is it not for many another word for revenge? Will killing Artie and Judd stop other sick boys from killing. No. Your honor, if you hang these boys, you are turning back to the past. I am pleading for the future. I plead not merely these boys but for all boys and for life itself when we can overcome hatred with love. When we can learn that all life is sacred and that many in the highest attribute of mankind?

Afterword

"In a common core curriculum, what is the value of studying 'the best that is known and thought in the world'?"

Victor J. Moeller

Matthew Arnold's question about Great Books deserves an answer. The most obvious reason has to be that stories are **entertaining** and amusing. With imaginative literature, there is something to satisfy everyone's taste—from romance, to gothic tales, to mystery, to westerns, to science-fiction, to whatever! Look around. Be a browser. Talk to a reader.

Reading stories also **educates our imaginations**. In fiction, anything can happen and an author does not have to prove anything. Our only obligation as readers is to understand the world that an author has placed us in—not to argue about the author's creation. If we do so, we can increase our enjoyment immensely. Unless we develop our imaginations, we will remain literal-minded and foolishly demand that all stories be true to life. How dull that would be.

On the other hand, the contrast between the real or actual and the extraordinary or the fanciful suggests two different uses that readers make of imaginative literature. Sometimes we **do** want to read about people like ourselves, or about places, things, experiences, and ideas that we are familiar with and make us feel comfortable. In the process of reading about situations related to our own lives, **we can learn more about ourselves and the world about us**. Realism will always have its appeal.

But at other times, the last thing that we want is a story about people like ourselves or experiences similar to those in our everyday lives. We might be accused of wanting **to escape**. We want something **different or strange**—like Stephen King stories. We want to get out of ourselves and the confining, all-too-familiar, and learn that there are other ways of looking at the world besides our own. In short, we want to read about exotic places, about other worlds that have never existed, or worlds that may never exist. The romantic spirit will always contend with realism's appeal.

Stories also prepare us for the unexpected and help us **to avoid projecting false hopes and fears** (such as superstitious zebras, who think that they are being preyed on by the ghosts of lions) and show us what we can actually expect in our everyday lives. Because some people never train their imagination to project any other "story" than their own, they cannot conceive of any other shape for their expectations. As a result, they remain stunted and naive about life.

Reading stories can also put us **in closer touch with our feelings**. Good stories, powerful stories, **revulse us** at what is ugly and cruel and mean in life. On the other hand, stories can also **inspire us** to marvel at what is good and wonderful, and beautiful in life. Recall George's devotion to Lennie or Nick Carraway's refusal to become as self-serving as those about him. In short, some stories can be so terrible that they may move us to tears and prompt us to say, "That's the way life must never be," while others are so poignant that we find ourselves saying, "That's the way life ought to be," or, "That's the way life could be!"

Most importantly and most profoundly, reading enables us to grasp our identity, **our own personal narratives**, because it requires us to overcome our infinite capacity for distraction and our culture of the present now which too many think demands or deserves immediate attention and response. In short, reflective, active, and close reading of good literature, of great books, enables us to discover our own narrative—who we are and who we want to be.

References

Adler, Mortimer J. (1940). "How to Mark a Book." *The Saturday Review* (July 6).

Adler, Mortimer J. (1940). *How To Read a Book: The Art of Getting a Liberal Education*. New York: Simon & Schuster.

Adler, Mortimer J. (1955). *A Guide for Leaders of Great Books Discussion Groups*. Chicago: Great Books Foundation.

Adler, Mortimer J. (1977). *Reforming Education: Opening the American Mind*. New York: Macmillan.

Adler, Mortimer J. (1981). *Six Great Ideas*. New York: Macmillan.

Adler, Mortimer J. (1982). *The Paideia Proposal*. New York: Macmillan.

Adler, Mortimer J. (1983). *Paideia Problems and Possibilities*. New York: Macmillan.

Adler, Mortimer J. (1984). *The Paideia Program*. New York: Macmillan.

Barthes, R. (1975). *The Pleasure of the Text*. New York: Hill and Wang.

Bloom, B. (Ed.) (1956). *Taxonomy of Educational Objectives*. New York: McKay.

Bloom, H. (2000). *How to Read and Why*. New York: Scribner.

Bruner, J. (1960). *The Process of Education*. New York: Alfred A. Knopf.

Burke, J. (2010). *What's the Big Idea: Question Driven Teaching Units*. Portsmouth, NH: Heinemann.

Dewey, J. (1997). *How We Think*. Mineola, New York: Dover Publications.

Frye, N. (1970). *The Educated Imagination*. Bloomington, IN: Indiana University Press.

Glaspey, Terry (2001). *Great Reading: A Guided Tour of Classic and Contemporary Literature*. Downers Grove, IL: InterVarsity Press.

Holst, S. (1993). *The Zebra Storyteller: Collected Stories*. Barrytown, NY: Station Hill Press.

Hutchins, R. M. (1952). *The Great Conversation*. Vol. 1 of Great Books of the Western World. Chicago, IL: Encyclopedia Britannica.

Jacobs, Alan (2001). *As Theology of Reading: The Hermeneutics of Love*. Boulder, CO: Westview Press.

Jacobs, Alan (2011). *The Pleasures of Reading in an Age of Distraction.* New York: Oxford University Press; Boulder, CO: Westview Press.

Kreeft, Peter (2002). *Socrates Meets Jesus.* Downers Grove, IL: InterVarsity Press.

Kubler-Ross, Elizabeth (1969). *On Death and Dying.* Macmillan Publishing Co. New York, NY.

Kutz, E., & Roskelly, H. (1991). *An Unquiet Pedagogy: Transforming Practice in the English Classroom.* Portsmouth, NH: Boynton/Cook.

Mann, T. (1969). *The Magic Mountain.* New York: Alfred A. Knopf, Vintage Books Edition.

Monaco, James (2000). *How to Read a Film: The World of Movies & Media.* New York: Oxford University Press.

Phillips, Christopher (2001). *Socrates Cafe: A Fresh Taste of Philosophy.* New York: Norton & Co.

Phillips, Christopher (2004). *Six Questions of Socrates.* New York: Norton & Co.

Postman, N. (1985). *Amusing Ourselves to Death: Public Discourse in the Age of Show Business.* New York: Penguin Group.

Quindlen, Anna (1998). *How Reading Changed My Life.* New York: Ballantine Books.

Richards, I. A. (1942). *How to Read a Page: Efficient Reading.* Boston, MA: Beacon Press.

Roberts, T. (1999). *The Paideia Classroom: Teaching for Understanding.* Larchmont, NY: Eye on Education.

Rosenblatt, Louise (1968). *Literature as Exploration.* New York: Noble and Noble.

Rosenblatt, Louise (1978). *The Reader, the Text, and the Poem.* Carbondale, IL: Southern Illinois University Press.

Rouse, W. H. (1995). *The Great Dialogues of Plato.* New York: Signet Classics.

Sanders, Norris (1966). *Classroom Questions: What Kinds?* New York: Harper & Row.

Teasley, Alan B., and Wilder, Ann (1997). *Reel Conversations: Reading Films with Young Adults.* Portsmouth, NH: Boynton/Cook.

Ulin, David (2010). *The Lost Art of Reading: Why Books Matter in a Distracted Time.* Seattle, WA: Sasquatch Books.

Warren, R. and Wellek, W. (1956). *Theory of Literature.* New York: Harcourt, Brace & Company.

Whitehead, A. N. (1929). *The Aims of Education.* New York: Macmillan.